TWENTY LESSONS IN READING AND WRITING PROSE

TWENTY LESSONS IN READING AND WRITING PROSE

by DONALD DAVIDSON
PROFESSOR OF ENGLISH
Vanderbilt University

CHARLES SCRIBNER'S SONS · NEW YORK

B-9.56[MH]

LIBRARY OF CONGRESS CATALOGUE CARD NO. 55-7293

PREFACE

THE PURPOSE of this textbook is to supply a group of prose selections which can be studied intensively both for their intrinsic value and for what is to be learned from them about how one may, or should, or perhaps should not write. The material provided, together with the usual theme assignments, will certainly occupy a class for a full term, or for a semester or more if supplemented, as is common, by collateral reading, handbook assignments, or other allied studies.

The principle of organization of the book is simple. It recognizes the fact that the teacher of writing and the student of writing are perpetually in the condition of crisis described by Julius Caesar when, on a famous summer evening in France, over two thousand years ago, he was attacked by the Nervii. Part of Caesar's army, protected by a cavalry screen, was pitching camp; and part, encumbered by the baggage train, was crossing a river. The Nervii, Caesar says, broke and tore up his cavalry screen and hit his legions at three points simultaneously. And then, Caesar tersely remarks, he had to do everything at once—*omnia uno tempore agenda.* And what he had to do all at once was the more difficult because lack of time and the onrush of the enemy were something of an obstacle to the performance of military duties.

So it is in any composition class—or in any act of writing. The Nervii are always attacking. Just as teacher or student is settling down to solve one isolated problem of sentence structure, or grammar, or usage, or rhetoric, it suddenly becomes necessary to fight all along the line. And the flag has to be raised, the trumpet sounded, the labor detail recalled, the engineer squad summoned back, the line of battle drawn up, the courage of the troops whetted, and the signal given to fight—*omnia uno tempore agenda.*

In a peaceful, leisurely, roomy, full-scale course in composition and rhetoric, the problems of writing can be taken up one by one, all the long way from punctuation to polemics. Achievement occurs, then, by a gradual coalescence of solutions of problems. Who will say that it is not possible for a student to start by being a comma-hound and end up by being Demosthenes? We are all patriotic Americans, and we like gadgets. A correction chart is a very convenient gadget; it permits themes to be processed *en masse.* Attention to correction symbols may well be the first step an American student takes towards becoming president of the United States.

All the same, a punctuator must have something to punctuate. He does not (we hope) insert commas into a vacuum. To write even one sentence is a large commitment. What textbook and teacher are always putting asunder, the act of literary creation is always joining, for better or worse. The grammar, the rhetoric, the thought, the diction, the general organization—all fly together with an instantaneous affinity that may be confusing or even frightful, yet is splendid if by accident or design a proper union is arranged.

At any rate, such things must be attended to all together. The act of writing is not a piecemeal but an all-together matter—a verbal-grammatical-rhetorical-logical-scientific-artistic act. It is impossible to write or speak any other way—though the quality of such acts may follow a range of bad-worse-worst or good-better-best, as the case may be.

This book assumes, first, that a student may profit by confronting the verbal, grammatical, rhetorical, logical, scientific, artistic aspects of written composition in their all-together-ness—that is, in their natural union within the context of an acceptable—or preferably excellent—piece of prose. Momentarily, it is true, any one given aspect of the prose must be abstracted for the sober purpose of paying close attention to it, recognizing it for what it is, and learning its applicability and use. But this kind of abstraction is slight and carries little risk. It is different from the kind of abstraction encountered in a rule book since the feature to be examined is seen in its living context; it is not a mere dry specimen with a label stuck on it, isolated from the tissue where it was meant to dwell and function.

Whatever virtue of necessity must be conceded to the rule

book, various difficult problems are best studied in the context where they are well solved, and in the different contexts where different solutions may appear. There is, for example, the problem of grammar, which can be most difficult and dull when the study of grammar is attempted in the purely abstract environment of the typical handbook. In this author's opinion, grammar cannot be fully mastered for writing purposes, or at least will not disclose its true nature and use, until it is studied in conjunction with rhetoric—or "stylistics," if the more special term is preferred. Grammar and rhetoric have a positive educational value only when studied and practiced in such conjunction. If kept in separate categories and divorced from each other during instruction, grammar and rhetoric both tend to lose their positive quality. The teacher finds himself seeking merely to "correct mistakes," the student thinks first of avoiding mistakes, and both become habituated to makeshift solutions.

The second assumption of this book is that the student who, with proper guidance, engages in such positive study of prose will be better prepared for writing than if he had not followed such a positive, organic method. He will be strengthened to meet the attack of the Nervii. He will be more capable of "doing everything at once" because, like Caesar's legions, he will have acquired *scientia et usus* through previous battle experience and so will be "no less able to tell himself what to do than to be taught by others." This assumption is a little dangerous, as every teacher knows. In the republic of letters the equalitarian principle does not hold good. Inevitably *aristoi* move to the top, and *hoi polloi* seem less movable than the benches they occupy. Still, from classic times to the present, no one has found a good way to teach writing without the use of models and of exercises and theme projects based on the models. The only question is as to methods of teaching, study, and practice.

No doubt there are perfectly good arguments for immersing the student in the destructive element and letting him swim as best he can. The present textbook, however, does not follow that large and daring conception. Lesson by lesson, it is intended to call the student's attention to whatever aspects of composition and rhetoric can be fruitfully examined in a single short selection or in a pair or group of selections. Although the selections vary in length, they have mostly been kept within relatively brief limits in order to insure intensiveness of study. The lessons are lessons, not "assignments." A lesson may include one or more assignments, according to the discretion of the instructor. The term *lesson* is used on the assumption that educational institutions actually are what they profess to be—places where teachers do teach and students do learn. Each lesson has its particular focus, but there is also some deliberate overlapping and repetition in the series of lessons, since the principles of grammar, rhetoric, and the like, however stable in theory, vary greatly in their application to different contexts. Each of the principal selections is accompanied by a set of questions—many of which are inevitably "leading" questions—together with some exercises, suggestions for themes, and other relevant material. This instructional apparatus is not intended to be prescriptive and can be used selectively, or supplemented, or passed by, as need and wish may decide. The selections have been chosen and the instructional material arranged so as to cover, during the "twenty lessons," the essentials of composition and rhetoric—and much besides, including some acquaintance with various strategies of writing and with the world of men and ideas, past and present.

Since some emphasis is placed in the instructional material upon sentence analysis, a part of Lesson XX is given to specimen analyses of sentences, followed by a selection of sentences upon which grammatical-rhetorical analysis may be practiced if the instructor wishes to make such an assignment. Also included in Lesson XX are a group of passages, mostly short, unaccompanied by questions or other instructional material. These passages are supplied with the thought that they may be useful for occasional supplementary studies, as the instructor may direct, which will be trials of the student's ability to proceed *without* the guidance elsewhere provided.

DONALD DAVIDSON

Vanderbilt University
Nashville, Tennessee

CONTENTS

PART ONE

SIMPLE NARRATIVE: AUTOBIOGRAPHY AND REMINISCENCE

For a man to write well, there are required three necessaries: to read the best authors, observe the best speakers, and much exercise of his own style.—Ben Jonson, *Timber: or Discoveries Made upon Men and Matter.*

LESSON I

Straight Narrative: Plain Prose.

ENCOUNTER WITH A RHEA *

by W. H. HUDSON

These rough plains were also the haunt of the rhea, our ¶ 1
ostrich, and it was here that I first had a close sight of this greatest and most unbird-like bird of our continent. I was eight years old then, when one afternoon in late summer just as I was setting off for a ride on my pony, I was told to go out on the east side till I came to the cardoon-covered land about a mile beyond the shepherd's ranch. The shepherd was wanted in the plantation and could not go to the flock just yet, and I was told to look for the flock and turn it towards home.

I found the flock just where I had been told to look for it, ¶ 2
the sheep very widely scattered, and some groups of a dozen or two to a hundred were just visible at a distance among the rough bushes. Just where these furthest sheep were grazing there was a scattered troop of seventy or eighty horses grazing too, and when I rode to that spot I all at once found myself among a lot of rheas, feeding too among the sheep and horses. Their grey plumage being so much like the cardoon bushes in colour had prevented me from seeing them before I was right among them.

The strange thing was that they paid not the slightest ¶ 3
attention to me, and, pulling up my pony, I sat staring in astonishment at them, particularly at one, a very big one and nearest to me, engaged in leisurely pecking at the clover

*From the book, *Far Away and Long Ago,* by W. H. Hudson. Copyright, 1946, The Royal Society for the Protection of Birds. Published by E. P. Dutton & Co., Inc. Reprinted by permission of the publishers. The text of Sen. 2, Par. 1, has been slightly altered.

plants growing among the big prickly thistle leaves, and as it seemed carefully selecting the best sprays.

LESSON I ¶ 4 What a great noble-looking bird it was and how beautiful in its loose grey-and-white plumage, hanging like a picturesquely-worn mantle about its body! Why were they so tame? I wondered. The sight of a mounted gaucho, even at a great distance, will invariably set them off at their topmost speed; yet I was within a dozen yards of one of them, with several others about me, all occupied in examining the herbage and selecting the nicest-looking leaves to pluck, just as if I was not there at all! I suppose it was because I was only a small boy on a small horse and was not associated in the ostrich brain with the wild-looking gaucho on his big animal charging upon him with a deadly purpose. Presently I went straight at the one near me, and he raised his head and neck and moved carelessly away to a distance of a few yards, then began cropping the clover once more. I rode at him again, putting my pony to a trot, and when within two yards of him he all at once swung his body round in a quaint way towards me, and breaking into a sort of dancing trot brushed past me.

Straight Narrative Plain Prose

¶ 5 Pulling up again and looking back I found he was ten or twelve yards behind me, once more quietly engaged in cropping clover leaves!

¶ 6 Again and again this bird, and one of the others I rode at, practised the same pretty trick, first appearing perfectly unconcerned at my presence and then, when I made a charge at them, with just one little careless movement placing themselves a dozen yards behind me.

¶ 7 But this same trick of the rhea is wonderful to see when the hunted bird is spent with running and is finally overtaken by one of the hunters who has perhaps lost the bolas with which he captures his quarry, and who endeavours to place himself side by side with it so as to reach it with his knife. It seems an easy thing to do: the bird is plainly exhausted, panting, his wings hanging, as he lopes on, yet no sooner is the man within striking distance than the sudden motion comes into play, and the bird as by a miracle is now behind instead of at the side of the horse. And before the horse going at top speed can be reined in and turned round, the rhea has had time to recover his wind and get a hundred yards away or more. It is on account of this tricky instinct of the rhea that the gauchos say, "El avestruz es el mas *gaucho* de los animales," which means that the ostrich, in its resourcefulness and the tricks it practises to save itself when hard pressed, is as clever as the gaucho knows himself to be.

EXERCISES

I. The simplest task in prose composition, it might appear, is to tell in plain, straight-forward language "what happened" in some particular situation. If a writer cannot do that much—if he cannot relate a simple happening in a clear and orderly way—then how can he be competent to discuss such perplexing subjects as the procession of the equinoxes, the pains of love, the ups and downs of politics? The task may turn out to be not quite as easy as it seems. At any rate it is a fundamental task— as fundamental for the writer as a simple charcoal drawing of an apple or a vase may be for the artist. Therefore it may well serve as a beginning here.

The component elements of W. H. Hudson's brief narrative are indeed simple and matter-of-fact: a boy, eight years old, is told to go and look for a flock of sheep; he does so, and finds not only the sheep and some horses, but also a flock of strange birds, rheas or ostriches; this is his first sight of the strange creatures; he observes them with amazement, while they, queerly enough, pay him little attention; with effortless unconcern, they elude his approaches, but he is able to study them carefully.

Consider, first, the *arrangement* or *order* of "Encounter with a Rhea." It obviously follows the arrangement or order of the events themselves as they actually occurred, without any juggling or distortion of their sequence. Furthermore, this sequence of events divides rather naturally into certain *stages of action,* in each of which there is more or less elaboration of detail. Without this elaboration of detail—this necessary dwelling upon particulars—the narrative would consist only of generalities. It would be only a bare summary such as is given in the preceding paragraph. Note also that the author devotes a greater amount of attention, proportionately, to one or two of these stages than to others.

The arrangement of the composition may be represented in a scheme or outline like the following:

I. My mission (Par. 1)
II. Finding the flock of sheep and, with them, the rheas (Par. 2)
III. In astonishment, I observe the rheas
  A. But they pay no attention to me (Par. 3)
  B. One rhea, in particular, attracts me
    1. I wonder why he is so "tame"
    2. I experiment by riding at him
    3. He evades me easily (Pars. 4, 5, 6)
IV. The trick of evasion is practiced by the rhea
  A. When closely pursued by a gaucho
  B. The gauchoes have a "saying" (Par. 7)

Note that, in the outline, Division I corresponds to Par. 1, and Division 2 to Par. 2. Division IV also covers but one paragraph. But Division III covers four paragraphs (3, 4, 5, 6); and the three "minor" subdivisions of Division III correspond to three paragraphs.

It is evident that the successive topics of the paragraphs, set down in sequence, accurately represent the *order* of the composition, but not its *logical organization*—that is, the inter-relationship of part to part.

With these points in mind, answer the following questions:

A. What is the most important "stage" or "part" of the series of events?

B. How is its relative importance indicated in the composition?

C. What is the function of the first sentence, Par. 1 ("These rough plains . . . our continent") in (1) the paragraph where it stands and (2) in the composition as a whole?

D. What is the function of Par. 1 in the composition as a whole?

E. How do you account for the brevity of Pars. 3, 5, 6 and, in comparison, the length of Pars. 4 and 7?

F. Are paragraphs in narrative writing subject to the same rules of development as paragraphs in expository and argumentative writing? That is, must narrative paragraphs have a "topic sentence" which is "developed" by various methods?

II. *Far Away and Long Ago,* from which the selection is taken, is the autobiography of W. H. Hudson, a great naturalist who was also one of the finest of modern writers. (He wrote, among other books, the famous novel, *Green Mansions.*) The autobiography was written in his later years, when, during a long illness, he discovered that recollections of his childhood on the Argentine pampas were entering his mind with unusual vividness. "It was," he says, "as if the cloud shadows and haze had passed away and the entire prospect beneath me made clearly visible. Over it all my eyes could range at will, choosing this point and that point to dwell on, to examine in all its details." Propped on a pillow, he wrote his book.

Here we have, then, a man past middle age, remembering his childhood and "examining" it point by point. The word "examine" is important in a study of Hudson's prose. He is writing not only as a mature man but as a naturalist—a scientist trained to observe and to record. We may well strive to discover how far such circumstances influence his prose—even matters that we habitually pass over without much notice. Bear in mind, for example, that the dominant tense of narrative is usually "past tense"; that the mature man is "reporting" the experience of a boy eight years old— *but not in the language such a boy would use;* and that the habits of the scientific observer will influence to some extent Hudson's attitude toward his subject, his general procedure, his sentence constructions, and his choice of words. Answer the following questions:

A. If the tense of narrative is "past" tense, explain the tense of the verb in: "where I had been told to look for it" (Par. 2); "will invariably set them off" (Par. 4).

B. Why is Par. 7 written in present tense? Is this paragraph so far out of relationship to the preceding paragraphs that it constitutes a violation of unity in the composition?

C. Or, on the other hand, are past tense, present tense, and other tenses used, correctly and appropriately, throughout the composition to reflect the inter-relationships of the events observed?

D. To what extent does this change of tenses reflect the different viewpoints of the eight-year-old boy and the mature naturalist? Are the two points of view blended or do they conflict? Do you find instances, other than tense-forms, in which the double-view is manifested?

III. In a simple, matter-of-fact narrative like Hudson's the movement of the sentences is "straight-forward" and free of subtle complications. One mark of such straight-forwardness is the prevalence of *normal word order:* i.e., the *subject—verb—object* (or *complement*) sequence of sentence elements that is characteristic of English syntax. Another mark of straight-forwardness is the tendency to link sentence elements in coördinate relationships—to join words, phrases, and clauses by *and* and *but*—and to avoid difficult subordinate constructions. The sentences "grow" by a process of "addition" and "move" easily and informally, as if the writer were not taking any particular trouble to shape them in varied rhetorical patterns. Study Hudson's use of coördinate constructions as indicated below.

A. Analyze the sentence beginning "The shepherd was wanted. . . ." (Par. 1, last sentence)

B. Beginning in Par. 4 with the sentence, "The sight of a mounted gaucho. . . .", identify all coördinate elements and describe their function in the structure of the sentence in which they appear. In describing their function, deal not only with their grammatical function, but also with their effectiveness.

C. Make similar identifications for both coördinate and subordinate elements in the sentences of Par. 7. Is there a good reason for the prevalence of subordinate constructions in this paragraph?

IV. It was said above that Hudson's composition is "matter-of-fact." That is to say, he avoids emotional coloring, and on the whole he is content to record physical details without expressing a personal reaction. He does not seek out words that will appeal to the senses. In general, he avoids "figurative" language. Study his prose with a view to discovering the extent to which Hudson's matter-of-factness is due to his avoidance of adjectival and adverbial expressions.

A. To what extent does Hudson tend to use nouns, pronouns, and verbs (the fundamental sentence elements) *without* accompanying modifiers? Note, for example, Sen. 3 in Par. 1. Are there many other sentences like this?

B. When Hudson uses adjective and adverb forms, does he prefer "colorful" expressions or expressions of a rather simple and general kind? In this connection, consider such expressions as *rough* plains", "*close* sight" (Par. 1); "these *furthest* sheep," "a *scattered* troop of . . . horses." "Their *grey* plumage" (Par. 2); "engaged in *leisurely* pecking," "*carefully* selecting the *best* sprays" (Par. 3). Make a list of adjectival and adverbial expressions that are "matter-of-fact" and another list of expressions that are more "imaginative." What do these lists reveal as to the nature of Hudson's diction?

C. Study Hudson's use of participial constructions (as, for example, "pulling" . . . "staring" . . . "engaged" in Par. 3). Does Hudson tend, here and elsewhere, to "add" participial constructions after his nouns and pronouns, instead of converting these expressions into clauses? Is this use of participles a characteristic feature of his prose style? Is it effective? (Do not confuse participles with gerunds. In Par. 3, for example, you should note that certain *-ing* forms are gerunds, not participles.)

D. Is the last sentence in Par. 4 a grammatically correct sentence? Is "when within two yards of him" a dangling elliptical clause, or not? If you consider the sentence faulty, how would you go about improving it?

E. Account for Hudson's use of such uncommon words as *gaucho, cardoon, bola.* Look these words up in your dictionary. Was it necessary and proper for him to use these words? Should he have used them without an accompanying explanation?

F. Look up the derivation and meaning of *plantation* (Par. 1), *cropping* (Par. 4), *quarry* (Par. 7). Are they familiar to you, in the meaning Hudson uses? Are they appropriate to his context? Would any of the possible synonyms of these words suit as well?

V. Write a theme in which you relate some "first encounter" that you have experienced. Follow Hudson's method. Try to be straight-forward, simple, unpretentious. Avoid the temptation to enlarge upon your special personal reactions in the situation you are dealing with. Be matter-of-fact. If you have become aware that Hudson produces an effect of strangeness, wonderment, and excitement even though he is matter-of-fact, try to decide how he obtains such an effect and see whether you, too, can achieve it.

THE BALANCE SHEET OF ROBINSON CRUSOE *

by DANIEL DEFOE

LESSON 1

Straight Narrative Plain Prose

¶ 1 After I had been there about ten or twelve days, it came into my thoughts that I should lose my reckoning of time for want of books, and pen and ink, and should even forget the Sabbath days from the working days: but, to prevent this, I cut it with my knife upon a large post, in capital letters; and making it into a great cross, I set it up on the shore where I first landed, viz., "I came on shore here on the 30th of September, 1659." Upon the sides of this square post I cut every day a notch with my knife, and every seventh notch was as long again as the rest, and every first day of the month as long again as that long one: and thus I kept my calendar, or weekly, monthly, and yearly reckoning of time.

¶ 2 But it happened, that among the many things which I brought out of the ship, in the several voyages which, as above mentioned, I made to it, I got several things of less value, but not at all less useful to me, which I found, some time after, in rummaging the chests: as, in particular, pens, ink, and paper; several parcels in the captain's, mate's, gunner's, and the carpenter's keeping; three or four compasses, some mathematical instruments, dials, perspectives, charts, and books of navigation; all of which I huddled together whether I might want them or no; also I found three very good Bibles, which came to me in my cargo from England, and which I had packed up among my things; some Portuguese books also, and, among them, two or three popish prayer-books, and several other books, all which I carefully secured. And I must not forget, that we had in the ship a dog, and two cats, of whose eminent history I may have occasion to say something, in its place; for I carried both the cats with me; and as for the dog, he jumped out of the ship himself, and swam on shore to me the day after I went on shore with my first cargo, and was a trusty servant to me for many years: I wanted nothing that he could fetch me, nor

* From *Robinson Crusoe.*

any company that he could make up to me, I only wanted to
have him talk to me, but that would not do. As I observed
before, I found pens, ink, and paper, and I husbanded them LESSON I
to the utmost; and I shall show that while my ink lasted, I
kept things very exact, but after that was gone, I could not;
for I could not make any ink, by any means that I could
devise.

And this put me in mind that I wanted many things, not- ¶ 3
withstanding all that I had amassed together; and of these,
this of ink was one; as also a spade, pickaxe, and shovel, to
dig or remove the earth; needles, pins, and thread; as for
linen, I soon learned to want that without much difficulty.

This want of tools made every work I did go on heavily; ¶ 4
and it was near a whole year before I had entirely finished
my little pale, or surrounded my habitation. The piles of
stakes, which were as heavy as I could well lift, were a long
time in cutting and preparing in the woods, and more by far,
in bringing home; so that I spent sometimes two days in cutting and bringing home one of those posts, and a third day
in driving it into the ground; for which purpose, I got a
heavy piece of wood at first, but at last bethought myself of
one of the iron crows; which, however, though I found it answer, made driving those posts or piles very laborious and
tedious work. But what need I have been concerned at the
tediousness of anything I had to do, seeing I had time enough
to do it in? nor had I any other employment, if that had been
over, at least that I could foresee, except the ranging the island to seek for food, which I did, more or less, every day.

I now began to consider seriously my condition, and the ¶ 5
circumstance I was reduced to; and I drew up the state of
my affairs in writing, not so much to leave them to any that
were to come after me (for I was like to have but few heirs),
as to deliver my thoughts from daily poring upon them, and
afflicting my mind: and as my reason now began to master
my despondency, I began to comfort myself as well as I
could, and to set the good against the evil, that I might have
something to distinguish my case from worse; and I stated

very impartially, like debtor and creditor, the comforts I enjoyed against the miseries I suffered, thus:

LESSON I

Straight Narrative Plain Prose

EVIL		GOOD
I am cast upon a horrible, desolate island, void of all hope of recovery.	¶ 6	But I am alive; and not drowned, as all my ship's company were.
I am singled out and separated, as it were, from all the world, to be miserable.	¶ 7	But I am singled out too from all the ship's crew, to be spared from death; and He that miraculously saved me from death, can deliver me from this condition.
I am divided from mankind, a solitaire; one banished from human society.	¶ 8	But I am not starved, and perishing in a barren place, affording no sustenance.
I have no clothes to cover me.	¶ 9	But I am in a hot climate, where, if I had clothes, I could hardly wear them.
I am without any defence, or means to resist any violence of man or beast.	¶ 10	But I am cast on an island where I see no wild beasts to hurt me, as I saw on the coast of Africa: and what if I had been shipwrecked there?
I have no soul to speak to, or relieve me.	¶ 11	But God wonderfully sent the ship in near enough to the shore, that I have got out so many necessary things, as will either supply my wants, or enable me to supply myself, even as long as I live.

¶ 12 Upon the whole, here was an unbounded testimony, that there was scarce any condition in the world so miserable, but there was something negative, or something positive, to be thankful for in it; and let this stand as a direction, from the experience of the most miserable of all conditions in this world, that we may always find in it something to comfort ourselves from, and to set, in the description of good and evil, on the credit side of the account.

Having now brought my mind a little to relish my condition, and given over looking out to sea, to see if I could spy a ship; having, I say, given over these things, I began to apply myself to accommodate my way of living, and to make things as easy to me as I could. ¶ 13

EXERCISES

At first glance, Daniel Defoe's classic account of Robinson Crusoe's "miserable condition" may seem as simple, matter-of-fact, and straight-forward as Hudson's "Encounter with a Rhea." Close inspection will reveal that, despite the simplicity of Defoe's style, he is much less matter-of-fact and straight-forward than Hudson. His narrative—whatever may have been its supposed basis in fact—is a fictional account. It does not represent Defoe's individual and personal experience, but the experience of an imaginary person who, being isolated from civilization by shipwreck on a desert island, uses his human "good sense," or his natural capacity for reason, to restore himself to something like a civilized condition. Robinson Crusoe is a *type* of the rational man rather than an *individual.* His "autobiography" becomes the instrument of Defoe's "thesis" or "argument." It is "impersonal" to the extent that Defoe uses Crusoe as the "reporter" of his outcast state. But though much is said in the narrative about the "hard facts" of Crusoe's experience, the emphasis is on the subjective or abstract side—on how the rational mind of the hero copes with disaster. It is Crusoe's rational attitude that makes the "hard facts" significant. Otherwise, the experience might have become merely a "sensational" affair—a startling account of an exciting adventure, as indeed it even now seems to childish or immature persons.

I. Make a topical outline of the selection. In planning your outline, take into consideration the following questions:

A. Is the true subject of the narrative stated in Par. 1? Or does this paragraph serve merely as an "introduction" which is intended to convey information as to time, place, and condition?

B. Does Defoe state, anywhere near the beginning, the subject (or "thesis") which dominates his narrative?

C. If this subject is not indicated near the beginning, where is it specifically set forth? Note that, while Hudson in his first sentence says, ". . . it was here that I first had a close sight of this greatest and most unbird-like bird," and then goes on to the details of that "first sight," Defoe's procedure is quite different.

D. After making your topical outline, compare it with the outline of the Hudson selection, on page 6. What conclusion do you reach as to the possible methods of organizing a composition? Under what circumstances is it preferable to proceed from the general to the particular, or the reverse? Are the two methods equally valid? Are the terms *deduction* and *induction* applicable as descriptions of the two methods?

II. Why does Defoe use present tense in the "dialogue" between Evil and Good? Does he use present tense for the same reason that Hudson used it in "Encounter with a Rhea"? Could the dialogue passage have been written with equal effectiveness in past tense? Before answering the question, write a passage, in a style as much like Defoe's as you can contrive, which puts the material of the dialogue into past tense.

III. Study carefully the sentence structure of Par. 1. In making your study, deal with the following questions:

A. What change in "normal order" is involved in the constructions referred to below? (Use grammatical terms in your identification and discussion of sentence elements.)

1. "After I had been there . . . it came into my thoughts that . . . ."
2. ". . . to prevent this, I cut it with my knife . . . ."
3. "Upon the sides of this square post I cut . . . ."
4. ". . . and thus I kept . . . ."

B. What sentences or parts of sentences are in normal order?

C. The paragraph, as punctuated by Defoe, contains only two "sentences," each elaborate in its construction but simple in language. What is the value of the following words or phrases in binding together the long and elaborate sentences: "to prevent *this*"; "of *this* square post"; "*every* day . . . *every* seventh notch . . . as the rest; *every* first day . . . *that* long *one* . . . and *thus* . . ." What do you conclude as to the value of pronouns, pronominal expressions, and repetitions in binding together the elements of sentences or paragraphs? Is "transitional expressions" a proper term for such constructions?

D. Study Defoe's use of *it* in Par. 1. Give the antecedent—if one appears—in each sentence where *it* is used.

IV. What distinction between *value* and *use* is implied in Par. 2? Note that the structure of this paragraph affords an instance of the simplest or most primitive use of "particulars" to support a general statement. The particulars are merely set down in a list or "inventory." What is the difference between such a use of particulars and the method followed in Hudson's Par. 7? Is it possible that Defoe used this very "primitive" kind of structure because his hero is thrown into a "primitive" or almost savage condition?

V. Defoe is in many ways the most English of English writers. His strongly English quality shows in his seemingly habitual use of small, familiar words, which are quite often of Saxon or North European origin. For example, *want, cut, post, packed, fetch.* Note, however, that his vocabulary becomes heavily Latinistic at some points.

A. In Par. 2, what words are of Latinistic or non-Saxon origin? Why is it necessary for Defoe to use these rather than more "English" or Saxon words?

B. Why is the diction of Pars. 5, 12, and 13, and of the dialogue, more abstract and Latinistic than the diction of other parts of the narrative?

C. Look up the following words in your dictionary and note *all* the meanings entered for each word: *reckoning* (Par. 1); *secured* (Par. 2); *eminent* (Par 2); *fetch* (Par. 2); *husbanded* (Par. 2); *want* (Par. 3); *pale* (Par. 4); *employment* (Par. 4); *testimony* (Par. 12); *relish* (Par. 13); *accommodate* (Par. 13).

Do you yourself use these words in the same meaning as Defoe does? If changes in meaning have occurred, from Defoe's day to ours, can you account for such changes? Are there any instances in which it would be useful to recall the *original* meaning of the word?

VI. Compare the following passage with Defoe's Par. 12:

> Little though I dreamed it, right then I was a thorough-going witness that there is no kind of wretchedness so painful but that a man may thank God either for being thus-and-so or for not being thus-and-so. Know, then, from one who has been through the worst pitch of wretchedness, that men can always take hope, no matter how bad off they may be, and can always find something to write on the good side of the sheet, if it comes to the pinch of weighing good against evil or evil against good.

Is the above better or worse than Defoe's paragraph? Give your reasons for your choice. Try a similar experiment of your own with Pars. 5 and 13.

VII. Write a paragraph, on a subject of your choosing, in which you follow the method of one of Defoe's paragraphs. Try to use both Defoe's simplicity of diction and his kind of sentence structure.

LESSON II

Matter-of-Fact Narrative.
Extraordinary and Ordinary Experience.
Patterns of Organization. Problems of Diction and Sentence Structure.

THE GREAT DECISION *

by AGNES DE MILLE

Sometime during the beginning of the sophomore year a ¶ 1
revue was put on in the college auditorium for the benefit of student victims of a campus fire. I volunteered and danced French *bergerettes* in the manner of Watteau and that was the first time in my life I stepped on a stage. The next day I was rushed by three sororities. I joined one which later became the Beta Xi chapter of Kappa Alpha Theta.

For four years this lovely life lasted. I continued in a happy ¶ 2
somnambulistic state, blousy, disheveled, dropping hairpins, tennis balls, and notebooks wherever I went, drinking tea with Dr. Lily Campbell and the professors, lapping up talk of books and history, drinking tea with classmates and Elizabeth Boynton, the librarian, having dates or nearly dates with the two *M*'s on either side of me, Macon and Morgan, having dates with Leonarde Keeler, who was working out campus thefts and misdemeanors with the first lie detector, falling asleep in all afternoon lectures, late for every appointment (once when I entered English history on time the whole class burst out laughing). With the smell of iris and budding acacia coming through the windows, the sound of scholasticism filling my dreams with a reassuring hum, I sank deeper and deeper into a kind of cerebral miasma as I postponed all

* From *Dance to the Piper,* by Agnes De Mille. Copyright 1951, 1952, by Agnes De Mille. Reprinted by permission of Little, Brown & Co., and the Atlantic Monthly Press.

vital decisions. I had some vague, soothing fantasy of living in Mother's garden indefinitely and studying until I slipped gracefully into old age while I wrote exquisitely about—what? No doubt it would all become apparent in time.

Matter-of-Fact Narrative . . .

¶ 3 Occasionally I staged dances for the student rallies, mostly to Chopin, mostly about yearning for beauty and always accompanied by sorority sisters who were not trained. Campbell shook her head. "This is not good," she said. "You simply haven't a dancer's body. I'd like you to write, but if you must go on the stage, act. I believe you're a tragic actress. Stop dancing. Look at yourself in the mirror."

¶ 4 In my junior year I presented a skit at the Press Club Vod based on the idea of how closely allied jazz dancing was to the jungle. I represented the jungle. Father for a wonder was in the house—he hadn't been up to this point—and was, along with the student body, markedly impressed. He told me next day with quiet gratification that my sketch made a real dramatic point, and that he thought it good enough to incorporate into his next picture. I went to bed dizzy. I lay awake hours planning each shot, thinking of lighting, rhythm, camera angles, experiments that I have never seen to this day. I prepared to write it all down and present it to him. But the next night he came home to dinner with the announcement that he had given the idea to Kosloff and told him to get to work on it. Kosloff thought it was good, he added.

¶ 5 I can't remember whether I left the table or not. Probably not. I probably ate as usual. But if he had slapped me I couldn't have been more stunned. And yet I was not wholly unprepared. Father simply could not consider any member of his household as a professional with professional rights. He must have noticed something of my bitter disappointment. He was extremely uncomfortable for a few hours, but he came home the next night with everything solved; he had decided not to use the dance after all.

¶ 6 I usually danced about Beauty and how one should be ready to die for it. I did a good number of Petrarch's sonnets at one football rally when the men got their letters. I suspect the student body must have had pretty nearly enough of me. But this last performance had one happy aspect. I dressed the girls exactly like Botticelli nymphs with draperies split to the crotch and was forthwith summoned into the director's office to explain why. Dr. Moore knew all about Botticelli; he was also acquainted with eighteen-year-old glands. I listened with profound respect but refused to alter a stitch.

¶ 7 In order to get back up on my numb points, I had started exercising again. At first only for a couple of weeks before each show, but gradually, with God knows what contingency in mind, because I swear I had banished from conscious intention all thought of going back on the stage, I got to practicing every day. It could not be for very long, and it was always late at night after I had finished studying. I used to fall asleep over my books, and then toward midnight force myself awake, and shaking with fatigue perform between the bureau and the closet mirrors, *relevés* in every position, on toes that went pins and needles with the unexpected pressure. I tried not to shake the floor out of concern for the sleeping family. Once, while I prodded along the upstairs hall in a particularly stumpy *pas de bourrée,* Father stepped out of his study, pipe in one hand, book in the other, and contemplated me. I kept going. I was in my petticoat, face blanched and wet with weariness. At length he spoke, "All this education and I'm still just the father of a circus." He went back in his room and shut the door.

¶ 8 At the Pasadena Playhouse, Margaret had spotted a young actor she thought she'd like to get better acquainted with. She engineered a meeting, that is, she gave out the order that he was to be brought to the house on a Sunday night, and he was brought. His name was Douglass Montgomery, and he turned out to have good manners and a pleasant husky charm. Mag liked him fine. She arranged to take him through the Fairbanks studio, which was the second step in her softening-up routine. He came the following Sunday. Mag was dressed to kill in white silk, a dazzling white coat, a white cloche on her sleek dark hair. She sported gardenias and fake pearls. I thought she looked, as always, just ravishing. I was dressed in a dirty red practice tunic, and I had all the living room rugs rolled back to the wall. Mag met him at the garden gate and whisked him around to the tennis court where the lively twanging of rackets and the yelping of our seven dogs gave evidence of Father's Sunday fun. "But what is that going on in the house?" said Douglass, turning his head. "Oh that," said Mag, "never mind about that. That is just my sister Agnes, who practices dancing on Sunday afternoon."

¶ 9 "I would like to see," said Douglass, and although she resisted, he maneuvered her back. There was no use in apologizing for the way I looked. Nobody looked the way I did who expected to be seen by anyone else. "Do you do this where people can watch you?" he asked.

¶ 10 "Well," I said with great misgiving. "This Friday . . . it's just amateur . . . ."

¶ 11 "I'll come," said Dug.

¶ 12 Dug came. He stood backstage at the Friday Morning Club and looked me hard in the face. He trembled a little. There were tears of excitement in his eyes. (Dug was only seventeen.) He spoke in a very low voice. He put a cigarette in his mouth, but his lips shook. "Look here. You're no amateur. You're a very great performer. You belong to the world. Get out of the university. Stop this nonsense. Get into the theater. You've got a calling. You've got a duty. It's hard to say. Are you listening to me? You're a great dancer."

¶ 13 No trumpets sound when the important decisions of our life are made. Destiny is made known silently. The wheels turn within our hearts for years and suddenly everything meshes and we are lifted into the next level of progress. In a crowd of fussing club-women, overdressed, chattering, impatient to get to their chicken patties and ice cream, the laborious battlements my father had erected with all the sincerity of his heart and life fell before one sentence. This boy simply said what I had waited all my life to hear.

EXERCISES

I. At first reading, "The Great Decision" may seem as casually arranged as the four years of college life described in Par. 2—the "happy, somnambulistic state" in which dates with the M's, talks with professors, and fantasies of the future are confusedly mixed. More careful reading should disclose that the composition has a definite *theme* or *central idea* and a form appropriate to the theme. "The Great Decision," however, is very different in style and method from the two preceding selections. Hudson and Defoe are, on the whole, objective, impersonal, matter-of-fact. Hudson proceeds from the general to the particular; Defoe from the particular to the general. Each writes in a plain, systematic, unemotional way. Agnes De Mille deals in surprises, ridiculous incongruities, anticlimaxes. Her procedure is to take the reader through a series of violent contrasts—jangling discords which only at the end are resolved in firm harmony. *Contrast*—the clash of opposites—dominates the composition until the "great decision" is made. Once that decision is made, it becomes clear that, as it was Agnes' avoidance of her true role that brought about uncertainty and hence disarrangement of life, so it is appropriate that the composition should reflect that disarrangement in its method and tone. The composition, however, only simulates this disarrangement. Actually, the composition is rather subtly organized.

A. What is the function of Par. 13 and, in particular, of the sentence beginning, "The wheels turn . . . ."?

B. Make a study of the incongruities and anticlimaxes that are depicted or suggested in "The Great Decision." For example, a ridiculous incongruity seems to be intended in the following sentences: "I . . . danced French *bergerettes* in the manner of Watteau. . . . The next day I was rushed by three sororities." (Par. 1) For complete understanding of the "contrast" here, you will need to know what *bergerettes* and *Watteau* mean and imply. Find other passages in which incongruities or contrasts, major and minor, are used for their effect rather than as mere items of fact.

C. Would the composition have been more effective if it had begun with some *explicit* statement like the following?

> My outward activities, during my college years, had nothing to do with my inner life. In fact, what I pretended to be, and had persuaded myself I truly wanted to be, was in grotesque contrast with my real purpose in life. I behaved like any other mixed-up undergraduate, but all the time, even though I would not admit it to myself, I was a ballet dancer at heart—an artist.

D. What is the difference between *explicit* interpretation of ideas or events and *implicit* representation of them? Give examples of passages in which Agnes De Mille makes an explicit interpretation or explanation and of other passages in which something is implied that is not stated or explained in an obvious, forthright manner.

E. In the general scheme of contrasts—which includes some arrayal of conflicting forces—what is the role of Dr. Campbell? Of Father (William C. De Mille)? Of Margaret? Of Douglass Montgomery? Of the students? Does Agnes De Mille give a complete account of her studies, friends, teachers, and activities, or does she select only those that best represent her own state of mind during the period described? How are the episodes placed in which "friends" and "foes" appear? That is, does the author follow a strictly chronological order of events or does she arrange incidents in such a way as to emphasize her theme and to point toward the conclusion? How is lapse of time indicated? How are the several episodes linked?

II. Make a study of how varied sentence patterns are used to depict the state of mind of a passively wavering, very much undecided undergraduate. "A," below, indicates how this study may be made.

A. Sen. 2, Par. 2, begins, "I continued in a happy, somnambulistic state. . . ." We might expect that this fairly simple assertion would be followed by a series of *sentences* of average length in which the details of the "somnambulistic state" would be set forth. Instead, a single sentence is extended to an abnormal length. The extension consists of an elaborate series of phrases, nearly all of which are organized around an *-ing* word (present participle). Before deciding on the appropriateness and effectiveness of this unusual sentence, be sure to observe its grammatical and rhetorical pattern. Note that the simple subject ("I") and the simple predicate ("continued"), though grammatically essential, constitute only a small and, rhetorically, an unimportant part of the sentence. From the standpoint of emphasis, the key phrase is "in a happy, somnambulistic state." It is a prepositional phrase, modifying the verb "continued" and therefore functions as an adverbial modifier. The real substance and force of the sentence lie in this phrase and in the series of phrases following, which support and elaborate its meaning.

1. Distinguish the *-ing* phrases and their subdivisions.
2. What do these phrases modify?
3. To what extent do they resemble each other in internal structure (parallelism)? To what extent do they differ in structure?

4. Does the parenthesis "(once when I entered . . . .)" constitute an admissible and effective sentence ending?

After you have finished your analysis of the sentence, give some reasons why it may be considered useful and effective at the point where it is used.

B. Make a similar study of the following sentences or groups of sentences:

1. "I had some vague, soothing fantasy . . . ." (Par. 2)
2. "Occasionally I staged dances . . . ." (Par. 3)
3. The two sentences beginning: "In my junior year . . . ." (Par. 4)
4. "I lay awake hours . . . ." (Par. 4)
5. "I usually danced . . . ." (Par. 6)
6. "I listened . . . ." (Par. 6)
7. "I used to . . . ." (Par. 7)
8. "In a crowd of fussing club-women . . . ." (Par. 13)

In each of the sentences analyzed, note any key-words or key-phrases that are of great rhetorical importance. Note all instances in which "minor" grammatical elements (elements other than subject, predicate, or object) assume major importance, from the viewpoint of rhetoric, in the sentence pattern.

C. Make a study of how variety of sentence pattern is obtained in Par. 7. For present purposes, you may concentrate on two factors: (1) variation in *length;* (2) variation in *order* of sentence elements. For example, note that the long sentence, "I used to . . . unexpected pressure," is followed by a sentence of no great length. In the sentence "I used to fall asleep," the simple subject and simple predicate stand at the beginning of the sentence; but in the sentence "At first . . . every day" the simple subject and simple predicate are preceded by modifiers. Apply a similar analysis to other sentences of Par. 7 and—at the direction of your instructor—to sentences of other paragraphs.

III. Make a study of the use of deliberate overstatement and understatement in the selection. For example, "late for every appointment" (Par. 2) is probably overstatement. "Father . . . was, along with the student body, markedly impressed" (Par. 4) may well be an intentional understatement, especially in its reference to the student body. Find other examples.

IV. When Agnes De Mille uses phrases such as "yearning for beauty" (Par. 3) and "danced about Beauty" (Par. 6) is irony intended, or is she simply stating "facts"?

V. The diction and tone of "The Great Decision" are to a large extent "informal." The informality is due to the occasional lightening of the prose by (1) use of words or phrases that are actually colloquial or that echo the rhythm or manner of conversation; (2) use of slang; (3) use of dialogue; (4) use of lively metaphorical expressions that seem "slangy" but are not actual slang. Classify the following under the headings just indicated:

"a revue was put on" (Par. 1)
"The next day I was rushed" (Par. 1)
"lapping up talk" (Par. 2)
"having dates or nearly dates" (Par. 2)
"a kind of cerebal miasma" (Par. 2)
"I presented a skit" (Par. 4)
"I went to bed dizzy" (Par. 4)
"that he had given the idea to Kosloff and told him to get to work on it" (Par. 4)
"to get back up on my numb points" (Par. 7)
"on toes that went pins and needles" (Par. 7)
"While I prodded along the upstairs hall in a particularly stumpy *pas de bourrée*" (Par. 7)
"All this education and I'm still just the father of a circus" (Par. 7)
"Margaret had spotted a young actor" (Par. 8)
"She engineered a meeting" (Par. 8)
"Mag liked him fine" (Par. 8)
"the second step in her softening-up routine" (Par. 8)
"Mag was dressed to kill" (Par. 8)
"I thought she looked. . .just ravishing" (Par. 8)
"whisked him around to the tennis court" (Par. 8)

Are any of the expressions that you have classified as slang so commonplace or otherwise objectionable that they should not have been used? Is the author lavish or restrained in her use of slang and colloquialisms? Point out any passages in which she gives the effect of informality without resorting to slang or colloquialisms.

Distinguish and define all expressions that belong to the *cant*—technical or professional language—of the stage or ballet. Would it have been possible to avoid entirely such terms?

VI. Look up the derivation and meaning of the following words: *somnambulistic, campus, scholasticism, cerebral, miasma, jazz, contingency, petticoat, twanging, university.*

SALT-RISIN' BREAD *

by DELLA T. LUTES

LESSON II

In the days when men wrested almost an entire living from the soil, there was little talk about dieting, and little need of it. People, old and young, worked and walked and had small occasion for reducing girth or girdle. They ate strong food, and bread was believed to be the staff of life. Flour was not as yet too refined, and milk, or the water in which potatoes had been boiled, was used as liquid, lard from the crock as shortening, and the whole, when baked, provided a rich, luscious, and nutritious food from infancy to old age. ¶ 1

My father did not like yeast bread, however, and would not eat it. He said there was nothing to get your teeth into, and that it wasn't fit for a dog. My mother said, be that as it may, she was not going to feed it to the dog; that she liked it, that I liked it, and she was going to make it. To which my father replied that she could make it if she wanted to, and eat it, too, but as for him he wanted salt-risin' bread and he wanted it fresh. ¶ 2

So twice each week the big elevated oven yielded three fat, brown-crusted loaves of salt-risin' bread, along with an equal or greater number of loaves in which yeast cakes were the leavening power. And no one living at that time could have dreamed that in a few years the dry yeast cake would have gone the way of pungs, cutters, and dried apple sauce. ¶ 3

My mother never became quite reconciled to what seemed an unnecessary demand. She thoroughly disliked making salt-risin' bread. It was temperamental, required longer "raising," and took more time to bake. On one occasion my father, grown unusually testy from argument, clumped about the kitchen waving his arms, shouting, "Jumpin' Christopher! What's your time *for?* I don't ask much of you, do I?" ¶ 4

*From *The Country Kitchen,* by Della T. Lutes. Copyright 1935, 1936, by Della T. Lutes. Reprinted by permission of Little, Brown & Co. and the Atlantic Monthly Press.

¶ 5 This superfluous question my mother met with an enigmatical silence doubtless harder to bear by one of a controversial nature than argument, but nevertheless she continued to make salt-rising bread.

LESSON II

Matter-of-Fact Narrative . . .

¶ 6 Three loaves went into the oven at about nine o'clock, and although my father, from long years of anticipatory watchfulness, knew to a moment the hour of their consignment and the length of time it took to bake, he would invariably appear at the kitchen door within fifteen minutes to ask, "What time do you think it ought to be done?"

¶ 7 Mother would reply, "Oh, in about an hour, I guess. But you can't cut it when it's hot, you know"—being perfectly well aware that when it was hot was exactly when he did want to cut it, and would.

¶ 8 A fat-cheeked old silver watch that kept him company throughout his life apprised him of the time, but he never waited for the hour to expire. Within the half he would again appear at the door, eager and expectant.

¶ 9 "Bread done yet?" Craftily he would peer past her toward the oven as if he never quite trusted her computation of time.

¶ 10 "Mercy, no," she would reply leniently. "I've only just put it in."

¶ 11 He had various ways of employing himself during the last few minutes of waiting. In the winter he would fill the woodbox to overflowing, or he would shell corn for the hens, an occupation generally accorded to the leisure of evenings, but sometimes anticipated in order to provide an excuse for a position near the oven door. In summer he would go to the garden, pick two or three crisp young cucumbers, throw them into a pan of cold water, and demand testily to know whether that bread wasn't done *yet.*

¶ 12 To satisfy him my mother would open the oven door a crack and peer inside, only to close it again with the verdict, " 'Bout fifteen minutes more," delivered in a professional tone.

¶ 13 "Jiminy *Christopher!*" The explosion was mild in word

but electric in effect. "Can't you hurry it *up?* You want some more wood?"

"No," Mother would reply to both inquiries, "the fire's ¶ 14
all right and if you'd eat yeast bread it wouldn't take so long. You can't hurry salt-risin' bread."

Then my father would snort and clump his feet down hard, ¶ 15
and say he didn't see why she didn't bake it every day and then a man could have it when he wanted it, fresh.

No matter where he happened to be at the time, he seemed ¶ 16
to know the moment the bread came out of the oven, if indeed he was not on hand. My mother tried to insist that the bread should be turned out upon a clean towel and covered with another until it had cooled at least a little—but this was beyond my father's endurance. The only concession he would make was a sufficient time to peel the cucumbers that were cooling and put them lengthwise on a plate with a salt-cellar. This, with another plate filled with huge slices of hot bread generously buttered, was then carried out to our accustomed position on the back steps, where he and I would feast our corporeal selves on the nutty richness of salt-risin' bread and stock our souls with memories against another day.

I regret that I cannot give my mother's rule for salt- ¶ 17
rising bread, but I can quote one that was printed by the *Detroit Free Press* in 1881 and is probably similar to hers. "In the evening scald two tablespoonfuls of corn meal, a pinch of salt and one of sugar with sweet milk and set in a warm place until morning. [With the charming insouciance of old-time recipes this does not state how much milk, but I should judge it means just enough to make a mush, perhaps a cupful.] In the morning scald a teaspoonful of sugar, one of salt, half as much soda, with a pint of boiling water; add cold water till lukewarm, then put in the mush made the night before and thicken to a batter with flour; put in a closed vessel and set in a kettle of warm water (not too hot); when light mix stiff [presumably with flour], adding a little shortening; mould into loaves and let rise again. Then bake."

¶ 18 This rule does not say at what particular time the decidedly unpleasant odor peculiar to this kind of bread made itself known, but I am sure it was there when the "empt'in's" were uncovered in the morning. In all my two hundred cookbooks I have not been able to find a satisfactory recipe for making salt-rising bread.

EXERCISES

I. The general purpose of Della Lutes' book, *The Country Kitchen,* from which the preceding selection is taken, is to depict country life in Michigan. The kitchen is here the central point of reference from which family life is viewed. A subordinate but by no means unimportant purpose is to give the recipes for many old-fashioned dishes that the family relished at various seasons. Della Lutes' prose is as quiet, direct, and unpretentious as the prose of Agnes De Mille is—. But at this point it may be profitable for you yourself to make the critical comparison and to say in what respects the two selections are like or unlike. Following the procedure used for the De Mille selection, set down the "points" on which you think it is fair to judge the two authors, if a comparison is to be made. Make an analysis of the Lutes selection, according to the scheme that you have decided on. Then write a critical review of the two selections in which you describe the methods of the two authors and attempt to arrive at an estimate of their merits or faults.

II. During the course of your study of "Salt-risin' Bread" you may have occasion to notice the features of usage, grammar, or rhetoric referred to in the following questions:

A. Why does Della Lutes use expressions "in pairs" in the first two sentences of Par. 1 ("little talk about dieting, and little need of it"; "old and young"; "worked and walked"; "girth or girdle")? Is this use of pairs effective?

B. What are the grammatical constituents of the four-member series out of which Sen. 4, Par. 1, is formed?

C. Why is the language of Father and Mother reported in indirect quotation in Par. 2, but at other points (as in Par. 4) in dialogue? Identify all passages in which indirect rather than direct quotation is used.

D. In Pars. 7-12, underline all words or phrases, other than conjunctions, that serve as connectives. Determine the grammatical function of each such connective. Note that, though your grammar may define a *conjunction* as "a word that joins other words, phrases, or clauses," conjunctions are by no means the only words that "connect" in a rhetorical sense.

E. Explain the tense and mood of the following verbs: *met, continued* (Par. 5); *knew, would appear* (Par. 6); *would reply, did want, would (cut)* (Par. 7); *waited, would appear* (Par. 8). Why does the author use the *would*-construction at some points but not at others? (That is, why does she not write "my mother would meet" and "my mother would continue" instead of "met" and "continued"?) Study the author's use of *would,* Pars. 9-15. Are there instances in which another verb form should be preferred?

F. Study the order of the sentence elements in the sentences referred to below.

1. "To satisfy him . . . ." (Par. 12)
2. "No matter where . . . ." (Par. 16)
3. "The only concession . . . ." (Par. 16)
4. "In all my two hundred cookbooks . . . ." (Par. 18)

In each sentence, identify simple subject, simple predicate, and their modifiers; give the syntax of all substantives and their modifiers.

III. Why are brackets used instead of parentheses in Par. 17? What is the verb-form used in the following: *scald, set, add, thicken, mix, let rise, bake?* To what extent is the language of the recipe elliptical? In what situations is such elliptical language permissible?

IV. Suggestions for themes. Draw upon your personal experience—in school, college, or elsewhere—for material for an autobiographical theme of one of the following types:

A. A theme dealing with "extraordinary" events. The narrative should be so constructed that the events, however unusual, will seem credible or at least not unreasonable, once they are brought into focus, perhaps through the meaning supplied (as in Agnes De Mille's account) at a decisive moment.

B. A theme dealing with some event or series of events of apparently only "ordinary" or every-day character into which you infuse more than ordinary interest by depicting (as in Della Lutes' account) a subdued clash of personalities or other kind of conflict.

LESSON III

Exposition of Typical and Individual Objects. The General and the Particular. Use of Source Material.

THE INNS OF ENGLAND IN THE SEVENTEENTH CENTURY *

by THOMAS BABINGTON MACAULAY

¶ 1 All the various dangers by which the traveller was beset were greatly increased by darkness. He was therefore commonly desirous of having the shelter of a roof during the night; and such shelter it was not difficult to obtain. From a very early period the inns of England had been renowned. Our first great poet had described the excellent accommodation which they afforded to the pilgrims of the fourteenth century. Nine and twenty persons, with their horses, found room in the wide chambers and stables of the Tabard in Southwark. The food was of the best, and the wines such as drew the company on to drink largely. Two hundred years later, under the reign of Elizabeth, William Harrison gave a lively description of the plenty and comfort of the great hostelries. The Continent of Europe, he said, could show nothing like them. There were some in which two or three hundred people, with their horses, could without difficulty be lodged and fed. The bedding, the tapestry, above all, the abundance of clean and fine linen was matter of wonder. Valuable plate was often set on the tables. Nay, there were signs which had cost thirty or forty pounds.

¶ 2 In the seventeenth century England abounded with excellent inns of every rank. The traveller sometimes, in a small village, lighted on a public house such as Walton has de-

* From *The History of England,* Chapter III, "State of England in 1685."

scribed, where the brick floor was swept clean, where the walls were stuck round with ballads, where the sheets smelled of lavender, and where a blazing fire, a cup of good ale, and a dish of trouts fresh from the neighbouring brook, were to be procured at small charge. At the larger houses of entertainment were to be found beds hung with silk, choice cookery, and claret equal to the best which was drunk in London. The innkeepers too, it was said, were not like other innkeepers. On the Continent the landlord was the tyrant of those who crossed the threshold. In England he was a servant. Never was an Englishman more at home than when he took his ease in his inn. Even men of fortune, who might in their own mansions have enjoyed every luxury, were often in the habit of passing their evenings in the parlour of some neighbouring house of public entertainment. They seem to have thought that comfort and freedom could in no other place be enjoyed with equal protection. This feeling continued during many generations to be a national peculiarity. The liberty and jollity of inns long furnished matter to our novelists and dramatists. Johnson declared that a tavern chair was the throne of human felicity; and Shenstone gently complained that no private roof, however friendly, gave the wanderer so warm a welcome as that which was to be found at an inn.

Many conveniences, which were unknown at Hampton Court and Whitehall in the seventeenth century, are in all modern hotels. Yet on the whole it is certain that the improvement of our houses of public entertainment has by no means kept pace with the improvement of our roads and of our conveyances. Nor is this strange; for it is evident that, all other circumstances being supposed equal, the inns will be the best where the means of locomotion are worst. The quicker the rate of travelling, the less important is it that there should be numerous agreeable resting places for the traveller. A hundred and sixty years ago a person who came up to the capital from a remote county generally required, by the way, twelve or fifteen meals, and lodging for five or ¶ 3 six nights. If he were a great man, he expected the meals and lodging to be comfortable, and even luxurious. At present we fly from York or Exeter to London by the light of a single winter's day. At present, therefore, a traveller seldom interrupts his journey merely for the sake of rest and refreshment. The consequence is that hundreds of excellent inns have fallen into utter decay. In a short time no good houses of that description will be found, except at places where strangers are likely to be detained by business or pleasure.

EXERCISES

I. We may assume that Macaulay drew upon many and varied sources of information when he wrote the three paragraphs given above. No doubt he had read diaries, letters, books of travel, literary works, biographies, and histories. Perhaps he had also consulted court records or other public documents. But since, in his famous Chapter III of his *History of England* —a "chapter" as long as an ordinary book—he was surveying cultural and social conditions in seventeenth-century England, he could deal with inns only in brief terms, under the general heading of transportation and travel. He presents, therefore, the *typical* inn, or inns in general. He does not, and cannot, linger to discuss any particular inn, no matter how famous. Macaulay's problem here is a problem of how to simplify and condense. He must dwell only upon the most significant features of English inns—the features that English inns had in common—and must exclude other features, however interesting they might be in themselves. His language necessarily has to be general in its cast, yet clear and unequivocal. His discussion is both descriptive and explanatory and presents us with an example of a type of writing that may be called either "expository description" or "descriptive exposition." Much historical, scientific, and journalistic writing is of this nature. It describes facts, phenomena, tendencies, personalities; and it explains as it describes. Macaulay's writing here is a model of clarity, of skill in selection of details, and of consistency and force of style.

II. Bearing in mind Macaulay's purpose—and the limitations under which he must work—deal with the following questions:

A. The material immediately preceding Par. 1 (in Macaulay's Chapter III) sets forth the "various dangers" that beset the English traveler. What, then, is the function of the first two sentences of Par. 1, in relation to the preceding material? In relation to Par. 1 as a whole? What is the *topic sentence* of Par. 1?

B. What two "authorities" on the inns of England does Macaulay refer to in Par. 1? Who was "our first great poet" and what is the source of the details given in Sens. 5 and 6 of this paragraph?

C. What is the function in Par. 1 of the phrases "From a very early period" and "two hundred years later"? What part of the paragraph is devoted to William Harrison's "lively description"? Could "William Harrison's Lively Description" be used as the title of a subdivision of Par. 1?

D. What is the relation between Par. 1 and Par. 2? If Macaulay is primarily concerned with the seventeenth century, why does he here write a paragraph which refers to inns of earlier times?

E. What is the topic of Par. 2? What subtopics are treated under the general topic? Identify all words, phrases, or sentences that mark the *transition* from one subtopic to the next. To what extent does Macaulay rely upon *conjunctions* to make his transitions and to connect sentence with sentence or subdivision with subdivision?

F. Why does Macaulay refer to Walton, Johnson, and Shenstone in Par. 2? Read the passage in Walton's *The Compleat Angler* to which Macaulay refers (Chapter II, "The Second Day"). Would the paragraph be improved if Macaulay had quoted extensively from Walton?

G. Look up "Hampton Court" and "Whitehall"—if you do not already know what these names refer to. Why does Macaulay refer to them here? (Sen. 1, Par. 3) What is the relationship between this sentence and the sentences preceding and following? What is the topic sentence of Par. 3?

H. What is the logical connection between Par. 3 and the preceding two paragraphs? Is Par. 3 made necessary because Macaulay must answer a question his reader may have in mind—a question which might be formulated as follows: "If the inns of seventeenth-century England were so numerous and wonderful, why does modern England no longer have such inns?" Remember that in Macaulay's Chapter III, as was said above, inns are discussed in connection with transportation and travel. Macaulay makes the point that the means of transportation in seventeenth century English were scanty, crude, and highly uncomfortable, even for the rich, and that travel was slow and dangerous.

III. Make a study of the tenses used in Par. 3. Identify each tense-form and explain why Macaulay uses a particular tense-form at the place where it appears. Give special attention to the tenses of Sen. 3: *will be . . . are.* What verb is omitted, but implied, in "the quicker the rate of travelling"? Explain both the mood and the tense of *should be* (Sen. 4) and *If he were . . . he expected* (Sen. 6).

IV. In the following sentences, tenses and moods are handled in an incorrect or ineffective way. Make whatever changes you consider necessary, and give your reasons for such changes:

A. I was apprehensive that the effect will be different, that his much talking should be misrepresented, that the partisan press are going to take notice of it and attack him. I am still apprehensive that he may be injuring his cause by the speeches he made during the past two weeks.

B. If he was as badly off, in a financial way, as he claimed during his recent appearances before the Board, he should never be making a large down payment on a house and own two automobiles.

C. You told me you have read it and desire more said. I could still have something to say; but I would much rather you would be able to form a judgment upon what I already said and wrote, as I dislike the job of writing, especially when it is made a task.

V. Identify and account for each use of the passive voice in the three paragraphs. For example, Sen. 1, Par. 1, contains two passives; *was beset* and *were increased.* Macaulay could have written the sentence as follows: "Darkness greatly increased all the various dangers which beset the traveller." Probably he did not use the active verb forms because he wished to give "all the various dangers" (to which he has just been referring) the first and most emphatic position in the sentence. He did not want to give that much emphasis to "darkness." Furthermore, "darkness" is the agent or promoting cause of danger. It is not the danger itself, in an active state. Use a similar method of analysis in studying other passives.

VI. To what extent does Macaulay use comparison and contrast in (1) the general organization of the composition and its component paragraphs; (2) single sentences? Macaulay has frequently been criticized for using "antithesis and balance" to an excessive degree, especially in his sentence structure. Does this criticism apply to the selection here presented?

VII. Since Macaulay is setting forth the typical and general character of English inns, it is to be expected that his diction will be prevalently general and to some extent abstract. It is a good rule of composition that general and abstract terms, when thus used, need to be supported by particulars and details. In Par. 1, for example, *excellent accommodation* is a general and abstract term. To what extent is it supported by particulars and details? Find other instances of general and abstract terms and note whether they are or are not thus supported. Would it be possible to express adequately the thought of the following sentences in anything but general and abstract language?

A. "They seem to have thought that comfort and freedom could in no other place be enjoyed in equal perfection." (Par. 2)

B. ". . . all other circumstances being supposed equal, the inns will be best where the means of locomotion are worst." (Par. 3)

C. "The quicker the rate of travelling, the less important is it that there should be numerous agreeable resting places for the traveller." (Par. 3)

VIII. Using Macaulay's description of inns—with whatever other information you can obtain—as a source of information, write a description of a particular, individual inn of the seventeenth century. See the following selection, "Pendergasses'," by Hervey Allen, as a model.

PENDERGASSES' *

by HERVEY ALLEN

LESSON III

Exposition of Typical and Individual Objects . . .

¶ 1 Whatever one might think of Bedford, whether one was a European or an American, there was only one single opinion about Pendergasses': it was a good place to be in, in this or in any other kind of world. Even Indians liked to come there, when allowed.

¶ 2 It would be hard to describe the establishment exactly. For Pendergasses' was its own peculiar self, and no such set terms as tavern, inn, trading post, ordinary, public house, mill, or general store could precisely apply; since it was all these things or any of them, depending upon what a man's bent or business might be. And it was all of them at once, and so proclaimed itself by the songs that emanated from the taproom, the hum of business about the store, the click of iron from the blacksmith shop at one end near the road, and the intricate voices of the men, women, and children that came from the hive—for it was that, too—and perhaps best described by Murray in a simple homely term as a "goin' consarn."

¶ 3 Its houses, for there were two of them, faced the road on one side and the river on the other. And the level riverbank between was covered with a medley of small buildings devoted to various domestic, business, and farm uses.

¶ 4 From the midst of these shacks and outhouses the two main buildings towered up like two swans leading a flock of cygnets to the water. But that is not to say there was anything fragile or graceful about them. On the contrary, they were massive and substantial, built of the materials at hand provided by the original clearing of the land.

¶ 5 The lower stories were of large river stones set in lime-puddled clay, and the upper of walnut logs, vast fellows, the remains of a grove cleared from the ground on which the houses stood.

* From *Bedford Village,* by Hervey Allen. Copyright, 1944, by Hervey Allen, and reprinted by permission of Rinehart & Company, Inc., publishers.

"Such trees will never grow here again," said Garret, ¶ 6
when he and his sons cut them down. "They are the kind the Lord makes when he works all alone"—and he had refused to have them burned as the general custom was when making a clearing.

Instead, he had made the frames of the houses out of the ¶ 7
mightiest of these trees and used the comparatively smaller ones to cabin him in. Nothing but adzes, axes; nothing but wooden pegs had been used in building. But they had been used skilfully, and both the massiveness and the neatness of the place were the pride, envy, and model for the whole neighbourhood and its inhabitants.

Not that many other settlers could profit by the example ¶ 8
set by the Pendergasses. Garret had seven sons and four daughters. His wife was a little woman. But great and small they had all laboured together upon the place. And a great deal can be accomplished when something is done every day by thirteen skilful and devoted people for twelve years.

Such in fact was the natural genesis and continuing rea- ¶ 9
son for Pendergasses', and why, perhaps, it was always named in the possessive plural. For it was a hive of family industry and a store of local plenty, one that inevitably attracted travellers; that overflowed with news, gossip, and the benefits of trade, sustenance and furnishings; a veritable well-spring of sociability and primary necessities to the town and garrison, and to the pioneers in the coves of the mountains and the valleys about. For many years Mrs. Pendergass, for instance, had been the main, if not the sole, source of seeds, eggs, yeast, kittens, puppies, and even of fire itself, as the settlement spread.

Prime and vital nucleus of the establishment was the long ¶ 10
room on the ground floor of the store building nearest the fort, known to the Pendergasses themselves and to all the older settlers as the "hearth room", and to others as the "taproom" or "general store". Combine the three, and a complete description of the function, indeed a history of the place, could be had, except for the fact that before the fort

was built the main dwelling had also served on several occasions as the blockhouse or rallying point of the whole Raystown neighbourhood for defence against the Indians. A few louvres and loopholes in the stone walls of its lower story and the heavy log section above, now all carefully stoned in or blocked up, was all that remained to tell of a time of precarious, private conflict with the savages, which had already passed.

¶ 11 Pendergass and his seven sons had built the hearth room originally for the ample living quarters and kitchen of an equally ample family, to which, seeing the capacity of his copious loins already increased by a Biblical number of sons, to say nothing of his daughters, Garrett had prophetically seen fit to provide the largest and widest proportions that the hugest specimens of his giant walnut trees would permit.

¶ 12 Hence, the beams supporting the ceiling were twice the thickness of a man's body. The floors were of mighty planks ground smooth by the passing of time, innumerable feet, and the action of clean, white river sand. The windows were not numerous, but enclosed by shutters, iron bars, and glass, the first to be brought into the community. If anything, the apartment suffered from a certain lack of light. But this was at least partially offset by the fact that the long walls were plastered and whitewashed, and that at one end of the place burned continuously and forever a fire that was never less than twelve feet long and might be nine feet high, depending upon the weather and the exigencies of cookery.

¶ 13 Indeed, the actual dimensions of the fireplace were even larger. A whole ox, a stag, or an elk could be roasted there, or a bear upon occasion. There were several stone ovens provided with separate flues in the body of the towering chimney, and the hearth itself, made of the whitest, smoothest, largest of boulders, rose a good two feet like a stage at one end of the apartment above the level of the rest of the floor.

¶ 14 To enter the hearth room therefore, was to become immediately, although perhaps unconsciously, a spectator of a comforting drama of life. And the spectacle at Pendergasses' seldom failed to be interesting, since not the eye and mind alone were engaged, but food, drink, appetizing odours, and lively company also made their appeal. Perhaps, more than anything else, *that* was the secret of the place.

EXERCISES

I. Since Hervey Allen's *Bedford Village* (in one of the early chapters of which occurs the description of "Pendergasses'") is a historical novel of the Pennsylvania frontier, we may assume that Allen, like Macaulay, has a thorough knowledge of his subject. For, although a historical novel is "fiction," not "history," it uses the same materials as history—the "facts" of life in the past. The historical novel, however, presents its "facts" in a different way. The historian can hardly ever do more than draw generalized patterns. He accents tendencies rather than episodes. He *explains* events in broad outline, but does not relate them in detail. He cannot linger very often to draw a sharp picture of a particular event, locality, or residence—all such are merged in his generalized pattern.

The historical novelist seeks out the particulars that have been obscured or maybe lost in the generalizing process of the historian. He restores their freshness and liveliness. He wishes to reconstruct imaginatively the events of the past and so give his reader the imagined experience of living in the past.

Hervey Allen's interest, therefore, is in recreating the inn (or, as he says, "tavern . . . trading post, ordinary, public house . . . or general store") as it appeared to the eyes of his hero, Salathiel Albine and other characters of the novel. Although his description generalizes to some extent, Allen is chiefly concerned with leading the reader to "see" the Pendergass establishment in terms of its physical arrangements and to enjoy the "sensations" of the traveler who stops there. Behind the description is the implication that, while "Pendergasses'" is a "peculiar" establishment, it also has some of the typical features of the frontier inn of Pennsylvania and perhaps of other states. In working out the method used in Hervey Allen's "Pendergasses'" we shall therefore explore the means used by Allen to achieve his blending of the particular with the general.

II. The following questions will serve to direct your study of the *organization* of "Pendergasses'":

A. What are the *main divisions* of the composition? Designate these main divisions by composing (or quoting) sentences or phrases.

B. What *sub topics* are treated under each main division? Designate these also by sentences or phrases.

C. What portions of the composition deal with the *general* or *typical* features of Pendergasses', as an inn?

D. What portions deal with its particular or "peculiar" features?

E. Designate portions of the composition in which Allen proceeds (1) from the general to the particular; (2) from the particular to the general. At what point in the composition does Allen deal with each of the following: location; external appearance; nature of building material used; interior features; craftmanship involved; social function; food and drink served; family and community life; relationship of inn to the surrounding frontier; reputation of inn?

F. What *point of view* does Allen use in describing Pendergasses'? That of a historian (like Macaulay)? A traveler previously unacquainted with the inn? A traveler to whom the inn is familiar? A person who has never seen an inn before? A member of the Pendergass family? The author himself? Do you find any relationship between "point of view" and the order of treatment that you may have discovered in your consideration of II,E?

G. Is there a thematic link between Pars. 1 and 2 and Par. 14?

III. Study the diction used in the selection. Consider and answer the following questions:

A. Assemble all the terms, other than *inn,* applied to the Pendergass establishment. (In Par. 1, for example, it is "a good place"; in Par. 2, "tavern, trading post, etc.") What is the appropriateness of these terms (1) in the sentence and paragraph where they appear; (2) in the composition as a whole? Question A,2 can best be answered by first considering the following question: Why are so many different terms used?

Which of the terms on your list are plain, matter-of-fact terms that merely *denote* some specific function or aspect of Pendergasses'? Which are *figurative* terms (metaphors or similes) that *connote* qualities of Pendergasses' not readily expressed in matter-of-fact language?

B. Comment on the meaning and effectiveness of the following:

1. "the intricate voices of the men, women, and children" (Par. 2)
2. "a medley of small buildings" (Par. 3)
3. "towered up like two swans leading a flock of cygnets" (Par. 4)
4. "a veritable well-spring of sociability" (Par. 9)

5. "seeing the capacity of his copious loins already increased by a Biblical number of sons" (Par. 11)
6. "the hearth . . . rose a good two feet like a stage" (Par. 13)

C. How many of the above (under III,B) might Macaulay have used if he had had occasion to write on the inns of frontier America in the eighteenth century?

D. Pick out at least six phrases or sentences—other than the above—that Macaulay might have used; six more that he definitely would not have used.

E. Work out and discuss the overtones of meaning intended in the following: "natural genesis" (Par. 9); "the main, if not the sole, source of seeds, eggs, yeast, kittens, puppies, and even of fire itself" (Par. 9); "Prime and vital nucleus" (Par. 10); "copious loins" (Par. 11); "burned continuously and forever a fire" (Par. 12); "a comforting drama of life" (Par. 14).

IV. Suggestions for writing:

A. Read Chaucer's "Prologue" to *The Canterbury Tales* (in the original or in a modern English version) and write an expository description of the Tabard Inn. If you find it necessary, consult some standard historical source for additional material.

B. After reading the passage in Walton's *The Compleat Angler* referred to by Macaulay (Chapter II, "The Second Day"), write a detailed description of the inn, with "ballads stuck about the wall," which was visited by Piscator (Fisherman) and Venator (Hunter).

C. Using the manner of Macaulay, write a three- or four-paragraph composition with the following title: "Inns of the American Frontier in the Eighteenth Century." Use the "facts" or "data" of Allen's Pendergasses'" and other relevant material. Or simply rewrite "Pendergasses'" in the style of Macaulay.

D. Write a theme of three or four paragraphs in which you develop the typical characteristics of some institution known to you. For example: The Typical Southern Motor Court; The Typical American Filling Station; The Typical Deer Hunters' Camp; The Typical Second-hand Bookstore; The Typical New England Antique Shop; The Typical Beauty Shop.

E. After writing your description of the type, reverse the procedure and write about some particular or "peculiar" establishment.

PART TWO

EXPOSITORY DESCRIPTION

The power of the artist and the completeness of his performance achieve a concentration and creative life that compel men to follow and to make a great work of art a part of themselves. Meantime, however, it is true, as Plato said, that most men are blind to the fact of their ignorance of the essential character of each individual thing. They do not see in each thing that which distinguishes it from every other; they do not see what, if the thing were freed from all but its own characteristic, would remain, and would be the point of it, and would define its existence in the midst of a multitude of things like and unlike. What men are least apt to do is to see the point.—Stark Young, "Seeing the Point," in *Glamour: Essays on the Art of the Theatre.* Reprinted by permission of Charles Scribner's Sons, publishers.

LESSON IV

Matter-of-Fact and Dramatic Methods Compared. Authenticity. Organization According to Central Principle. Point of View. Tense in Relation to Levels of Narrative. Problems of Paragraph Structure, Sentence Structure, and Diction.

A ROUNDUP *

by DEE BROWN and MARTIN F. SCHMITT

Roundups for assembling a trail herd were begun early in the spring, with every cattleman eager to hit the trail first in order to insure plenty of grass along the route to Kansas. At the beginning of a "gather," the roundup boss would assemble an outfit of about twenty cowhands, a horse wrangler to look after the mounts, and, most important of all, a camp cook. ¶ 1

On range or drive, the chuckwagon was home, and a good cook was supposed to be proficient at more than the culinary arts. He had to be a combination housekeeper, morale builder, and expert wagon driver or "bull whacker." The cowhands usually referred to the cook as the "Old Lady," but they were careful not to offend him. He had too many subtle ways of evening the score. The cook was the aristocrat of the roundup and trail drive, a man who prized his dignity, was seldom a good rider, and had slight use for the temperamental cattle. ¶ 2

As for the chuckwagon, it was a work of utilitarian art, an invention of a master cattleman, Charles Goodnight. The chuckwagon was a commissary on wheels, a stout wagon ¶ 3

* From *Trail Driving Days,* by Dee Brown and Martin F. Schmitt. Copyright, 1952, by Charles Scribner's Sons. Reprinted by permission of the publishers, Charles Scribner's Sons.

covered with canvas and equipped with a box at the rear for storing tin dishes, a Dutch oven, a frying pan, kettle, and coffee pot. The standard staples also had their exact places: green-berry coffee, salt, pork, corn meal, flour, and beans. For fresh meat, of course, there was always plenty of beef handy. A folding leg was usually attached to the chuck box lid, so that it formed a table when lowered for action. The main body of the wagon was packed with bedrolls, slickers, extra clothing. Fastened securely in the front was a water barrel with a convenient spigot running through the side of the wagon. Beneath the bed was a cowhide sling for transporting dry wood, kindling, or buffalo chips. And in a box below the driver's seat, the cook usually kept necessary tools such as axes, hammers, and spades.

¶4 The first day of a roundup, the men would be up before dawn to eat their breakfasts hurriedly at the chuckwagon, and then in the graying light they would mount their best ponies and gather around the range boss for final instructions.

¶5 As soon as he had outlined the limits of the day's roundup, the boss would send his cowhands riding out in various directions to sweep the range. When each rider reached a specified point, he turned back and herded all the cattle within his area back into the camp center. All day the men worked the animals back, seeking them out in brush thickets and in arroyos. By evening a restless, noisy herd would be assembled beside the camp. As darkness fell, the cattle usually quieted and gathered close together to rest or sleep on the ground, and the roundup boss assigned night herders to hold the herd in place by patrolling its borders.

¶6 After supper in a cow camp, while the cook was washing the pots and pans, the cowboys who were free of duties liked to assemble around the fire for some singing. If they were lucky, a fiddler would be among them. They sang rollicking songs, sad songs, unprintably ribald songs, but usually ended with a sacred hymn. Soon afterward, all except the night herders would be in their bedrolls; the next day's work would begin before the sun was up.

The second operation of a roundup began as soon as a ¶ 7
herd had been collected. This next step was to separate from the herd the mature animals which would be driven north to market, and the calves which were to be branded for return to the range.

"Cutting out," it was fittingly called, and this perform- ¶ 8
ance was, and still is, the highest art of the cowboy. Cutting out required a specially trained pony, one that could "turn on a dime," and a rider who had a sharp eye, good muscular reflexes, and who was an artist at handling a lariat.

After selecting an animal to be separated from the herd, ¶ 9
the rider and his horse would begin an adroit game of twisting and turning, of sudden stops and changes of pace. Range cattle were adept at dodging, and if a cowboy's pony was not a "pegger" the chased animal would soon lose itself in the herd. Some horses never learned the art of cutting out; others seemed to sense instinctively what was demanded of them. For the latter the work was pure sport and show. Working with the best type of cutting pony, a cowboy could drop his reins over the saddle horn and by pressure of a knee indicate the cow he wanted, leaving the rest of the action to his mount.

If calves were being cut out, the objective was usually the ¶ 10
mother cow. The calf would follow her out of the herd into the open where it could be roped with ease.

Roping, the final act of the cutting out process, also re- ¶ 11
quired close cooperation between pony and rider. As soon as a steer or calf was clear of the herd, the cowboy lifted his coiled lariat from its place beside the saddle horn, quickly paid out an oval-shaped noose six or seven feet in diameter, and spun it out over his head with tremendous speed. An instant before making the throw, he would draw his arm and shoulder back, then shoot his hand forward, aiming the noose sometimes for the animal's head, sometimes for its feet.

As the lariat jerked tight, the rider instantly snubbed it ¶ 12
tight around the saddle horn. At the same moment, the pony stopped short, practically sitting down. The position of a

pony at the moment of the throw was important; balance in motion is a delicate thing, and a sudden jerk of a taut lariat could quickly spill horse and rider.

LESSON IV

¶ 13 *Matter-of-Fact and Dramatic Methods Compared . . .*

Forefooting was found to be particularly effective with calves, the noose catching the animal by the feet and spilling it in a belly slide, with no damage done. If roped around the neck, a lusty calf would usually have to be forced to the ground, by "bulldogging" it. Bulldogging is a sort of cow *jiujitsu,* and as seen today is a more modern technique than was used in trail driving days. Old-time "doggers" used no ropes, but were clever enough to select fast-moving animals for their victims. By throwing one arm over a calf's head and quickly twisting its neck, an experienced cowhand could unbalance the animal and drop it to the ground like a surprised wrestler—if it was moving swiftly enough.

¶ 14 Tail-twisting was sometimes an effective method of downing calves, and some of the tougher breed of cowboys thought nothing of grabbing a full-grown Longhorn by the tail, twisting the appendage around a saddle horn, and dumping the luckless animal to the ground. But most working cowboys preferred ropes, leaving bulldogging and tail-twisting to rodeo exhibitionists.

¶ 15 As soon as an unbranded animal was roped, it was immediately dragged or herded to the nearest bonfire, where the branding irons were being heated to an orange red. In Texas, all branding was done in a corral, a legal requirement devised to prevent hasty and illegal branding by rustlers on the open range.

EXERCISES

I. In "A Roundup" the purpose of the authors is evidently to give a clear, compact, and, above all, an authentic explanation of the process of rounding up and branding cattle. The authors are not concerned with the supposed romance of cowboy life. They do not bother to set down any visual impressions of the range, of horses and cattle, of cowboys. They do not dwell upon the picturesque, humorous, or tragic aspects of western life during the trail-driving days. Like the actual cowboys of the range, they are interested in getting their work done as quickly and efficiently as possible. Their task is to give a careful and economical explanation of a rather complex process, and they perform it in a plain, businesslike manner.

A. Would "A Roundup" have been more interesting or impressive if Brown and Schmitt had "injected romance" or "added color" to their account? If you think that such changes would improve the composition, what changes, exactly, would you make, and where?

B. Is the process of the roundup, on the other hand, so interesting in itself that it needs no "added" color or spice? Could the authors assume that American readers would be interested in their account, if it were plain and clear, no matter how plain and "unliterary" the prose? What subjects can you list, chosen from familiar American life, that are inherently interesting?

C. How much knowledge of cowboy life, trail-driving, and western cattle-herding could Brown and Schmitt assume that their readers would already have? Would previous knowledge of the subject by the readers simplify or complicate the task of a writer dealing with that subject? From what common sources would the average reader derive a knowledge of cowboy life? How correct would his knowledge be? How reliable would the sources of his information be? After considering such questions, you will be in a position to understand the purpose of the authors as stated above: "to give a clear, compact, and, above all, an *authentic* explanation."

II. Throughout "A Roundup" the authors use various "technical" or "cant" terms that relate to the specialized work of the cowboy. For example, in Par. 1, we have "roundup boss," "outfit," "cowhands," "horse wrangler."

A. List all expressions of this type that you find in "A Roundup." Then make a group-classification of them under the following headings:

1. Words or phrases that you understand without recourse to the dictionary but do *not* commonly use in speaking or writing.
2. Words or phrases that you understand without recourse to the dictionary and that you yourself use, either commonly or occasionally.
3. Words or phrases that you had to look up.

B. Make a separate list (selecting from your first list) of words from the cowboy vocabulary that have a particular and special meaning on the range, but another meaning—either technical, matter-of-fact, or metaphorical—in some other field of application.

C. Out of the words you have listed under "A," how many, in your opinion, are current in the vocabulary of the average American?

D. From what sources have you acquired the words that you can familiarly use (list A, 2, above)? From reading "western" stories or novels? From movies, radio, television? Folk-songs and stage songs? Conversation?

E. Using the material you have accumulated in the preceding analysis, write a brief article on the influence of cowboy life on the American vocabulary.

III. Pars. 2 and 3, dealing with the chuckwagon, form in themselves a small composition—a model explanation of what might be called a mechanism. Generally a mechanism is explained with reference to the *central principle* by which it operates. What is the central principle of the chuckwagon? Do the authors use any single phrase or sentence which indicates or states that principle? Are all the details of the explanation closely related to that central principle?

IV. What other "small compositions" form integral parts of the general explanation contained in "A Roundup"? Distinguish each, give it a title, and analyze its organization.

V. Study the authors' use of *would* in Par. 5. Would the prose of this paragraph be improved, or not, if, instead of the forms they now have, the authors had written: "each rider *would reach* . . . ."; "he *would turn* back and *herd* . . . ."; the men *would work* the animals back . . . ."; "the cattle *would* usually *quiet* and *gather* . . . ."; "the roundup boss *would assign* . . . ."? Would the paragraph be better prose, on the other hand, if the authors had nowhere used *would?*

VI. In Pars. 10 and 11, are the words "objective" and "coöperation" both appropriate and correct?

VII. Explain a complex process with which you are familiar, taking care to write in plain and economical language. Like Brown and Schmitt, you will have to ask yourself how much knowledge of technical or cant terms you can assume that your reader possesses; also what terms you may leave unexplained and what terms need to be accompanied by some explanation. Note how Brown and Schmitt deal with this problem.

ILLINOIS BUS RIDE*

by ALDO LEOPOLD

LESSON IV

A farmer and his son are out in the yard, pulling a cross- ¶ 1
cut saw through the innards of an ancient cottonwood. The tree is so large and so old that only a foot of blade is left to pull on.

Time was when that tree was a buoy in the prairie sea. ¶ 2
George Rogers Clark may have camped under it; buffalo may have nooned in its shade, switching flies. Every spring it roosted fluttering pigeons. It is the best historical library short of the State College, but once a year it sheds cotton on the farmer's window screens. Of these two facts, only the second is important.

The State College tells farmers that Chinese elms do not ¶ 3
clog screens, and hence are preferable to cottonwoods. It likewise pontificates on cherry preserves, Bang's disease, hybrid corn, and beautifying the farm home. The only thing it does not know about farms is where they came from. Its job is to make Illinois safe for soybeans.

I am sitting in a 60-mile-an-hour bus sailing over a high- ¶ 4
way originally laid out for horse and buggy. The ribbon of concrete has been widened and widened until the field fences threaten to topple into the road cuts. In the narrow thread of sod between the shaved banks and the toppling fence grow the relics of what was once Illinois: the prairie.

No one in the bus sees these relics. A worried farmer, his ¶ 5
fertilizer bill projecting from his shirt pocket, looks blankly at the lupines, lespedezas, or Baptisias that originally pumped nitrogen out of the prairie air and into his black loamy acres. He does not distinguish them from the parvenu quack-grass in which they grow. Were I to ask him why his corn makes a hundred bushels, while that of non-prairie states does well to make thirty, he would probably answer that Illinois soil is better. Were I to ask him the name of that white spike of

pea-like flowers hugging the fence, he would shake his head. A weed, likely.

¶ 6 A cemetery flashes by, its borders alight with prairie puccoons. There are no puccoons elsewhere; dog-fennels and sow-thistles supply the yellow *motif* for the modern landscape. Puccoons converse only with the dead.

¶ 7 Through the open window I hear the heart-stirring whistle of an upland plover; time was when his forebears followed the buffalo as they trudged shoulder-deep through an illimitable garden of forgotten blooms. A boy spies the bird and remarks to his father: there goes a snipe.

¶ 8 The sign says, "You are entering the Green River Soil Conservation District." In smaller type is a list of who is co-operating; the letters are too small to be read from a moving bus. It must be a roster of who's who in conservation.

¶ 9 The sign is neatly painted. It stands in a creek-bottom pasture so short you could play golf on it. Near by is the graceful loop of an old dry creek bed. The new creek bed is ditched straight as a ruler; it has been "uncurled" by the county engineer to hurry the run-off. On the hill in the background are contoured strip-crops; they have been "curled" by the erosion engineer to retard the run-off. The water must be confused by so much advice.

¶ 10 Everything on this farm spells money in the bank. The farm-stead abounds in fresh paint, steel, and concrete. A date on the barn commemorates the founding fathers. The roof bristles with lightning-rods, the weathercock is proud with new gilt. Even the pigs look solvent.

¶ 11 The old oaks in the woodlot are without issue. There are no hedges, brush patches, fencerows, or other signs of shiftless husbandry. The cornfield has fat steers, but probably no quail. The fences stand on narrow ribbons of sod; whoever plowed that close to barbed wires must have been saying, "Waste not, want not."

¶ 12 In the creek-bottom pasture, flood trash is lodged high in the bushes. The creek banks are raw; chunks of Illinois have sloughed off and moved seaward. Patches of giant ragweed mark where freshets have thrown down the silt they could not carry. Just who is solvent? For how long?

The highway stretches like a taut tape across the corn, ¶ 13
oats, and clover fields; the bus ticks off the opulent miles; the passengers talk and talk and talk. About what? About baseball, taxes, sons-in-law, movies, motors, and funerals, but never about the heaving ground-swell of Illinois that washes the windows of the speeding bus. Illinois has no genesis, no history, no shoals or deeps, no tides of life and death. To them Illinois is only the sea on which they sail to ports unknown.

EXERCISES

I. Aldo Leopold (1887–1948), a native of Iowa, had a notable career as forester, conservationist, and wild life expert. Out of his long experience he developed, late in life, a profound interest in ecology—the science which deals with "the mutual relations of organisms and their environment." His book, *A Sand County Almanac,* reflects his conviction that civilized society is often blindly destructive of the natural environment upon which it must depend—even when that society thinks it is practicing "conservation." "Illinois Bus Ride" is one of various sketches and diary-like observations in which Leopold applies his views.

No doubt this particular sketch may be a record of some actual bus ride. But though, in its brevity and terseness, it resembles an entry in a personal journal, it is no mere hasty jotting. "Illinois Bus Ride" is tightly organized and highly purposeful. Leopold makes an assessment of a personal experience while he is in process of relating that experience. The bus ride becomes a device for *dramatizing* both the narrative details of the experience and the meaning Leopold finds in them.

By the term *drama* we mean, fundamentally, a conflict of forces presented in the form of a play, with actors speaking "lines" and "acting" the story. A drama has a minimum amount of explanation. It conveys a strong sense of immediacy—of the presence of the action before our watching eyes. "Illinois Bus Ride," of course, is not an actual drama; it is a combination of description, exposition, and narration. But it is *dramatic* in that (1) it begins abruptly, without explanation of any "antecedent action" (we do not know where the narrator came from or where he is going); (2) all material not essential to the theme is relentlessly excluded; (3) a sharp sense of *present action* is conveyed from beginning to end; (4) the bus and the prairie constitute a "stage," and they also have both a matter-of-fact and a symbolic meaning; (5) the characters—i.e., the narrator and the passengers—suggest an array of conflicting forces (or ideas).

This dramatic method enables Leopold to use words, phrases, and sentences that are "packed" with meaning—that, in fact, often contain double meanings or operate at more than one level of meaning. Indeed, the entire sketch is virtually an extended metaphor. The "bus ride" becomes, in Leopold's mind, a symbol of the "march" of civilization. For these and other reasons, "Illinois Bus Ride" is in every way different from "A Roundup," and it must be studied in a different way.

II. The following questions are suggested by way of assisting your study:

A. In which paragraph does Leopold "orient" the reader—that is, tell him, by way of information, that the narrator is taking a bus ride through the old prairie country of Illinois? Is the information thus given elaborated to any extent? Is it sufficient for the purpose of the sketch? Why does Leopold *not* give this information in the first paragraph?

B. Par. 1 is a good example of an "abrupt" beginning which uses the "dramatic" principle. A significant image is flashed upon the reader's eye but is not at once interpreted. What is this image, and why does Leopold use this particular image? Since we do not as yet "know" (except from the title) that the narrator is taking a bus ride, is it legitimate ("fair" to the reader) for Leopold to use this image? What bearing does it have on the theme of "Illinois Bus Ride"?

C. Are Pars. 2 and 3 part of the "action" proper or merely the "thoughts" of the narrator, considered apart from the action? Can "thoughts" have a place in a narrative action?

D. What point of view is established in the first four paragraphs? How is it indicated?

E. What two "levels" of time are established in these same paragraphs? Why does Leopold begin in the present tense, then change to past tense, then revert to present? What is the dominant tense of the narrative as a whole? Would it be advisable to follow Leopold's method in the use of tenses for all narratives or only for special kinds of narrative?

F. Trace out (Pars. 5–7) the emergence of other "characters." Note the terse and striking means used by Leopold to make known their parts in the "drama"—their opinions and points of view.

G. Are the various natural and man-made objects also "characters" in a sense? If "Nature" is here represented as contending with "Society," which are the representatives of "Nature"? Which of "Society"?

H. Leopold's paragraphs are short. Is this shortness a fault? Or does the brevity of the paragraphs suit the rapidity of the very modern 60-miles-per-hour bus ride and enhance the sharpness of the general effect?

I. The sketch permits us, as readers, to use what may be called "double vision." The passengers "see" one series of objects during the ride; the narrator "sees" a different series, even though passengers and narrator are looking at the same landscape. Why, do you think, does Leopold use this particular method of rendering his experience? Is it an effective method? What other methods could he have used?

III. Par. 2 begins with a metaphor: "that tree was a buoy in the prairie sea." This is the first of many metaphors used by Leopold. As indicated above, the entire sketch is in principle a long metaphor, in which the "bus ride" may signify the "march" (or "voyage") that American civilization is taking through its natural environment, heedless—according to the implications of this sketch—of both past and future, but very intent upon present convenience. The narrator is a passenger on the bus, too; perhaps he had no other choice. But he knows what the "ride" means.

Make a study of all figurative expressions (metaphors, similes, etc.) in the sketch. Analyze at least five of Leopold's figures of speech in terms of: (1) appropriateness in the passage where they appear and in the sketch as a whole; (2) the extent to which they intensify the effect or reveal truth; (3) the extent to which they enable Leopold to write in terse, economical language, "packed" with meaning.

IV. Distinguish between Leopold's use of images that are merely images and images that are also metaphors. For example, Par. 1 conveys the image of two men sawing an ancient cottonwood tree. In the next paragraph the tree becomes a "buoy."

V. In Par. 2 the word "important" (Sen. 5) has not one meaning but two. The double meaning arises out of the context in which "important" is used. What are the two meanings of "important" in this passage? Find other examples of relatively colorless words which, because of their use in a certain context, take on more than one meaning.

VI. Make a grammatical and rhetorical analysis of Sen. 3, Par. 4. Why does Leopold arrange the sentence elements as he does?

VII. What is the meaning of the sentence (Par. 11): "The old oaks in the woodlot are without issue"? Does Sen. 2, in this paragraph, imply that Leopold approves "shiftless husbandry"?

VIII. Does Leopold mean *literally* what he says in Par 13: "Illinois has no genesis, no history, no shoals or deeps, no tides of life and death"? Is this observation intended as a "criticism" of Illinois? Of American civilization? Of modern agricultural methods?

IX. In the clause "buffalo may have *nooned* in its shade" (Par. 2) we have an example of a deliberate transfer of a word from one grammatical function to another. The dictionary lists *noon* as a noun only; Leopold makes it into a verb. This kind of transfer is a common feature of metaphorical language. Many expressions now considered quite ordinary originated in metaphorical transfers that may once have seemed daring or improper. The use of *camp* as a verb is a good illustration of this tendency, which a skilful writer may turn to his advantage. Find other examples.

X. Suggested theme topics: The Five O'Clock Rush; Fisherman's Luck; Trout Streams and Automobiles; Skyline Drive; Lake Shore Drive; Downstream from the City; Tourist Guide; Life Guard on the Beach; Highways and Trees; Throughway Ends Here; Bicycling to School; Campus Walk.

AN AIR VIEW OF THE AMERICAN IDEA*

by WOLFGANG LANGEWIESCHE

LESSON IV

The air view is an honest view: "You can't kid *me*" is your ¶ 1
attitude as you look down. "So *that's* how it is." For example, the great, famous dams—Hoover, Norris, Grand Coulee. In the ground view, the thing you marvel at is how big they are. The glamour photographs show them that way—small human figures, dwarfed by the gigantic wall behind them. Well, from the air, it's the other way round. It strikes you how small they are. Hoover Dam especially—it's actually hard to find! The eye sweeps all over the naked rock and the shores of Lake Mead before you find it—hidden down in a gulch. It makes you smile. Some boy has jammed a rock into this stream at just the right spot—and has managed to dam up one hell of a big lake. Small cause, big effect: clever little devil. And that, I'm sure, is the correct view. An engineer would say so. He would always try to build the smallest possible dam, not the biggest.

Or, New York City. What's it all about? On the ground, ¶ 2
why you know: *Time, Life, Look, Quick,* and *Harper's;* Batten, Barton, Durstine, and Osborn; Merrill, Lynch, Pierce, Fenner and Beane; NBC, CBS, ABC; words, ideas, paper of all sorts. But, from the air, I regret to state, New York looks like a place where steamships tie up to piers. The piers catch your eye, not Radio City or the Wall Street skyscrapers. Manhattan, with all those tentacles sticking out into the water, looks like some biological exhibit—some organ specially developed to draw nourishment from the sea.

The foreground doesn't hide the background. Looking ¶ 3
down at a place from the air, you see everything, literally, that's there. You may not notice everything; you may not understand the half of it; but at least you've seen it. What's this? Why does it look so odd? It's been amusing, for example, to watch the college campuses: the old fake, ivy-

* From *A Flier's World,* by Wolfgang Langewiesche. The McGraw-Hill Book Company, Inc. Copyright, 1951, by Wolfgang Langewiesche. Reprinted by permission of the author.

covered Gothic; the stadium with its vast parking space; the new research factory; the rows of Quonset huts. 'Tain't Oxford, brother. You run your own private census all the time. This thing—why do I see more and more of this? Not much can happen in the country that you don't notice, often ahead of the papers and magazines. For example, much will be written soon about our cities, how they have grown in area, not to say exploded; how the FHA town, way out on the potato fields, is taking the place of the tenement; and so on. Why sure: pilots have seen that grow for years.

¶4 Everything people do, and perhaps everything they think, makes its mark sooner or later on the ground. (That's what Reconnaissance is all about.) I used to amuse myself, looking down at Washington, by tracing the idea of Checks and Balances in the city plan and the shape of buildings. I've seen, in the South, a little country church with a swimming pool behind it: a fine point of theologic doctrine—baptism by total immersion—clearly written into the landscape! That is the kind of writing you try to read.

¶5 The American landscape is a palimpsest. Underneath what is written in it now, in concrete and barbed wire, there is older writing.

¶6 To bring out old writing, a man might photograph a document under trick light. The same in flying. Over the forests of New England, winter light is best. The trees must be bare, so the eye is not stopped at the treetop level. There must be snow on the forest floor, because that lights up the inside of the forest and makes it easier to look down into it.

¶7 Then you see, underneath the present-day forest, the farms of long ago. They did have decent fields there after all! Not decent to land on, but lovingly made, cleared out of the forest, carefully fenced by stone walls. Each rock once was picked up by hand, carried out of the field, carefully placed. It's said they made their children do that, to make them hard-working and God-fearing. Stern stuff. It's all under the forest. The forest is still only scrubby; but already it is full of dead trees helter-skelter, like virgin forest. The 1938 hurricane put them down, and nobody cares. History did a high-speed job here.

The second layer in this palimpsest is in strong plain writ- ¶ 8
ing: those section lines are the main part of it.

I believe this was written by Jefferson and perhaps Rous- ¶ 9
seau, but I don't know. About this, the main feature of the United States landscape, it is curiously hard to find anything in books. But I have often admired this scheme. Remember, it was drawn up on paper before the country had ever been explored. The lines were run before the people came; so it was literally a blueprint for a future society. I think it is a diagram of the idea of the Social Contract: homestead by homestead, men would sit each in his own domain Free and Equal: each man's domain clearly divided from his neighbor's.

I mean, it wasn't the only way they could have parceled out ¶ 10
the country. They could have gone out there with manor-houses, each with a bunch of cottages around it. (You do see some of that in the South.) They could have built villages nestling around a commons and a church. They might have built forts. Today, I think, we would build a headquarters first. There would be a row of houses; a communal water tower, "housing" for bachelor workers, a hospital, a recreation area. Radiating out, I imagine, would be roads, and off the roads would be the fields. The whole "development" would be star-shaped, and right in the center would be of course the Administration Building.

But they picked the layout where every man is his own ¶ 11
boss. Even now, this is the main feature of the American landscape: the square-cornered parcels, big in the West, small in the East, big in the country, small in the cities, of which each means a man. I realize they rent 'em, they are mortgaged, they grow the stuff by government subsidy, all that; but it is still true—the *design* of the landscape, seen from the air, is a design for independent men.

EXERCISES

I. Langewiesche's "An Air View of the American Idea," like Leopold's "Illinois Bus Ride," is a study in *perspective,* or use of point of view. Leopold shares with his fellow-passenger the same *physical* point of view—a seat in the bus—and differs from them in having his own *mental* point of view, which is scientific and philosophical and includes a farther range of time. Langewiesche emphasizes the difference between two physical points of view—the air view and the ground view. Out of the application of these two points of view he develops two contrasting interpretations of the American scene. The mental interpretation, in each instance, derives from the "angle of vision" afforded by the physical point of view. Leopold's method is *indirect* and *subtle.* His interpretation of the American scene is dramatic and symbolic. The sharp contrasts that Leopold "sees" are "represented" in concrete terms, but not explained. The reader is left to make his own social or political interpretation of the "views" developed in Leopold's succession of images. Langewiesche's method is *direct* and *obvious.* He speaks directly to the reader. His tone is conversational and instructive. He sows his discourse thickly with explanations and illustrations so clear that his meaning cannot be missed. It is interesting to note, however, that the two writers do not differ very greatly in their fundamental interpretation of the American scene. In his airplane, far above the American landscape, Langewiesche observes a pattern broadly similar to that which Leopold "sees" from the mental elevation of the wisdom he has attained.

II. Make an outline of Par. 1. What relationship does the first sentence have to this paragraph? To the composition as a whole? Why does Langewiesche state and illustrate the "ground view" before he presents the "air view"? If he had reversed this order, would the paragraph be equally effective? Why does Langewiesche, at this point, emphasize the matter of size? Does the statement "The air view is an honest view" imply that the ground view is a dishonest view? Or that the ground view invites false impressions which are easily corrected by an air view? Which of the following statements best expresses the generalization implied in Par. 1?

A. Size is only relative.

B. Objects are "large" or "small" only in their relationship to each other.

C. The air view brings the relationship between the natural terrain and the works of man into a very clear and revealing perspective.

In view of your study of this paragraph and of your reading of the composition as a whole, is "honest" the best possible adjective Langewiesche could have used in Sen. 1, Par. 1?

III. In Pars. 1 and 2, why does Langewiesche use certain famous dams and the physical arrangements of New York City as the concrete illustrations of the points he wishes to make? Looking at his illustrations only, one finds that they are arranged in the following order, in the composition: (1) the great dams—Hoover, Norris, Grand Coulee; (2) New York City; (3) college campuses; (4) the FHA town; (5) Washington; (6) little country church with swimming pool—in the South; (7) the forests of New England—old farms beneath; (8) section lines; (9) homesteads; (10) modern "star-shaped" developments.

The order of discussion is evidently not consistently from large to small; or from one compass point to another; or merely what may be seen along a particular air route. Are the illustrations, then, arranged according to the *logical development* of Langewiesche's thought? If so, what are the steps in his process of reasoning? Devise outline headings that represent those steps; then place under them the illustrations listed above.

You are now in a position to trace out the process of reasoning by which Langewiesche developed his opinions as to what an air view reveals and the logical plan that he chose to present his process of reasoning.

Perhaps Langewiesche's observation led him, first, through air views of particular objects (Hoover Dam, New York City, etc.) to correct his ground views of such objects; and next, to limited generalizations about the objects; for example, that great dams and great cities disclose their relationship to the natural terrain, under human occupation, more clearly from the air than from the ground. With this observation and limited generalization he correlates another observation: that the American past of small farms and section lines is disclosed from the air although it may be completely obscured to the ground observer. Then Langewiesche reasons his way to his large generalization: that the old "idea" of American life ("the idea of the Social Contract") is still the dominant feature of our landscape. His conclusion is that our landscape, despite modern changes, is still "a design for independent men."

Do you think that these steps of logical thought appear in the composition in the same arrangement that they may have had in Langewiesche's mind during the early stages of his thinking about the American scene? Go back now to the tentative outline that you made at the beginning of III and draw up, in a final form, a clear logical outline of the composition as it now stands.

LESSON IV

Matter-of-Fact and Dramatic Methods Compared . . .

IV. Langewiesche gives his discussion the form of an *interior monologue*—that is, not an actually spoken piece, but a discussion or quasi-argument that he carries on with himself, in his thoughts, as he views America from the pilot's seat. This monologue is not, apparently, the product of any single flight by airplane, but is the fusion of thoughts developed on many different journeys by air. It is the epitome of many such journeys and of his reflections and memories. The following questions relate to this peculiarity of form.

A. Is the interior monologue justifiable merely on grounds of verisimilitude? Does the solitariness of the pilot's occupation necessarily stimulate observations and reflections of the kind set forth?

B. Does the use of monologue justify the informality of the language used? Note the instances in which Langewiesche represents himself as having a lively and rather slangy conversation with himself. Would this slang informality be justified if Langewiesche had not used the monologue form?

C. What person is referred to in the *you* so frequently used by Langewiesche? The pilot himself? The reader? Is this use of *you* grammatically correct? Is it grammatically correct but rhetorically doubtful? Is it allowable and suitable in a colloquial context but not in a formal context?

D. Langewiesche's use of a chatty, conversational idiom permits him at certain points to set forth his ideas in a clipped, "short-hand" type of symbolical reference. Thus in Par. 2 the reply to the question "What's it all about?" is a series of magazine titles and proper names. The mere mention of these titles and names, Langewiesche assumes, will arouse in a reader's mind the group of inferences that he wishes the reader to make. In view of Langewiesche's general purpose and the style he uses, is this an appropriate and effective device?

If the inferences referred to above were set forth in full, Langewiesche's intended point might be developed in a paragraph beginning as follows:

> The inhabitant of New York—or for that matter the visitor to New York—rarely or never sees the great city in its totality and certainly not in its true relationship to the American continent. To him New York is just about what it is continually represented to be in the news columns, the pictures, the advertisements contained in *Time, Life,* and other publications . . . .

E. Make similar expansions of at least one of the passages indicated below:

1. "It's been amusing . . . to watch the college campuses. . . . 'Tain't Oxford, brother." (Par. 3)
2. ". . . how the FHA town . . . is taking the place of the tenement." (Par. 3)
3. "I used to amuse myself . . . the shape of buildings." (Par. 4)
4. "Today, I think . . . the Administration Building." (Par. 10)

V. Look up the word "palimpsest" (Par. 5). The figure of speech, "The American landscape is a palimpsest," gives Pars. 5–11 a definite, though not always explicit, thematic organization. Work out all the "correspondences," both explicit and implicit, that Langewiesche uses to carry out his metaphorical comparison of the American landscape with a palimpsest. Is this figure of speech effective? Would it be more effective, or less effective, if Langewiesche had everywhere tried to express explicitly the respects in which the American landscape "is a palimpsest"? A critic might possibly charge that Langewiesche here runs off into "allegory." At what point does metaphor become allegory? Would there be any objection to the use of allegory in a piece of writing like Langewiesche's?

VI. In what respects would Leopold and Langewiesche agree about the American landscape? Point out passages of which Leopold would approve and others of which he might disapprove. Which of the two writers is more optimistic? Is there any inherent reason why Leopold should be less optimistic about America's future than Langewiesche?

VII. *Suggestions for writing.* The studies made in the preceding lesson lead naturally to various kinds of theme projects:

A. Themes in which the defects of a "short-sighted" or "close-up" view are corrected by the use of a perspective in time. For example, historical reasons for the founding of a city on some site that seems undesirable from a modern point of view (Washington, New Orleans, etc.); failure of a town or city to plant young oaks or elms to succeed old trees that have provided shady streets for past generations; defects in residential design due to lack of understanding of climatic or other conditions; the problem of water supply and increase of population.

B. Themes in which the defects of a local or provincial point of view are corrected by use of a perspective in space. For example, themes in which a travel experience is used to bring home to an Iowan the realities of the Civil War in the South, or to a Southerner the relationship between some Great Lakes port and world trade; or the relationship between the Imperial Valley of California and the New Yorker's breakfast table.

C. Themes in which a too generalized or abstract view is balanced by an emphasis on particular values.

LESSON V

Scientific Description

WATER STRIDERS *

by L. J. and M. J. MILNE

When a substance attracts water molecules more strongly ¶ 1
than water molecules attract each other, the water wets the surface. The liquid creeps along, invading every crevice, clinging tightly to each irregularity. But some materials, such as waxes and oils, attract water molecules so little that the water draws away, pulling back into itself and leaving the surfaces dry. Aquatic birds take advantage of these differences by regularly adding oil to their outer plumage, thereby keeping their feathers from becoming water-soaked. The many creatures that walk on the water do so by means of well-waxed, hair-booted feet that the water cannot wet.

Best known of all the animals that walk dry-shod on ponds ¶ 2
and streams are the water striders—insects with four long legs stretching out to the sides and a shorter pair held under the head. Texans call them "Jesus bugs" while in Canada they are "skaters." Their slender feet are covered with a short pile of greasy hairs that the water fails to invade. Each foot presses the water surface and makes a dimple there, but the water does not let the foot fall through the surface film as it would if the fine waxy bristles were absent. Instead the insect's weight is supported, partly by the buoyant force of the water displaced from the dimples, partly by the surface tension that tends to erase the depressions and bring all the water film to the same level. The strider stands chiefly on its

* Reprinted by permission of Dodd, Mead & Company from *A Multitude of Living Things,* by L. J. and M. J. Milne. Copyright, 1947, by Lorus J. Milne and Margery J. Milne.

hind- and foremost legs, while with the middle pair, as oars, it sculls along, its body well above the smooth and slippery surface of the pond. Mirrored in the water film below the bug is its image—a reflected "double" seldom seen except by small creatures close to the water surface. Below the strider, on the bottom of a shallow stream, are dark shadows cast not only by the insect, but also by the dimples in the surface film where its feet press downward. Sometimes, on sunny days, these shadows on a sandy bottom are more conspicuous than the insect making them. They drift along and follow every movement of the rowing strider on the film above.

¶ 3 A considerable *length* of surface must be called upon to support an insect as heavy as a full-grown water strider. If its hair-booted feet pressed on the film at only six small points, the bug would penetrate into the water and sink at once. But the strider's legs are spread so widely as to be almost parallel to the surface, and its feet make elongated dimples which are really furrows in the water film. So secure is the insect on a quiet pond or stream that it can shift its weight freely among its feet. Most spectacular are the demonstrations of this when a strider cleans itself. Drawing its rowing legs far back, it stands with its head almost in the water, while its hind legs are raised well above the surface and rubbed one on the other much in the manner of a housefly. Then the insect rests on forefeet and one hind foot, with the rowing leg on that side as an outrigger, while the middle and rear feet of the opposite side are elevated into the air and rubbed free of clinging particles by a similar fiddling movement. To accomplish this contortion the bug practically lies down on its side. The water film stands the strain, but the shadows cast on the bottom shift and spread as the pressures on the fewer surface furrows are increased. Finally the strider stands on rowing feet and rear pontoons while its body and forelegs are raised high above the water. The insect washes itself much as a kitten does, transferring dust particles from feelers, beak, and body to the forefeet. Then it rubs these together until they are satisfactorily clean. If uninterrupted, such a complete toilet operation may take ten minutes, and the bug seems to give great care to every detail. At last, with antennae brushed, the insect rows forth alertly to seek its fortune.

Water striders dive upon occasion, but only under threat of serious danger. They have difficulty breaking through the film, but once below, they sink to the bottom. Afterwards they crawl out, wet and obviously miserable, to dry and comb themselves into respectability. All active stages in a water strider's life are spent on the water surface, but for winter they fly or crawl (some are wingless even as adults) under leaves on the shore. ¶ 4

EXERCISES

I. "Water Striders" is an example of what is sometimes called "scientific writing." That this term is inexact and misleading is at once evident when we consider that the Milnes, in their explanation of a certain peculiar insect, are using not only the special knowledge and skill that they, as scientists, have acquired, but also the knowledge and skill that belong to the art of writing in general. If their writing here were strictly scientific, it would be comprehensible only to specialists in entomology. It would appear in some technical periodical, read only by entomologists and scientists working in allied fields, and would never be used in a college textbook intended for students in writing. The selection comes, in fact, from a book intended for the general reader, not for scientists as scientists.

Here we encounter one of the most difficult problems of our scientific age. In order to extend the sphere of scientific knowledge, science has steadily multiplied its special fields of research and at the same time has consistently narrowed each particular field as it comes under more and more intense scrutiny. The result is a continually increasing number of "specialties," each of which develops its peculiar technique and its own technical vocabulary. An expert in a special field finds it difficult to communicate his knowledge except to specialists who share his knowledge and use his vocabulary. As a pure scientist, he may find it impossible to write for the layman. But, since scientists cannot be pure scientists all the time and for various reasons may find it desirable, now and then, to communicate their special knowledge, or part of it, to laymen in some form or other, the problem arises of how they may communicate this knowledge without so distorting or diluting it that the communication may do more harm than good. "Popular science"—science watered down to the point where it may be "understood" by any and all literate persons, generally very badly—may become a kind of quackery, a quasi-science that is either frivolous or positively dangerous. The necessity of communicating scientific knowledge is nevertheless obvious, if it is to become any significant part of the body of our general culture.

The way to solve the problem is to deal with it as a problem in writing, not as a problem in "scientific writing." The scientist can fortunately assume that educated persons know *some* of the common terms and basic principles of physical science. If he can succeed in giving clear expression to the scientific principle that operates in the particular instance that he is discussing, and if he can apply that principle as any other good writer would, he will have no great difficulty in solving his problem. If Euclid could formulate in beautifully clear language the axiom, "Things equal to the same thing are equal to each other," there would seem to be no good reason for the modern technician to quail or flounder. A truth sufficiently valuable to be worth communicating must surely have its right and clear form of expression. If it cannot be clearly and definitely communicated, then we as laymen may be justified in regarding it with suspicion.

II. Bearing in mind the above discussion, apply the following test questions to the Milne selection:

A. Is a basic scientific principle stated? Is it expressed in a form clear and intelligible to the general reader?

B. If the principle is so stated, is it properly placed in the discourse?

C. Is the principle applied, illustratively, to other instances than the instance under discussion, or only to that instance?

D. If the special instance—here, the "water strider"—is something that an ordinary observer may have noticed, though with only a layman's interest and knowledge, does the writer take care to establish a link between that kind of interest and knowledge and the more exact and intensive knowledge of the scientific specialist?

E. If the composition passes all these "tests," what principle or principles of composition, already known to you as a student of writing, have been applied?

F. Is the explanation constructed upon this principle—or these principles—clear, systematic, and intelligible?

G. Are technical terms used to excess? Or is the language in general within the comprehension of the educated reader? Is the language at any point too abstract? Is it "pedantic"?

III. Examine the structure of Par. 3. What is the relationship between the group of sentences beginning "A considerable *length* of surface..." and the group beginning "So secure is the insect...that..."? Would you prefer to divide this paragraph into two or three paragraphs? If so, where would each new paragraph begin and end?

IV. In an ideal scientific discourse, language would be entirely *denotative.* All words would be chosen for their strictly logical meaning. Words having a *connotative*—or suggestive—value would be excluded.

A. In Par. 1, underline once all words that are used for their denotative quality alone. Underline twice those words used not only for the meaning they denote, but also for their connotative quality. Encircle those words used *only* for their connotative value. Apply the same test elsewhere in the composition—as your instructor may direct. After analyzing the results of this examination, state the conclusion that you would draw as to the kind of diction used by the authors.

B. How does the language used by the Milnes compare with that used in your textbook in mathematics? In chemistry or physics? In some applied science, such as engineering? In one of the social sciences?

V. To what extent do the Milnes resort to figures of speech? Are the figures of speech used for purposes of illustration? Or to "add color" and make the prose more "beautiful"? Is it possible to write an effective composition of this sort *without* using figures of speech?

VI. What is the meaning of the terms "buoyant force" and "surface tension"? (Par. 2)

VII. If the water strider can be viewed as a "living mechanism," what is the central principle of the "mechanism"? What functional use does this principle have in the organization of the composition?

VIII. What is the function of Par. 4?

IX. Suggestions for writing:

A. Using the method exemplified in "Water Striders," write a theme on one of the following topics or a similar one: Chimney Swifts; Land Crabs; Freshwater Mussels; Rock Lichens; The Seventeen Year Locust; The Common Angleworm.

B. Read an article in a technical or scholarly journal. Review it in such a way as to bring its essential points clearly and interestingly before a general reader.

PART THREE

HISTORICAL EXPOSITION: RESEARCH AND CRITICAL ANALYSIS

And with reference to the narrative of events, far from permitting myself to derive it from the first source that came to hand, I did not even trust my own impressions, but it rests partly on what I saw myself, partly on what others saw for me, the accuracy of the report being always tried by the most severe and detailed tests possible. My conclusions have cost me some labour from the want of coincidence between accounts of the same occurrences by different eye-witnesses, arising sometimes from imperfect memory, sometimes from undue partiality for one side or the other. The absence of romance in my history will, I fear, detract somewhat from its interest; but if it be judged useful by those inquirers who desire an exact knowledge of the past as an aid to the interpretation of the future, which in the course of human things must resemble if it does not reflect it, I shall be content. In fine, I have written my work, not as an essay which is to win the applause of the moment, but as a possession for all time.

—THUCYDIDES, *The Peloponnesian War* (CRAWLEY TRANSLATION).

LESSON VI

Two Ways to Use Source Materials.
Methods of Authentication. Statement of a Problem.
False Solutions and True.
Interpretation and Personal Judgement.
Summary and Direct Quotation.
Verb Forms, Moods, Sentence Structure.

HOW CHAMPOLLION DECIPHERED THE ROSETTA STONE *

by FLETCHER PRATT

Scientific history is filled with the strangest repetitions, as ¶ 1
though new ideas float into the world on some invisible medium and are caught through senses attuned by study in many places at once. The planet Uranus was discovered twice within a month; the periodic law which forms the basis of modern chemistry was propounded separately by two men who had never heard of each other and were working along different lines. Similarly, at about the time that Georg Friedrich Grotefend was painfully spelling out the names of forgotten kings, another archaeological cryptographer was using the same methods to work out the other great puzzle of antiquity—the Egyptian hieroglyphics.

He was Jean François Champollion, an infant prodigy, ¶ 2
whose father had been an archaeologist before him and had talked shop over the dinner table so entertainingly that at the age of fifteen the boy was already publishing a learned essay on "The Giants of the Bible" which won the applause of the bewigged professors at the French Institute.

Champollion's problem in dealing with hieroglyphic was ¶ 3
radically different from the one Grotefend of Göttingen had

* From *Secret and Urgent: The Story of Codes and Ciphers,* by Fletcher Pratt. Copyright, 1939, by Fletcher Pratt. Reprinted by permission of the author.

faced. The latter had before him various combinations of markings which were altogether meaningless except as the letters of an unknown language. Champollion was trying to read verbal sense into long strings of pictures which were considered by many very good scientists to have no more than a mystic religious sense, like the work of certain savage races which draw a picture of a deer when they feel hungry, expecting the gods to send them the real article in exchange for the pictured image.

¶ 4 Again, Niebuhr had identified forty-two different alphabetic signs, or letters in ancient Persian; but the scientists who had already held hieroglyphic under investigation for centuries had discovered over a hundred and sixty signs—far too many to constitute any alphabet, beside which they were unmistakably conventionalized pictures. Moreover Grotefend had plunged into a new field, where all thought was independent thought; Champollion entered a domain already strewn with the wreckage of hypotheses, where it would be fatally easy to accept the errors along with the logic of some previous failure.

¶ 5 Particularly since the discovery of the famous Rosetta Stone. That celebrated chunk of crockery had been found by the scientists who accompanied Napoleon's expedition to Egypt, and was surrendered to the English with the remains of that expedition. It bore an inscription in Greek, together with two other inscriptions, one in hieroglyphic and one in a third form known as Egyptian Demotic, then as unreadable as hieroglyphic. No great intelligence was required to make the supposition that all three inscriptions said essentially the same thing; but some of the best brains in Europe had spent years trying to resolve the hieroglyphic into an intelligible language, and even with the aid of the Greek texts it had proved impossible. The general conclusion was that the problem was insoluble.

¶ 6 For everything seemed to indicate that if the hieroglyphic were a language at all (and not a series of mystical pictures) it was that extremely rare thing, a purely syllabic tongue. For example, in the place where the word *king* appeared in the Greek text, the hieroglyphic had a picture of an extraordinarily tall man with a sword in his hand. This was a logical symbol for *king;* a whole word in one picture-letter. And if this were true, many of the other symbols stood for entire words or syllables; there would be no clue from the interrelation of letters as to how the language had been pronounced, and it would be forever unreadable.

There was also another difficulty. The British scientists ¶ 7
who first handled the Rosetta Stone had taken the obvious step of making parallel lists of Greek words and the hieroglyphics that supposedly represented them. To their dismay they discovered that Greek words which appeared more than once in the inscription were represented on these different appearances by wholly unrelated sets of hieroglyphics, and that the same hieroglyphics were sometimes used to represent different words of the Greek text. Even the names, through which Grotefend was even then breaking ancient Persian, were of no help in this case. The only personal name in the Greek text was that of King Ptolemy V; in the hieroglyphic it was represented by four symbols—too few to spell it out with letters, too many to spell it in syllables. There seemed no conclusion but that the hieroglyphics were purely symbolical; and they had been generally abandoned as such when Jean François Champollion, the boy wonder, entered the lists.

His first step was to count the total number of symbols in ¶ 8
the Greek and hieroglyphic texts, a method which is now a commonplace of decipherment, but which Champollion seems to have been first to take in this science. The count revealed that there was something radically wrong with all previous efforts to solve hieroglyphic; for there were three times as many Egyptian as Greek letters. If the hieroglyphics were, then, either symbols for syllables or for ideas expressed as directly as the cave man's deer, the Egyptian inscription must be more than three times as long as the Greek. But the very basis of any deduction must be that the

inscriptions say the same thing; and the nature of the Greek text (a hymn of praise to Ptolemy V by a corporation of priests) made it seem unreasonable that there could be any great difference. If the inscriptions were identical, then the hieroglyphics must, after all, be letter-symbols. There were too many of them for any other theory.

¶ 9 On the other hand an alphabet of 160 letters remained inadmissible. But since other scientists had allowed themselves to be hung up on the horns of this dilemma, Champollion neglected it and plunged ahead on the alphabetic theory, attacking the names as Grotefend had in Persian. The name of Ptolemy was neatly enclosed in an outline, preceded by the symbol the English investigators had taken to represent the word for *king.* Now "Ptolemy" is a Greek word; Champollion made the reasonable deduction that in Egyptian it would have to be spelled phonetically. If the four symbols that stood for the name on the Rosetta Stone were letters, some letters in the name must have been omitted—which? The vowels, Champollion answered himself, remembering that Hebrew, which had a considerable Egyptian heritage, also omitted the vowels. The four symbols of the name were the letters pronounced *P, T, L,* and *M.*

¶ 10 At this point the investigator turned to some older hieroglyphic inscriptions to check his conclusions. He had at hand a couple whose origin in the reigns of Kings Rameses and Thutmoes were proved by portraits and other evidence. The symbol he had adopted as *M* appeared in both names, and the *T* twice, in the proper places, in the second name. Thus it checked and, checking, gave him values for *R* and *S;* and with six letters to work on the scientist-cryptographer began to work through all the Egyptian inscriptions containing known names, obtaining new letter values at every step.

¶ 11 Very rapidly as scientific processes go—that is, in a matter of a few years—he accumulated enough data from names to provide the correct symbols for every possible consonant sound. There remained many letters of the impossibly extended alphabet for which he had no values; letters which never appeared as part of a name. Of these Champollion formed a separate list.

¶ 12 Returning to the Rosetta Stone inscriptions, he noted that one of these unidentified symbols appeared before every noun in the hieroglyphic text, and a few of them appeared before verbs. Now one such symbol was the picture of a tall man that had preceded King Ptolemy's name. Later, where a temple was mentioned the word was preceded by a conventionalized picture of a building, and when the sun-god Ra's name appeared there was a conventionalized solar disc. Champollion therefore reasoned that such characters were "determinatives"—special signs placed in the text by the Egyptian writers to indicate the character of the object they were talking about.

¶ 13 He died at the age of thirty-four without having worked out all the alphabet, and without having accounted for the remainder of the enormous surplus of letters, for even with the determinatives taken out, most of the words were far too long. It remained for later investigators to show that the Egyptians, in writing words, were never satisfied by expressing a sound in a single letter, but must repeat the same sound in three or four other ways to make certain the reader got the idea. It is as though one were to write the word "seen" as S-C-SC-EE-IE-EA-N. In a cryptological sense hieroglyphic was thus a substitution cipher with suppression of frequencies and the introduction of a prodigious number of nulls; and Champollion's great merit as a decipherer was that he held to the main issue without allowing these things to throw him off the track.

EXERCISES

I. A *reader* of Fletcher Pratt's "How Champollion Deciphered the Rosetta Stone"—especially if he is reading for entertainment or general instruction—will be fascinated by the unfolding of the puzzle of Egyptian hieroglyphics. The *writer* will find in it two important foci of study: first, the skill with which Fletcher Pratt has digested an obscure and complex subject; second, the ease and clarity of his presentation, which reduces an intricate problem to its essential elements.

The word *digested,* as used above, refers to the manner in which Fletcher Pratt uses the materials of research. He does not authenticate his source material through footnotes, as a professional scholar does (see Louise Pound, "Audience and Authorship As Mirrored in the Ballads," pp. 150–154), but follows the procedure of journalists and magazine writers. Except when quoting, as in reports of interviews and similar instances, journalists do not invariably give the specific source of the information they present; and when they do give the source, they skilfully imbed their reference to it in the body of the text. Magazines like *Harper's* and the *Atlantic* do not use footnotes, and even the literary quarterlies keep footnotes to a minimum. Fletcher Pratt is therefore following accepted journalistic practice in omitting a "scholarly apparatus." Possibly he used note cards or notebooks as the scholar does, but none of the tool marks of that type of craftsmanship appear in his discourse. Instead, we get a feeling of the author's complete familiarity with his subject. He has steeped himself in books, no doubt; but he has absorbed them, not they him. He may have written his piece, one feels, with only an occasional glance at the pile of books around him. In this good sense the piece is a digest—a distillation in highly readable form of knowledge that expert researchists had previously set forth, no doubt in very technical terms.

To gain such knowledge from a reading of scholarly works and to digest it was, however, only one part of Fletcher Pratt's task. His original contribution is in his method of presenting Champollion's solution of the problem of Egyptian hieroglyphics. Pratt's interest in codes and ciphers gives him an angle of approach that the trained Egyptologist would not be likely to use. To the Egyptologist, the Rosetta Stone is a problem in linguistics and archaeology. To Fletcher Pratt it is a problem in cryptography. Therefore this account of Champollion's feat is included in Fletcher Pratt's book, *Secret and Urgent,* along with discussions of military codes and ciphers and various other examples, historic and recent, of cryptological devices.

II. What is the function, in the composition as a whole, of Pars. 1–3? Is the phrase "another archaeological cryptographer" one that would be used by an archaeologist, Egyptologist, or philologist? (Before answering these questions, look up the meaning and derivation of *archaeology, cryptography, Egyptology, philology.)* Does the term "archaeological cryptographer" foreshadow any later specific references to cryptography? What other specific terms indicate that Pratt views Champollion's work as a problem in cryptography?

III. Examine the way in which Pratt reviews the work of Champollion's predecessors and contemporaries. Look up Grotefend and Niebuhr in an encyclopedia. Are Pratt's references to them and his summary of their accomplishments sufficiently extensive and clear for his purposes? In the absence of quoted material and footnotes, does this part of Pratt's discussion serve as an "authentication" of the material presented? Point out any passages in Pars. 1–4 which are Pratt's own contribution to the discussion, as distinguished from summaries of what others have said.

IV. Who discovered the planet Uranus and "the periodic law which forms the basis of modern chemistry"? What is the purpose of such references? Explain the phrase, "the bewigged professors of the French Institute."

V. When a complex subject needs clarification, it is often highly important to give a "statement of the problem" before developing a solution of the problem. Such a statement of the problem is a form of *analysis,* in that it narrows the area of discussion by reducing the subject to its central and basic features. The discussion can then be held "in focus," and the reader will not be confused by treatment of minor or non-essential matters. In what paragraphs does Pratt make a statement of the problem? To what extent does this statement of the problem determine his subsequent discussion?

VI. In such a discussion it is also logical and useful (as well as rhetorically effective) to set off false solutions of a problem against the true one, or unsuccessful attempts at solution against the successful one. At what point does Pratt treat false or unsuccessful solutions? Would it have been logically and rhetorically preferable to give the true solution (Champollion's) first—at least in broad outline—and then to compare it with the preceding failures? Note that correct statement of a problem may be the most important single step in its solution. Does Pratt anywhere take into account correct and incorrect statements?

VII. What important division in the composition is indicated by the sentence (Par. 8): "His first step was to count . . . ." Outline, by topical indications, the subsequent "steps" taken by Champollion.

VIII. In the sentence referred to above, what is the importance of "a method which is now a commonplace of decipherment, but which Champollion seems to have been the first to take in this science"? Why does Pratt use the term *commonplace?* What is the grammatical relationship between "to count" and "a method which . . . but which . . . in this science"? Is there a *rhetorical* reason why Fletcher Pratt should have used this particular grammatical construction instead of making two sentences, as follows: "His first step was to count the number of symbols . . . . This method is now a commonplace of decipherment, but Champollion seems to have been the first to take it in this science"?

IX. Determine and explain the mood and tense of all verbs in the four-sentence passage (Par. 8) beginning "If the hieroglyphics were" and ending "for any other theory." The forms of the verbs here should follow the rule for certain types of conditions used in English. Identify the types of conditions used by Pratt and determine whether or not he has followed standard practice in his use of mood and tense. Could the subject-matter of this passage be adequately conveyed without the use of conditional sentences? Would there be any rhetorical reason for preferring to use conditional sentences here, even though one might contrive to avoid them?

X. In the same passage, consider the last two sentences (from "if the inscriptions" to "any other theory"). One of these sentences is rhetorically classifiable as "loose," the other as "periodic." Which is loose? Which is periodic? Give reasons for preferring two different types of sentence structure in this particular passage. Consider also the function of these sentences in the paragraph as a whole. Do they acquire emphasis both from their structure and from their placing?

XI. Look up the derivation of *hieroglyphic* (Par. 1), *prodigy* (Par. 2), *mystic* (Par. 3), *hypotheses* (Par. 4), *inscription* (Par. 5), *decipherment* (Par. 8), *phonetically* (Par. 9).

XII. Discuss the appropriateness and effectiveness of the following phrases: "that celebrated chunk of crockery" (Par. 5); "was even then breaking ancient Persian" (Par. 7); "hung up on the horns of this dilemma" (Par. 9); "thus it checked, and checking, gave him values for" (Par. 10); "suppression of frequencies," "a prodigious number of nulls" (Par. 13); "held to the main issue without allowing these things to throw him off the track" (Par. 13).

XIII. What is the meaning of the word *value* as Pratt uses it in Pars. 10 and 11? Identify and define all terms that have a technical meaning peculiar to the science of cryptography.

XIV. Write a theme in which you discuss the solution of a problem. Organize your theme around a "statement of the problem." Give, if possible, false solutions to compare with a true solution. Develop your discussion in the way used by Pratt.

A. Suggested topics based on reading or research:

Lee's Strategy at the Battle of Chancellorsville (See Douglas Southall Freeman's *R. E. Lee,* Vol. II)

How the Wrights Solved the Problem of the Airplane (See Wolfgang Langewiesche's *A Flier's World)*

Schliemann and the Excavation of Troy

The Homeric Problem (i.e., Were the *Iliad* and *Odyssey* Composed by One Author?) (See Scott, *The Unity of Homer)*

How Were Shakespeare's Plays Acted in Shakespeare's Day?

B. Suggested topics to be discussed on the basis of your personal knowledge:

How to Manage a Sailboat in a Squall
How to "Break" a Saddlehorse
How to Train a Hunting Dog
How to Do "Parlor Magic"
How to Take Color Photographs of Wild Animals
How to Plan a Trip to Europe

THE FREE TRAPPER'S WINTER DIET *

by BERNARD DeVOTO

LESSON VI

Two Ways to Use Source Materials...

¶ 1 Squaws were good cooks and the Indian diet, which the wintering trapper took over entire when he had a wife or lived among Indians, was by no means so sparse or monotonous as the books say, if the camp was in good country. Its basis was the pot of meat which was always stewing over the fire in the middle of the lodge and a portion of which was set before every visitor as soon as he entered. (Indians had no fixed hours for meals; they and the trappers ate when they were hungry.) This was replenished with whatever fresh-killed meat came in. Roasted and boiled, baked in kettles or the ground, other meat dishes were standard. All were flavored with herbs, roots, leaves, and grasses which the squaws dried and whose properties they knew. The edible roots already mentioned were prepared in various ways. Roots, leaves, and buds that made good salads could be found under the snow.[8] In short, trappers and Indians lived high when food was abundant, and winter camps were pitched in places where it was expected to be abundant.

¶ 2 Protracted storms or the migration of game would produce shortages. And hunting was a daily job. The boys ranged through the woods, hillsides, and plains, usually on snowshoes. If the snow was too soft or deep for horses, they had to carry their take on their backs. There were problems of keeping the surplus from wolves. If the meat could be hung in trees it was safe from them but not from animals that could climb. Russell tells of burying some under three feet of snow and burning gunpowder on top to add another deterrent to the man-scent, but it did not work. No device worked for very long.

¶ 3 Protecting the meat from large or small vermin was a constant problem, winter or summer, in camp or on the trail. From porcupines to grizzlies the entire fauna liked to have their meals killed for them, as the modern camper knows. The modern camper, however, seldom if ever is troubled by the most skilful of all thieves, the wolverine. This pest is not considered by modern students to have any extraordinary animal intelligence.[9] But they could not have convinced the mountain men. To them the 'carcajou' was literally demoniac: he had an infernal ancestry. He would even steal beavers from traps and he regularly made a bloody garbage of the winter trap line that was run for fine furs. No cache of meat was safe from him and he did not work on shares. Few ever saw him, so his supposed size varies in the annals. Our painter, Alfred Miller, who claims to have seen one, makes him the size of a St. Bernard dog, which is too big, and adds that his body was shaped like a panther.[10] Osborne Russell saw one at work. Russell had killed a couple of bighorns for meat. He took some cuts back to camp and hung the rest in a tree. Next morning he went back for it and found a wolverine at the foot of the tree. 'He had left nothing behind worth stopping for,' Russell says. 'All the traces of the sheep I could find were some tufts of hair scattered about the snow. I hunted around for some time but to no purpose. In the meantime the cautious thief was sitting on the snow at some distance, watching my movements as if he was confident I had no gun and could not find his meat and wished to aggravate me by his antics. He had made roads in every direction from the foot of the tree, dug holes in the snow in a hundred places, apparently to deceive me.'

Russell conceded that 'a wolverine had fooled a Yankee,' ¶ 4
but halfbreeds and voyageurs had a different explanation: Ruxton reports them as believing that the carcajou was a 'cross between the devil and a bear.' Ruxton's companion in Colorado, a Canadian, said that he had once fought with one for upwards of two hours and had 'fired a pouchful of balls into the animal's body, which spat them out as fast as they were shot in.' Later when Ruxton drew a bead on one

the Canuck shouted so loud that he missed; in fact, he missed with both barrels of his rifle, and his companion refused to let him waste more powder. If he had shot fifty balls, 'he not scare a damn.'

EXERCISES

I. "The Free Trapper's Winter Diet" is a small portion of a long chapter in Bernard DeVoto's *Across the Wide Missouri.* It is given here for comparison with the preceding selection.

While Fletcher Pratt, in *Secret and Urgent,* reviews various famous puzzles always from the point of view of cryptology and writes in the manner of the good journalist, DeVoto, in *Across the Wide Missouri,* is writing as a historian very intent upon recovering and stating the true history of the trans-Mississippi fur trapper during the mid-nineteenth century. Once the facts are recovered, the problem for DeVoto is mainly a problem of selection and arrangement, with due regard also to emphasis and tone. From the mass of data gathered from a wide range of sources DeVoto as historian must choose items that are authentic, representative, and revealing. He must bring together scattered bits of information and work them into a coherent pattern. Because DeVoto is dealing with a historical subject and, like any other historian, knows that his treatment is open to critical scrutiny, he must authenticate his material in the orthodox way. His book is therefore provided with notes referring to sources, as also with maps, numerous illustrations, and an extensive bibliography. In the selection as here printed, DeVoto's numerals are printed to identify those passages which, in his book, are accompanied by notes.

The part of the chapter preceding our selection deals with the winter life of the "free trapper"—that is, the trapper not employed by a company, but trapping "on his own." We may assume that DeVoto took pains to assemble material relating to "winter diet" because he was conscious that other writers had treated the subject scantily or made errors that needed correction.

II. Identify all parts of DeVoto's discussion which, so far as you can tell, represent data drawn from research, and all parts which represent DeVoto's own interpretation, opinion, or general knowledge. To what parts could the term *objective* be properly applied? To what parts, the term *subjective?* What other terms would you suggest, in addition to *objective* and *subjective,* as accurately describing DeVoto's writing in this selection?

Why does DeVoto summarize at some points and give direct quotations at other points? Is there a particular reason why DeVoto would quote directly from Ruxton in Par. 4?

Is DeVoto so objective as to be neutral or characterless in his style? Do you feel, as you read, the impact of the personality of the writer? If so, how do you account for that feeling?

III. What is the purpose of the clauses, "As the books say" (Par. 1) and "as the modern camper knows" (Par. 3)?

IV. Justify or criticize the order in which DeVoto discusses the items of diet of the trapper family. Why is it pertinent to introduce the "problem" of the surplus meat? Is this the kind of problem for which a logical analysis should be made, accompanied by a "statement of the problem" (as in Fletcher Pratt's article) and a discussion of false and true solutions? How are the details of the general discussion grouped?

V. Are the following repetitions deliberate or accidental? If deliberately intended, are they effective? If accidental, do they constitute a defect of style?

A. "In short, trappers and Indians lived high when food was *abundant,* and winter camps were pitched in places where it was expected to be *abundant.*" (Par. 1)

B. ". . . but it did not *work.* No device *worked* for very long." (Par. 2)

C. ". . . shouted so loud that he *missed;* in fact, he *missed with both barrels. . . .*" (Par. 4)

VI. Would Sens. 3, 4, and 6 of Par. 2 be improved if the verbs were changed to the forms indicated; "The boys *would range. . . .* If the snow *were . . .* they *would have to. . . .* If the meat *could be . . .* it *would be.*" Compare DeVoto's use of verb-forms here with Pratt's in Par. 8 of "How Champollion Deciphered the Rosetta Stone." (See questions, under IX.) Explain the differences of form in terms of grammatical necessity or rhetorical effectiveness.

VII. Look up a subject on which you will need to do a limited but not an extensive amount of research. Then write a theme in which—following DeVoto's method—you use both summarized and quoted data, properly annotated.

LESSON VII

Critical Analysis

TWO VIEWS OF SCIENCE AND NATURE *

by ALFRED NORTH WHITEHEAD

¶ 1 Wordsworth was passionately absorbed in nature. It has been said of Spinoza, that he was drunk with God. It is equally true that Wordsworth was drunk with nature. But he was a thoughtful, well-read man, with philosophical interests, and sane even to the point of prosiness. In addition, he was a genius. He weakens his evidence by his dislike of science. We all remember his scorn of the poor man whom he somewhat hastily accuses of peeping and botanising on his mother's grave. Passage after passage could be quoted from him, expressing this repulsion. In this respect, his characteristic thought can be summed up in his phrase, 'We murder to dissect.'

¶ 2 In this latter passage, he discloses the intellectual basis of his criticism of science. He alleges against science its absorption in abstractions. His consistent theme is that the important facts of nature elude the scientific method. It is important therefore to ask, what Wordsworth found in nature that failed to receive expression in science. I ask this question in the interest of science itself; for one main position in these lectures is a protest against the idea that the abstractions of science are irreformable and unalterable. Now it is emphatically not the case that Wordsworth hands over inorganic matter to the mercy of science, and concentrates on the faith that in the living organism there is some

* Reprinted by permission of The Macmillan Company, the publishers, from *Science and the Modern World,* by Alfred North Whitehead. Copyright, 1925, by the The Macmillan Company.

element that science cannot analyze. Of course he recognizes, what no one doubts, that in some sense living things are different from lifeless things. But that is not his main point. It is the brooding presence of the hills which haunts him. His theme is nature *in solido,* that is to say, he dwells on that mysterious presence of surrounding things, which imposes itself on any separate element that we set up as an individual for its own sake. He always grasps the whole of nature as involved in the tonality of the particular instance. That is why he laughs with the daffodils, and finds in the primrose thoughts 'too deep for tears.'

Wordsworth's greatest poem is, by far, the first book of *The Prelude.* It is pervaded by this sense of the haunting presences of nature. A series of magnificent passages, too long for quotation, express this idea. Of course, Wordsworth is a poet writing a poem, and is not concerned with dry philosophical statements. But it would hardly be possible to express more clearly a feeling for nature, as exhibiting entwined prehensive unities, each suffused with modal presences of others: ¶ 3

> 'Ye Presences of Nature in the sky
> And on the earth! Ye Visions of the hills!
> And Souls of lonely places! can I think
> A vulgar hope was yours when ye employed
> Such ministry, when ye through many a year
> Haunting me thus among my boyish sports,
> On caves and trees, upon the woods and hills,
> Impressed upon all forms the characters
> Of danger or desire; and thus did make
> The surface of the universal earth,
> With triumph and delight, with hope and fear,
> Work like a sea? . . .'

In thus citing Wordsworth, the point which I wish to make is that we forget how strained and paradoxical is the view of nature which modern science imposes on our thoughts. Wordsworth, to the height of genius, expresses the concrete ¶ 4 facts of our apprehension, facts which are distorted in the scientific analysis. Is it not possible that the standardized concepts of science are only valid within narrow limitations, perhaps too narrow for science itself?

¶ 5 Shelley's attitude to science was at the opposite pole to that of Wordsworth. He loved it, and is never tired of expressing in poetry the thoughts which it suggests. It symbolizes to him joy, and peace, and illumination. What the hills were to the youth of Wordsworth, a chemical laboratory was to Shelley. It is unfortunate that Shelley's literary critics have, in this respect, so little of Shelley in their own mentality. They tend to treat as a casual oddity of Shelley's nature what was, in fact, part of the main structure of his mind, permeating his poetry through and through. If Shelley had been born a hundred years later, the twentieth century would have seen a Newton among chemists.

¶ 6 For the sake of estimating the value of Shelley's evidence it is important to realise this absorption of his mind in scientific ideas. It can be illustrated by lyric after lyric. I will choose one poem only, the fourth act of his *Prometheus Unbound.* The Earth and the Moon converse together in the language of accurate science. Physical experiments guide his imagery. For example, the Earth's exclamation,

> 'The vaporous exultation not to be confined!'

is the poetic transcript of 'the expansive force of gases,' as it is termed in books on science. Again, take the Earth's stanza,

> 'I spin beneath my pyramid of night,
> Which points into the heavens,—dreaming delight,
> Murmuring victorious joy in my enchanted sleep;
> As a youth lulled in love-dreams faintly sighing,
> Under the shadow of his beauty lying,
> Which round his rest a watch of light and warmth
> doth keep.'

This stanza could only have been written by someone with a definite geometrical diagram before his inward eye—a diagram which it has often been my business to demonstrate to mathematical classes. As evidence, note especially the last line which gives poetical imagery to the light surrounding night's pyramid. This idea could not occur to anyone without the diagram. But the whole poem and other poems are permeated with touches of this kind. ¶ 7

Now the poet, so sympathetic with science, so absorbed in its ideas, can simply make nothing of the doctrine of secondary qualities which is fundamental to its concepts. For Shelley nature retains its beauty and its colour. Shelley's nature is in its essence a nature of organisms, functioning with the full content of our perceptual experience. We are so used to ignoring the implication of orthodox scientific doctrine, that it is difficult to make evident the criticism upon it which is thereby implied. If anybody could have treated it seriously, Shelley would have done so. ¶ 8

Furthermore, Shelley is entirely at one with Wordsworth as to the interfusing of the Presence in nature. Here is the opening stanza of his poem entitled *Mont Blanc:* ¶ 9

> 'The everlasting universe of Things
> Flows through the Mind, and rolls its rapid waves,
> Now dark—now glittering—now reflecting gloom—
> Now lending splendour, where from secret springs
> The source of human thought its tribute brings
> Of waters,—with a sound but half its own,
> Such as a feeble brook will oft assume
> In the wild woods, among the Mountains lone,
> Where waterfalls around it leap for ever,
> Where woods and winds contend, and a vast river
> Over its rocks ceaselessly bursts and raves.'

Shelley has written these lines with explicit reference to some form of idealism, Kantian or Berkeleyan or Platonic. ¶ 10

But however you construe him, he is here an emphatic witness to a prehensive unification as constituting the very being of nature.

LESSON VII

Critical Analysis

¶ 11 Berkeley, Wordsworth, Shelley are representative of the intuitive refusal seriously to accept the abstract materialism of science.

¶ 12 There is an interesting difference in the treatment of nature by Wordsworth and by Shelley, which brings forward the exact questions we have got to think about. Shelley thinks of nature as changing, dissolving, transforming as it were at a fairy's touch. The leaves fly before the West Wind.

> 'Like ghosts from an enchanter fleeing.'

In his poem *The Cloud* it is the transformations of water which excite his imagination. The subject of the poem is the endless, eternal, elusive change of things:

> 'I change but I cannot die.'

¶ 13 This is one aspect of nature, its elusive change: a change not merely to be expressed by locomotion, but a change of inward character. This is where Shelley places his emphasis, on the change of what cannot die.

¶ 14 Wordsworth was born among hills; hills mostly barren of trees, and thus showing the minimum of change with the seasons. He was haunted by the enormous permanences of nature. For him change is an incident which shoots across a background of endurance,

> 'Breaking the silence of the seas
> Among the farthest Hebrides.'

¶ 15 Every scheme for the analysis of nature has to face these two facts, *change* and *endurance.* There is yet a third fact to be placed by it; *eternality,* I will call it. The mountain endures. But when after ages it has been worn away, it has gone. If a replica arises, it is yet a new mountain. A colour is eternal. It haunts time like a spirit. It comes and it goes. But where it comes, it is the same color. It neither survives nor does it live. It appears when it is wanted. The mountain has to time and space a different relation from that which color has. In the previous lecture, I was chiefly considering the relation to space-time of things which, in my sense of the term, are eternal. It was necessary to do so before we can pass to the consideration of the things which endure.

EXERCISES

I. In "Two Views of Science and Nature" Whitehead is not undertaking literary criticism of the type now current (as in the so-called "New Criticism"), but is writing, instead, a kind of critical interpretation. He directs attention to the fundamental ideas of the two poets, not to the form and style of their poetry. The form and style may or may not be closely related to the fundamental ideas; but Whitehead is not here interested in that aspect of the poetry which he is considering. No doubt we should expect a philosopher like Whitehead to be interested first of all in the ideas. The remarkable feature of his interpretation is that Whitehead the philosopher, who in so many ways is the interpreter and defender of science, is here the interpreter and defender of poetry. More remarkably still, Whitehead seems not only to give poetry an equal rank with science —as scientists themselves rarely do in our time—but also to accept the judgments of the two poets on science as being competent and valid.

After reading the selection, answer the following questions:

A. How does critical interpretation, as here exemplified, differ in its methods from writing based on research—as in the selections from Fletcher Pratt and Bernard DeVoto?

B. Who was Spinoza? Read the poem of Wordsworth's referred to in Par. 1 ("The Tables Turned"). Does it sustain the point Whitehead makes? Do you know—or can you find—other poems by Wordsworth which express "this repulsion" toward science? What phrase in Sen. 7, Par. 1 is quoted from Wordsworth? Why does Whitehead not put it in quotation marks?

C. What does Whitehead mean by "the abstractions of science"? Give examples of such "abstractions." State in your own words your understanding of Wordsworth's allegations against science. Is it an "abstraction" for a scientific investigator "to peep and botanise upon his mother's grave"? What is your understanding of Wordsworth's statement (Par. 1):

"We murder to dissect"? Is the dissection practiced by zoologists, anatomists, and others a form of abstraction?

D. Explain the last two sentences of Par. 2 in relation to the preceding sentences of the paragraph.

E. Explain the passage, "entwined prehensive unities, each suffused with modal presences of others," in its application to the ideas of Par. 3 and the passage of poetry that follows.

F. What defect or limitation of science is Whitehead stating in Par. 4? Explain what Whitehead means by "the concrete facts of our apprehension." In what way does scientific analysis "distort" such concrete facts?

G. What known facts in the life of Shelley support Whitehead's statement about Shelley's passion for the chemical laboratory (Par. 5)? Why does Whitehead *not* give a biographical reference here to support his statement? How does the sweeping comparison of Shelley with Newton support the thought of this paragraph, and bring it to a powerful climax?

H. In Pars. 6 and 7, what evidence does Whitehead give to show that Shelley's poetry is written "in the language of accurate science"? Refer to Shelley's *Prometheus Unbound,* Act IV, and find other lyrics which support Whitehead's view of Shelley's language. Are there lyrics or passages which do *not* support Whitehead's view? Why does Whitehead give only two quotations from Shelley at this point?

I. The language of Par. 8 is "philosophical" and difficult. Can you, nevertheless, interpret the paragraph? Is this difficulty here due merely to the language used, or to the brevity, compression, lack of development and illustration of this particular paragraph?

J. What is "idealism" (Par. 10)? Who were Kant, Berkeley, Plato? What is the meaning of the terms "intuitive refusal" and "abstract materialism of science" (Par. 11)?

II. Make a list of the transitional words, phrases, clauses, or sentences used by Whitehead. To what extent are these the type of connectives that would be used in a *formal* lecture, to be delivered orally? Is there any difference between the kind of transitional expressions used in *speaking* and those used in *writing?*

III. Note all general statements of Whitehead that are immediately followed by illustrative references. For example, in Par. 1, "He weakens his evidence . . . ." is followed by "his scorn of the poor man . . . ." Find similar examples.

IV. Are the longer passages of poetry quoted as mere illustrative material or does Whitehead offer them as *evidence* leading to *proof* of his contentions?

V. Whitehead's critical interpretation of Wordsworth and Shelley is highly unorthodox as coming from a philosopher. It is even more unorthodox, considered as "literary criticism," since it has been the fashion among literary critics not to take the poetry of Wordsworth and Shelley quite as seriously as Whitehead does.

Write a critical interpretation of some writer with whom you are already well acquainted—either a poet or a prose writer. Develop an "unorthodox" critical interpretation, but take care to sustain it with appropriate illustrations and valid evidence. Remember that it is much more difficult to take an affirmative position, as Whitehead does, and support it, than to indulge in negative criticism or "fault-finding." The best criticism—whether literary or philosophical—is, like Whitehead's, dispassionate and firm.

Suggested topics:

Is the Poetry of ——(some supposedly difficult poet) Really Obscure?

A Defense of Rudyard Kipling (or some other writer not now popular)

Detective Stories Also Interpret "Real Life" (Use Conan Doyle, Erle Stanley Gardner, or some similarly substantial writer of detective stories)

Grand Opera Is Drama, Too (show that some opera by Wagner, Puccini, Menotti, or other composer deserves to rank with the best in drama)

The Modernity of ——(use some literary work of a past age which you think is highly relevant to present issues)

LESSON VIII

Analysis of a Historical Problem.
Dramatic Presentation.

THE DILEMMA OF 1688 *

by THOMAS BABINGTON MACAULAY

¶ 1 It was not merely by arguments drawn from the letter of Scripture that the Anglican theologians had, during the years which immediately followed the Restoration, laboured to prove their favourite tenet. They had attempted to show that, even if revelation had been silent, reason would have taught wise men the folly and wickedness of all resistance to established government. It was universally admitted that such resistance was, except in extreme cases, unjustifiable. And who would undertake to draw the line between extreme cases and ordinary cases? Was there any government in the world under which there were not to be found some discontented and factious men who would say, and perhaps think, that their grievances constituted an extreme case? If, indeed, it were possible to lay down a clear and accurate rule which might forbid men to rebel against Trajan, and yet leave them at liberty to rebel against Caligula, such a rule might be highly beneficial. But no such rule had ever been, or ever would be, framed. To say that rebellion was lawful under some circumstances, without accurately defining those circumstances, was to say that every man might rebel whenever he thought fit; and a society in which every man rebelled whenever he thought fit would be more miserable than a society governed by the most cruel and licentious despot. It was, therefore, necessary to maintain the great

* From *The History of England,* Chapter IX, "Change in the Opinion of the Tories Concerning the Lawfulness of Resistance."

principle of nonresistance in all its integrity. Particular cases might doubtless be put in which resistance would benefit a community; but it was, on the whole, better that the people should patiently endure a bad government than that they should relieve themselves by violating a law on which the security of all government depended.

¶ 2 Such reasoning easily convinced a dominant and prosperous party, but could ill bear the scrutiny of minds strongly excited by royal injustice and ingratitude. It is true that to trace the exact boundary between rightful and wrongful resistance is impossible; but this impossibility arises from the nature of right and wrong, and is found in every part of ethical science. A good action is not distinguished from a bad action by marks so plain as those which distinguish a hexagon from a square. There is a frontier where virtue and vice fade into each other. Who has ever been able to define the exact boundary between courage and rashness, between prudence and cowardice, between frugality and avarice, between liberality and prodigality? Who has ever been able to say how far mercy to offenders ought to be carried, and where it ceases to deserve the name of mercy and becomes a pernicious weakness? What casuist, what law-giver, has ever been able nicely to mark the limits of the right of self defence? All our jurists hold that a certain quantity of risk to life or limb justifies a man in shooting or stabbing an assailant: but they have long given up in despair the attempt to describe, in precise words, that quantity of risk. They only say that it must be, not a slight risk, but a risk such as would cause serious apprehension to a man of firm mind; and who will undertake to say what is the precise amount of apprehension which deserves to be called serious, or what is the precise texture of mind which deserves to be called firm? It is doubtless to be lamented that the nature of words and the nature of things do not admit of more accurate legislation: nor can it be denied that wrong will often be done when men are judges in their own cause, and proceed instantly to execute their own judgment. Yet who would, on that account, interdict all selfdefence? The right which a people has to resist a bad government bears a close analogy to the right which an individual, in the absence of legal protection, has to slay an assailant. In both cases the evil must be grave. In both cases all regular and peaceable modes of defence must be exhausted before the aggrieved party resorts to extremities. In both cases an awful responsibility is incurred. In both cases the burden of the proof lies on him who has ventured on so desperate an expedient: and if he fails to vindicate himself, he is justly liable to the severest penalties. But in neither case can we absolutely deny the existence of the right. A man beset by assassins is not bound to let himself be tortured and butchered without using his weapons, because nobody has ever been able precisely to define the amount of danger which justifies homicide. Nor is a society bound to endure passively all that tyranny can inflict, because nobody has ever been able precisely to define the amount of misgovernment which justifies rebellion.

¶ 3 But could the resistance of Englishmen to such a prince as James be properly called rebellion? The thoroughpaced disciples of Filmer, indeed, maintained that there was no difference whatever between the polity of our country and that of Turkey, and that, if the King did not confiscate the contents of all the tills in Lombard Street and send mutes with bowstrings to Sancroft and Halifax, this was only because His Majesty was too gracious to use the whole power which he derived from Heaven. But the great body of Tories, though, in the heat of conflict, they might occasionally use language which seemed to indicate that they approved of these extravagant doctrines, heartily abhorred despotism. The English government was, in their view, a limited monarchy. Yet how can a monarchy be said to be limited, if force is never to be employed, even in the last resort, for the purpose of maintaining the limitations? In Muscovy, where the sovereign was, by the constitution of the state, absolute, it might perhaps be, with some colour of truth, contended that, whatever excesses he might commit, he was still entitled to demand, on Christian principles, the obedience of his subjects. But here prince and people were alike bound by the laws. It was therefore James who incurred the woe denounced against those who insult the powers that be. It was James who was resisting the ordinance of God, who was mutinying against that legitimate authority to which he ought to have been subject, not only for wrath, but also for conscience' sake, and who was, in the true sense of the words of Jesus, withholding from Caesar the things which were Caesar's.

Moved by such considerations as these, the ablest and most enlightened Tories began to admit that they had overstrained the doctrine of passive obedience. The difference between these men and the Whigs as to the reciprocal obligations of kings and subjects was now no longer a difference of principle. There still remained, it is true, many historical controversies between the party which had always maintained the lawfulness of resistance and the new converts. The memory of the blessed Martyr was still as much revered as ever by those old Cavaliers who were ready to take arms against his degenerate son. They still spoke with abhorrence of the Long Parliament, of the Rye House plot, and of the Western insurrection. But whatever they might think about the past, the view which they took of the present was altogether Whiggish; for they now held that extreme oppression might justify resistance, and they held that the oppression which the nation suffered was extreme. ¶ 4

EXERCISES

I. With masterly skill, Macaulay analyzes the state of mind of the English Tories just prior to the Revolution of 1688, when James II fled England to claim the protection and support of Louis XIV of France and when William of Orange, after entering England with an army recruited in the Netherlands, was seated, with Mary, on the throne of England. Macaulay is depicting the dilemma of the Tories, who were obliged to find reasons for reversing their former position of "passive obedience" to the Stuart dynasty. During the English Civil War the Tories had upheld Charles I and the "divine right of kings," but lost to their bitter enemies, the Whigs.

By 1688 Tories and Whigs found themselves in agreement, at least as to the desirability of dispossessing James II.

In setting forth the dilemma of the Tories, Macaulay not only summarizes and interprets the arguments by which the Tories justified their reversal of position, but also creates the impression of an argument actually in progress at the time when the somewhat embarrassed Tories were deciding that expediency rather than principle might be the best policy. Nowhere in this passage does Macaulay use direct quotation. Nevertheless, by echoing what were undoubtedly the arguments and what may have been the very language of the Tories, Macaulay conveys the impression of men arguing intimately with one another—or perhaps with their own consciences.

In the Defoe selection (pp. 10–13) we had a rather simple example of a dramatized conflict in a single individual's mind. Defoe, in comparison with Macaulay, may seem naive if not crude. Macaulay, however, is applying the same basic method as Defoe. The difference is that the situation depicted in Macaulay's account is highly complex. Many great people, including statesmen and clerics, are involved in an agony of debate, private and public.

Macaulay attacks his problem with zest and energy and evidently finds pleasure in using his opportunities for dramatization. The dramatization allows Macaulay as historian to assume the role of a seemingly detached observer who is merely reporting, with rather sardonic interest, the logical contortions by which the Tories could decide that it was utterly wrong for the Puritans to overthrow Charles I, but perfectly reasonable for the Tories of 1688 to combine with their former opponents and dispossess James II. The tone of irony that underlies Macaulay's dramatization gives a clue as to where lie the sympathies of Macaulay, the Victorian "liberal." Gibbon was the first English historian to cultivate this tone of seemingly detached irony. In the twentieth century, Lytton Strachey used it in his *Eminent Victorians* and other works. Strachey thus made history and biography as "dramatic" as fiction. Among American historians, Charles A. Beard, in *The Rise of American Civilization,* has used the technique of Macaulay and Strachey with great skill.

II. In his first paragraph, as a preliminary to his main discussion, Macaulay recapitulates the "old" arguments of the English Tories in favor of the principle of "nonresistance" to the established government. Make an outline or summary of the *thought* of this paragraph. Pass over for the time being all interesting features of style and confine yourself to stating the logical steps of the "old" argument of the Tories.

Before constructing your outline or summary, examine Par. 1 in the light of the following questions:

A. Is Macaulay here giving arguments drawn from Scripture or arguments drawn from reason? Are the two in conflict?

B. Does Macaulay represent the Tories as arguing that resistance to established government is *never* justifiable? If an exception is allowed, what is the nature of the exception, and where is it stated?

C. What is the relationship between the phrases in the following pairs?

> "except in extreme cases"—"some discontented and factious men"
> "forbid men to rebel against Trajan"—"leave them at liberty to rebel against Caligula"

D. Why does Macaulay refer to Trajan and Caligula? Are these monarchs cited as "proof" of an argument, or is Macaulay only illustrating a *hypothetical* possibility? If you do not know who Trajan and Caligula were, look them up. Would Macaulay's readers have had to look up these names?

E. Does the conclusion of the paragraph ("It was therefore necessary, etc.") follow logically and inevitably from the chain of argument preceding?

F. Is the following general statement a fair statement of the "old" Tory argument?

> Stability is the most desirable feature of government and takes precedence over abstract ideas about liberty. Grievances of individuals and parties should therefore never be permitted to disturb the stability of a government.

III. Make a similar outline or summary of Pars. 2 and 3. Again concentrate on the steps of thought, ignoring other matters. Note that these two paragraphs constitute the *argument proper*—as Pars. 1 and 4 do not, although they are a part of the *composition.*

A. Note that in Par. 1 the Tories seem to be drawing the line "between extreme cases and ordinary cases." But in Par. 2 they are drawing the line between "rightful and wrongful resistance"; "right and wrong"; "a good action" and "a bad action."

Does the change of terms signify a shift in the *basis* of the argument? Does this shift constitute a logical inconsistency in the "new" argument of the Tory party? Is a fallacy of logic involved?

B. The "proof" supporting the argument in Par. 2 consists largely of a series of *analogies.* Examine each of these analogies and determine whether it applies to the case of the subject resisting his King. Since Macaulay devotes special attention to the analogy of the individual acting in self-defense, give particular attention to this part of the paragraph. An analogy, to be logically acceptable, must constitute a true "parallel example." Is individual self-defense, in this instance, such a true parallel example? Is the argument effective regardless of whether this and other analogies used are logically acceptable?

C. Are the analogies of Par. 2 used in the same way as the examples of Trajan and Caligula in Par. 1?

D. What distinction is made (Par. 3) between "the thoroughpaced disciples of Filmer" and "the great body of Tories"?

E. The "new" argument as to the implications of "a limited monarchy" reveals an apparent contradiction in the "old" position of the Tories. What is the nature of this contradiction? Does Macaulay explicitly point out the contradiction? Does he expect the reader to be conscious that it is there?

F. What is the purpose of the contrast between Muscovy (Tsarist Russia) and England?

G. In what way does the "new" argument contrive to shift the onus of blame to James II?

H. Is it consistent for the Tory party to argue that "prince and people were alike bound by the laws" and also "It was James who was resisting the ordinance of God"? Are "the laws" and "the ordinance of God" the same thing? (Compare the first two sentences of Par. 1.)

IV. After making the suggested outlines and answering the questions asked above, determine whether the conclusion indicated in Par. 4 logically follows from the argument given in Pars. 2 and 3.

V. Whether or not the argument is logically perfect, does Macaulay, in presenting the argument, correctly interpret the fundamental nature of the English government?

VI. The *rhetorical question*—which Macaulay uses freely in this selection—is one of the chief devices through which Macaulay achieves his ironic dramatization—that is, as was said above, creates the impression of an argument actually in progress. A rhetorical question is "a question designed to produce an effect and not to draw an answer" *(The American College Dictionary).* The first of the rhetorical questions appears in Par. 1: "And who would undertake . . . ?" Identify all other rhetorical questions in the four paragraphs and discuss the degree of their effectiveness. To what extent is Macaulay simply reporting the argument of the Tories and to what extent is he deliberately infusing an element of irony?

VII. Much of the effectiveness of Macaulay's style depends upon his control of sentence structure. Each sentence is devised so as to deliver an emphatic blow, and though the sentences are prevalently elaborate in organization, there is never the slightest haziness of meaning. The blow falls, with real force, exactly where Macaulay intends. He takes care to place the word or phrase that carries the impact at the point in the sentence where it will count most heavily. The features of sentence structure that require special study are (1) Macaulay's use of "periodic" structure, and (2) his even more profuse use of the "balanced" construction, often with the parts in antithetical relationship.

A. Would Sens. 1, 2, and 3 of Par. 1 be equally effective if Macaulay had written as follows:

> During the years which immediately followed the Restoration, arguments drawn from the letter of Scripture were not the only means by which the Anglican theologians labored to prove their favorite tenet. According to their attempts at justification of their position, reason would have taught wise men the folly and wickedness of all resistance to established government, even if revelation had been silent. Such resistance was universally admitted to be unjustifiable except in extreme cases.

Before answering the question, make a close comparison between the arrangement of the elements of the three sentences as given above and as written by Macaulay.

B. In a similar manner, rewrite the sentences referred to below. Substitute the "loose" type of sentence for the "periodic." Eliminate the balanced constructions and antitheses as far as possible. Then compare your rewritten sentences with Macaulay's and decide whether you have improved his prose style.

1. "It was universally admitted . . . ." (Par. 1)
2. "But no such rule . . . ." (Par. 1)
3. "It is doubtless to be lamented . . . accurate legislation" (Par. 2)
4. "But the great body of Tories . . . ." (Par. 3)
5. "But whatever . . . view . . . Whiggish." (Par. 4)

VIII. In the following sentences, identify the grammatical elements that are placed in a balanced relationship. If the relationship is both balanced and antithetical, so indicate.

1. "If, indeed, it were possible . . . highly beneficial." (Par. 1)
2. "To say that . . . licentious despot." (Par. 1)
3. ". . . but it was, on the whole, . . . all government depended." (Par. 1, last sentence)
4. "A good action . . . from a square." (Par. 2)
5. "The right which . . . slay an assailant." (Par. 2)

Sentences or clauses framed in a balanced structure will also generally be formed according to the rhetorical-grammatical principle of *parallelism.* Point out all instances of parallelism in the sentences referred to above. Give the grammatical construction of the elements linked in parallel structure. Note also any instances in which Macaulay *varies* slightly the constituency of the parallel elements. Why does such variation occur? Find also at least five instances in which Macaulay uses parallel structure in sentences that are *not* "balanced."

IX. Macaulay frequently uses words in pairs (*e. g.,* "folly and wickedness," "discontented and factious men," "cruel and licentious," Par. 1). The habit of coupling words in pairs may easily become a mannerism of style. Some critics might hold that in Macaulay's style it is a mannerism, indeed a vice. Richard M. Weaver, however, in his *The Ethics of Rhetoric* (p. 158), argues that a similar use of pairs in John Milton's prose is a virtue: ". . . what the pairs create," says Mr. Weaver, "is the effect of dimension. . . . If he (Milton) used two words where another author would use one, that fact affords presumption that his second word had its margin of meaningful addition to contribute."

Collect at least ten of Macaulay's pairs. Examine them in the passages where they appear and decide whether Macaulay had better have used one word instead of two, or whether the second word contributes a "margin of meaningful addition."

X. Theme topics: Analyze the state of mind of some political, regional, national, or college group which arrives at a crisis and finds itself looking for "good reasons" to reverse old arguments and adopt a view it had formerly scorned. The title of your theme might well be "Politics (or Economics, Fashion, War, etc.) Makes Strange Bedfellows"—or something of the kind.

PART FOUR

REFLECTIVE THINKING
INTERPRETATION
ARGUMENT

I believe that man will not merely endure; he will prevail. He is immortal, not because he alone among creatures has an inexhaustible voice, but because he has a soul, a spirit capable of compassion and sacrifice and endurance. The poet's, the writer's, duty is to write about these things. It is his privilege to help man endure by lifting his heart, by reminding him of the courage and honor and hope and pride and compassion and pity and sacrifice which have been the glory of his past.—William Faulkner, *Nobel Prize Award Speech.*

LESSON IX

Analysis Applied to a Historical or Social Subject.
Obsolete and Archaic Words. Words in Pairs.
Tautology. Redundance.
Grammatical-Rhetorical Analysis of Sentences.

VICISSITUDE IN WARS *

by FRANCIS BACON

The changes and vicissitude in wars are many; but chiefly in three things; in the seats or stages of the war; in the weapons; and in the manner of conduct. Wars, in ancient time, seemed more to move from east to west; for the Persians, Assyrians, Arabians, Tartars, (which were the invaders,) were all eastern people. It is true, the Gauls were western; but we read but of two incursions of theirs; the one to Gallo-Graecia, the other to Rome. But East and West have no certain points of heaven; and no more have the wars, either from the east or west, any certainty of observation. But North and South are fixed; and it hath seldom or never been seen that the far southern people have invaded the northern, but contrariwise. Whereby it is manifest that the northern tract of the world is in nature the more martial region: be it in respect of the stars of that hemisphere; or of the great continents that are upon the north, whereas the south part, for aught that is known, is almost all sea; or (which is most apparent) of the cold of the northern parts, which is that which, without aid of discipline, doth make the bodies hardest, and the courage warmest. ¶ 1

* From "Of Vicissitude of Things," *The Essays of Francis Bacon.*

** Spelling and punctuation in the main follow A. W. Pollard's edition of *The Essays, Colours of Good and Evil, Advancement of Learning, of Francis Bacon,* Library of English Classics, Macmillan and Co., Ltd., 1925.

¶2 Upon the breaking and shivering of a great state and empire, you may be sure to have wars. For great empires, while they stand, do enervate and destroy the forces of the natives which they have subdued, resting upon their own protecting forces; and then when they fail also, all goes to ruin, and they become a prey. So was it in the decay of the Roman empire; and likewise in the empire of Almaigne, after Charles the Great, every bird taking a feather; and were not unlike to befall to Spain, if it should break. The great accessions and unions of kingdoms do likewise stir up wars: for when a state grows to an over-power, it is like a great flood, that will be sure to overflow. As it hath been seen in the states of Rome, Turkey, Spain and others. Look when the world hath fewest barbarous peoples, but such as commonly will not marry and generate, except they know means to live, (as it is almost everywhere at this day, except Tartary,) there is no danger of inundations of people: but when there be great shoals of people, which go on to populate, without foreseeing means of life and sustentation, it is of necessity that once in an age or two they discharge a portion of their people upon other nations; which the ancient northern people were wont to do by lot; casting lots what part should stay at home, and what should seek their fortunes. When a warlike state grows soft and effeminate, they may be sure of a war. For commonly such states are grown rich in the time of their degenerating; and so the prey inviteth, and their decay in valour encourageth a war.

¶3 As for the weapons, it hardly falleth under rule and observation: yet we see even they have returns and vicissitudes. For certain it is, that ordnance was known in the city of the Oxidrakes in India; and was that which the Macedonians called thunder and lightning, and magic. And it is well known that the use of ordnance hath been in China above two thousand years. The conditions of weapons, and their improvement, are, First, the fetching afar off; for that outruns the danger; as it is seen in ordnance and muskets. Secondly, the strength of the percussion; wherein likewise ordnance do exceed all arietations and ancient inventions. The third is, the commodious use of them; as that they may serve in all weathers; that the carriage may be light and manageable; and the like.

For the conduct of the war: at the first, men rested ex- ¶ 4
tremely upon number: they did put the wars likewise upon main force and valour; pointing days for pitched fields, and so trying it out upon an even match: and they were more ignorant in ranging and arraying their battles. After they grew to rest upon number rather competent than vast; they grew to advantages of place, cunning diversions, and the like: and they grew more skilful in the ordering of their battles.

In the youth of a state, arms do flourish; in the middle ¶ 5
age of a state, learning; and then both of them together for a time; in the declining age of a state, mechanical arts and merchandise. Learning hath his infancy, when it is but beginning and almost childish: then his youth, when it is luxuriant and juvenile: then his strength of years, when it is solid and reduced: and lastly, his old age, when it waxeth dry and exhaust. But it is not good to look too long upon these turning wheels of vicissitude, lest we become giddy. As for the philology of them, that is but a circle of tales, and therefore not fit for this writing.

EXERCISES

I. The *Essays* of Lord Bacon (1561–1626) were perhaps not esteemed by Bacon himself as among his profound and ambitious works. In the earlier, more literal meaning of the word "essay," they were "trials" or "experiments" in reflection upon various subjects, mostly of a practical, utilitarian nature. "Observations" or "notes" might be a fair rendering of "essays" as Bacon used the term, with the implication that an essay was limited, informal, and tentative in character. Bacon's *Essays* were in effect his notebook, in which he set down his thoughts without bothering to give them extension or finality. Since in his eyes they were no great matter, he wrote them in English, but his great philosophical works he wrote in Latin, the language of the world of learning, the familiar instrument of communication among men of letters, jurists, clergy, and statesmen in the Europe of Bacon's time.

To us, looking back, Bacon's *Essays* seem remarkable achievements in English prose. They may not have the wonderful finish and subtle elaboration of the writings of Cicero (as in the *De Amicitia*) which may well have influenced Bacon's style as it did that of other men. But the clearness, economy, and strength of Bacon's prose set a standard we might well aspire to emulate. A study of Bacon's prose is a good corrective for vagueness and diffuseness in composition. It may not, of course, be desirable for a modern writer to cultivate the particular kind of epigrammatic terseness in which Bacon excels. But though Bacon's prose is less persuasive and lofty in its influence than the prose of the King James Version of The Bible, his sayings are sometimes mistaken for Biblical utterances, and indeed the *Essays* do have, as John Livingston Lowes says of the King James Version, "apt and telling turns of expression, the phrases of homely vigor or happy pregnancy, which have become a part of our linguistic stock in trade."

II. The scope and plan of "Vicissitude in Wars" is firmly indicated in the first sentence. What is Bacon's subject? Wars in general? Or a single aspect of wars? Look up the derivation and meaning of *change* and *vicissitude.* Why are the two words coupled in the first sentence but not in the title? Mark the three divisions of the essay that correspond to the three divisions of the subject. Is Bacon's division of his subject into three parts a complete *logical analysis,* or is it an *informal analysis*—that is, a selection, for discussion, of three salient divisions or aspects of the subject? Be sure that you understand Bacon's terms: "seats or stages"; "manner of conduct." Here, as in other instances, Bacon's meaning lies close to the old, basic meaning of the words, which in our time may have acquired later or "derived" meanings. "Stages" does not here refer to "degree of progression," and "conduct" does not refer to a "code of behavior."

III. Bacon's first paragraph, after the first sentence, deals with "the seats or stages of the war." He passes to a discussion of this topic without making a transition. But elsewhere in this paragraph he is careful to bind closely the parts of his discussion. Underline all connective expressions in Par. 1.

A. What modern terms could be substituted for Bacon's "seats or stages"? Would "geographic pattern" serve as a synonym?

B. Interpret precisely, by paraphrasing in your own words, the following: (1) "have no certain points of heaven"; (2) "any certainty of observation"; (3) "North and South are fixed"; (4) "is in nature the more martial region."

C. Bacon is careful to give specific examples to support and illustrate his statement that wars in ancient times moved from east to west. What historic invasions are indicated in his references to the Persians, Assyrians, Arabians, Tartars, and Gauls?

D. Bacon does not cite any invasions from the north, other than of the Gauls. What "incursions" could he have cited? What support does he give his statement that "the northern tract of the world is in nature the more martial region"? Explain the phrase "in respect of the stars of that hemisphere."

E. In view of the events of the past half century, are Bacon's speculations as to "the seats and stages" of wars out of date? Give the reason for your answer. In this connection, look up the newly coined word *geopolitics.*

F. Would the Moorish invasions of southern Europe be an exception to Bacon's statement that "the far southern people" have seldom or never invaded the northern countries?

G. Make a grammatical-rhetorical analysis of the last sentence of Par. 1. Explain the syntax (grammatical construction) of "be it" and its relationship to the elements that follow in series. Are the elements of this series in *exactly* parallel form, or is there variation? After completing your analysis, write a sentence in which you follow Bacon's structure as closely as possible, but in which you substitute modern terms for Bacon's pithy Elizabethan form of expression. For example, your sentence might begin as follows: "It is clear that northern Europe must have seemed, to a Renaissance historian, more warlike than southern Europe . . . ." What does your paraphrase reveal as to the changes in the English language and in English prose style and usage since Bacon's time?

IV. Using the procedure developed in III, above, make analyses of the structural organization of Pars. 2 and 3. In Par. 2, is Bacon still discussing the "seats and stages" of wars? Devise modern terms that would serve as adequate headings for the subdivisions of Pars. 2 and 3. Explain all historical references.

A. What figure of speech is involved in "become a prey"? (Sen. 2, Par.

LESSON IX

Analysis Applied to a Historical or Social Subject . . .

2.) How is this figure further applied in the sentence following? Is the figure re-echoed elsewhere?

B. What reservation as to weapons does Bacon make in "it hardly falleth under rule and observation"? (Par. 3)

C. Is Bacon's analysis of "the conditions of weapons, and their improvement" applicable to modern conditions?

D. Give the derivation and meaning of *ordnance, percussion, arietations, commodious* (applied to *use*), *carriage.* Give modern synonyms for these terms.

V. Does Par. 4 give an accurate historical description of the development of military science? In this paragraph Bacon supplies no historical instances to exemplify his statements. Can you cite any?

VI. Does Bacon's description (Par. 5) of the youth, middle age, and declining age of a state fit the history of any country that you can cite? Does it apply to the United States? Does Bacon's description of the development of "learning" properly belong in this paragraph? Why does he say *his* youth, *his* strength, etc., instead of *its*? Look up *his* and *its* in the *New English Dictionary.* What does Bacon mean by saying that "the philology of them . . . is but a circle of tales"?

VII. Study Bacon's use of words in pairs. For example: "seats or stages" (Par. 1); "breaking and shivering," "marry and generate" (Par. 2); "main force and valour" (Par. 4); and the series in Par. 5: "beginning and almost childish," "luxuriant and juvenile," etc.

In what instances is a pair of words needed for exactness of meaning? In what instances do the words of the pair have a closely similar or identical meaning? In the latter case, does Bacon's use of a pair give some desirable richness or sonority of language? Test Bacon's sentences by omitting words that seem tautological or redundant. Is it a good principle of composition, as some argue, never to use two words when one will do?

To what extent is Bacon's use of pairs a familiar idiomatic practice in English? Is it the same kind of idiom that we find in such expressions as *give and bequeath, to have and to hold,* and the like?

LESSON X

Analysis and Argument Combined.
Use of Hypothetical Example.
Inductive-Deductive Thinking.
Analogy As Proof.

ORIGIN OF TYRANNY *

by GEORGE SANTAYANA

The inertia which physics registers in the first law of motion, natural history and psychology call habit. In society it takes the form of custom, which when codified is called law and when enforced is called government. Government is the political representative of a natural equilibrium, of custom, of inertia; it is by no means a representative of reason. But like any mechanical complication it may become rational, and many of its forms and operations may be defended on rational grounds. ¶ 1

Suppose a cold and hungry savage, failing to find berries and game enough in the woods, should descend into some meadow where a flock of sheep were grazing and pounce upon a lame lamb which could not run away with the others, tear its flesh, suck up its blood, and dress himself in its skin. All this could not be called an affair undertaken in the sheep's interest. And yet it might well conduce to their interest in the end. For the savage, finding himself soon hungry again, and insufficiently warm in that scanty garment, might attack the flock a second time, and thereby begin to accustom himself, and also his delighted family, to a new and more substantial sort of raiment and diet. Suppose, now, a pack of wolves, or a second savage, or a disease should attack these ¶ 2

* Reprinted by permission of the publishers, Constable & Co., Ltd., London, from *Little Essays,* by George Santayana.

unhappy sheep. Would not their primeval enemy defend them? Would he not have identified himself with their interests to this extent, that their total extinction or discomfiture would alarm him also? And in so far as he provided for their well-being, would he not have become a good shepherd? If, now, some philosophic wether, a lover of his kind, reasoned with his fellows upon the change in their condition, he might shudder indeed at those early episodes and at the contribution of lambs and fleeces which would not cease to be levied by the new government; but he might also consider that such a contribution was nothing in comparison with what was formerly exacted by wolves, diseases, frosts, and casual robbers, when the flock was much smaller than it had now grown to be, and much less able to withstand decimation. And he might even have conceived an admiration for the remarkable wisdom and beauty of that great shepherd, dressed in such a wealth of wool; and he might remember pleasantly some occasional caress received from him and the daily trough filled with water by his providential hand. And he might not be far from maintaining not only the rational origin, but the divine right of shepherds.

¶ 3 Such a savage enemy, incidentally turned into a useful master, is called a conqueror or king. His government is nothing but a chronic raid, mitigated by the desire to leave the inhabitants prosperous enough to be continually despoiled afresh. At first an army is simply a ravenous and lusty horde quartered in a conquered country; yet the cost of such an incubus may come to be regarded as an insurance against further attack, and so what is in its real basis an inevitable burden resulting from a chance balance of forces may be justified in afterthought as a rational device for defensive purposes. Such an ulterior justification has nothing to do, however, with the causes that maintain armies or military policies: and accordingly those virginal minds that think things originated in the uses they may have acquired, have frequent cause to be pained and perplexed at the abuses and overdevelopment of militarism. The constant compensation tyranny brings, which keeps it from at once exhausting its victims, is the silence it imposes on their private squabbles. One distant universal enemy may be less oppressive than a thousand unchecked pilferers and plotters at home.

EXERCISES

I. In his discussion of tyranny Santayana affords us an illuminating example of the possibilities and the dangers inherent in the use of rhetorical devices. In Par. 1 Santayana gives us his thesis: government is not a representative of reason, but of other forces (natural equilibrium, custom, inertia); however, it may *become* rational and to some extent may be then defended as rational.

In support of this general statement Santayana sets up a *hypothetical example.* We are to suppose a flock of sheep set upon by a savage who at first preys upon them mercilessly in his own interest. Soon it becomes also his interest to protect them, in order that he may have a secure provision of mutton and wool. The sheep multiply and become fat and contented, and they presently rationalize their condition and argue that the savage is acting in their interest, even though they must still yield him a ceaseless tribute of mutton and wool. From these circumstances "some philosophic wether" may thereupon develop a theory about "not only the rational origin, but the divine right of shepherds."

After brilliantly setting forth this hypothetical example, Santayana proceeds, in Par. 3, to apply it to a more definitely human situation. A conqueror or king, or presumably any governmental kind of tyranny, is the political parallel to the "savage enemy" of the hypothetical example. The citizens held in such a tyranny are the parallel to the "sheep." If the citizens think that the tyranny, because of its incidental benefits to them (for example, the tyrant's army that protects them against external aggression) is justified, they are thinking as badly as the sheep and are as fatally wrong. Their rational justification of the tyranny is "afterthought." They may suffer from the folly of this shallow rationalization—for example, in "the abuses and overdevelopment of militarism." But, sheeplike, they endure for the sake of the compensation that tyranny brings—i.e., relief from internal disorder ("private squabbles").

At first reading, Santayana's logic seems perfect, his argument impregnable. After making a clear general statement, he immediately supports it with a convincing hypothetical example, worked out in full detail. He then applies it to real circumstances, sufficiently familiar to all of us, and demonstrates its relevance, thus completing within small compass an inductive-deductive process of thinking which leads to a reaffirmation of his original generalization in a different form. Furthermore, Santayana's style is suave and artful. If we have momentary doubts, they are lulled by the delightful ingenuity of his talk about the sheep and the shepherd. We find ourselves saying, "Yes, it must have been like that!" The account of the sheep and the shepherd may remind us of something we know about the attitude of people toward government. And, recalling such bits of historical knowledge as we command, we may say, "It must have been like that from the very beginning of government." We are tempted to think—and in fact seem to be invited to think—that Santayana is giving a very plausible account not only of the origin of tyranny but of human government itself.

II. But it is also evident that Santayana's case rests heavily upon his hypothetical example. If it is not a valid example—if he does not use it in right relation to his process of reasoning—why, then, a very distinguished philosopher has been using the art of rhetoric to deceive us! Or if, on the other hand, the example may be valid enough, but is not intended to mean what we have taken it to mean (in "I," above), then the distinguished philosopher is writing obscurely, and not as clearly as we thought, or is mocking us, is talking "over our heads."

It is therefore necessary to ask and answer certain critical questions. The questions are asked below—and you may think of other questions. It is your task to answer them. Before answering them, however, you should understand that the hypothetical example is one of the common resources of all who engage in speculative thinking, of philosophers especially, but of scientists too, and others. It is in fact difficult to think speculatively without using the word "suppose," as Santayana does. The hypothetical example is not an actual example, taken from real life, present or past, but an imagined or supposititious example. The dictionary definition of "hypothetical" is: "assumed without proof, for the purpose of reasoning and deducing proof, or of accounting for some fact." *(Webster's New Collegiate Dictionary)* The hypothetical example, like any other example, must really exemplify. It is a fiction, and may be a fable, but it is valid and acceptable if it correctly *represents* the general pattern of known facts. It partakes of the nature of analogy; it must be sufficiently *like* what we know to carry conviction. The scientist can test the validity of his hypothetical example by laboratory experiment. The philosopher—or any other person relying upon reason alone—must depend wholly upon the process of reason applied to existing knowledge. Remember also that, while the philosopher may use the hypothetical example as a part of his proof, he may, on the other hand, use it only for illustration, and the illustration may be interpretative, even symbolical. Here, then, are the questions:

A. In the first two sentences of Par. 1, Santayana offers what is apparently a highly condensed theory of the *origin* of government. In the next two sentences Santayana emphasizes a certain *aspect* or *characteristic* of government: that it is not representative of reason but may be thought so. To which of these two theses is the example of Par. 2 to be related? Would the first three sentences of Par. 3 lead a reader to think that the example of sheep and shepherd is an account of the *origin* of government (or tyranny)? At what point, in Par. 3, does Santayana relate his example to the other idea embodied in Par. 1?

B. If you conclude that Santayana is really talking about how men can find excuses for accustoming themselves to tyranny rather than about the remote origin of government or of tyranny, how do you account for the title of the piece—"Origin of Tyranny"? Would any of the following titles be preferable: "Misconceptions about Tyranny"; "Is Tyranny a Reasonable Form of Government?"; "People Can Get Used to Anything"? Do you have an alternative title to propose, and, if so, what are your reasons for proposing it? In justice to Santayana, you should remember that this particular selection, though included under this title in *Little Essays* (Logan Pearsall Smith, ed.), is really but a small excerpt from Santayana's book, *Reason in Society,* which is Volume 2 of his six-volume work under the general title, *The Life of Reason, or Phases of Human Progress.* You are therefore considering this small selection out of its general context.

C. Is the hypothetical example of sheep-and-shepherd really applicable in Santayana's argument? What defects of analogy and application can you find? Is it realistic and fair to suppose a savage as imposing a government, similar to human government, upon sheep? The example requires us to think of the governor—the tyrant—as human, but of the governed as animals (sheep). Would it be more plausible to think of the tyrant as an ambitious sheep who seizes the power in a nation of sheep? Or a savage who rises to tyrannic position in a nation of savages?

D. Is Santayana's example sufficiently representative of known historic circumstances of the origin of government and the rise of tyranny? Look up Aristotle's theory of the beginnings of government in his *Politics (Modern Library,* Max Lerner, ed.). Does it support or contradict Santayana? Would Santayana's hypothetical example serve as a fair and true description of the origin of the government of the United States or of any government formed on the principle that governments derive their powers from the consent of the governed? If Santayana's example does not fit the case of the United States, in what ways would his tale of sheep-and-shepherd have to be changed to make it fit? Would you, in your fable, prefer some animal other than the sheep, or no animal at all? Why? Do not forget that the use of birds, animals, and other creatures to represent human behavior is a common and ancient device. See, for example, Aesop's fable, "King Log and King Stork."

E. If Santayana intends his example not as "proof" but merely as "illustration," what is he illustrating? Is he then using the terms "sheep," "savage," "good shepherd," "philosophic wether," and the like in a derogatory and satirical meaning? If so, why? Is the satirical meaning sufficiently clear for Santayana's purpose? Can he be justly charged with obscurity? With writing with a divided purpose? In this connection, explain (Par. 3) "may be justified in afterthought as a rational device," and "virginal minds that think things originated in the uses they may have acquired." Is the title, "Origin of Tyranny," itself composed with satirical intent?

III. After completing the study suggested above, you should be ready to explore the possibilities of the use of the hypothetical example, and to avoid the dangers. Write a theme—on one of the subjects suggested below or one of your own choosing—in which you make a general statement, support it by a hypothetical example, and then apply the example to known circumstances.

A. Read Homer's famous description of the Shield of Achilles (*Iliad, XVIII,* 497–508. See *Loeb Classical Library* for original text and prose translation) and pay particular attention to Homer's description of the judges hearing a dispute in what seems to be a primitive court of law. Construct an argument in which you base a conception of the origin of courts of law upon this passage of Homer's *Iliad* as your hypothetical example.

B. Using Aristotle's theory of the family as the possible origin of government (see his *Politics*), imagine a hypothetical example to fit his theory, and write a theme that would fit theory and example.

C. Assuming that college fraternities in their first foundation represent an ideal of brotherly fellowship rather than social aggrandizement, write a defense of fraternities in which you make use of a hypothetical example. Avoid statistical evidence, local history, personal opinion, and try to construct your case in terms of objective reason.

D. Following the method employed by Santayana, write a theme in which you endeavor to show, through the use of a hypothetical example, that the ideal of brotherhood upheld by fraternities is a "rational device" or "afterthought" rather than an inherent feature of fraternities.

E. Take for your subject some conflict between public and private interests. Find some issue of grave importance that may be obscured by the arguments of the contending parties and, by the use of a hypothetical example, develop an argued position on the pertinence of this issue. Present controversies over labor unions, public education, social security, and the like offer a fertile field for a well-reasoned discussion such as you are asked to write.

LESSON XI

Definition and Analysis in Combination.
Discussion of Technical Subject in Non-technical Terms.
Right and Wrong Views Examined.
Classification As a Feature of Analysis.
Proceeding "from the Known to the Unknown."
Definition in Terms of Origin.
Technical and Metaphorical Language.
Reasonable Conjecture and Proof.

SCIENCE AT ITS BEST *

by ANTHONY STANDEN

¶ 1 The various sciences can all be arranged in order, going from fairly good through mediocre to downright bad. Allowing the scientists to put their best foot forward, we may as well begin with the best of the sciences, which is physics.

¶ 2 Physics is, in a very general way, the study of all the material things in the world that are not alive. Looking at it this way, chemistry becomes a branch of physics—the distinction between conventional "chemistry" and conventional "physics" is largely one of convenience, and you can always call both of them together "physical science." Astronomy, geology, meteorology and some others are derivatives of the physical sciences, for they take the generalizations of physics and chemistry and apply them to certain particulars, the stars, the rocks and the weather. The next general division of the sciences is biology, which takes up things that *are* alive. Then comes psychology, which does not confine itself to material things, but deals with thought—or attempts to do so—while last comes a hodgepodge of studies, dealing with men's relations with one another, that some enthusiasts

*From the book, *Science Is a Sacred Cow,* by Anthony Standen. Copyright, 1950, by Anthony Standen. Published by E. P. Dutton & Co. Reprinted by permission of the publishers.

(but by no means all scientists) have dignified by the name "social sciences."

¶ 3 Physics is the most highly developed of all the sciences, and it is also the oldest, for it got well under way as early as the seventeenth century. The other sciences followed later, and their proponents like to think that the reason they haven't got so far is that they haven't been at it so long. Actually there are other reasons, as we shall see later, but at least they are right in paying deference and respect to physics, which is unquestionably science at its best.

¶ 4 The first thing to realize about physics, a thing which very few physics teachers make really clear, is its extraordinary indirectness. It appears to begin with very straightforward questions, but there are catches in it right from the start. Every high-school student is told that according to Aristotle the heavier of two weights would fall faster, but that Galileo, by dropping two different weights from the leaning tower of Pisa, "proved" that Aristotle was wrong, for the weights were found to fall in exactly the same time. And yet Aristotle was right. The heavier body does fall faster, because of air resistance, which slows up the lighter body more than the heavier. Only a very little faster, it is true, and the difference may not be detectable, but since scientists claim that they use words with such great precision, it is fair to hold them to it. If you press a physicist on this point, he will readily admit that what he means is that the two bodies would fall equally fast *in a vacuum*. If you press him further, he will very reluctantly admit that nobody has ever made a vacuum, and the closest to a vacuum anybody has ever made still contains millions of gas molecules per cubic inch. And so it turns out that the physicist's statement, that the two bodies fall at the same rate, refers to an entirely hypothetical, unreal state of affairs, whereas what Aristotle said refers to the actual world that we live in. This is characteristic of physics, all the way through. Yet it is because of this, and not in spite of it, that physics is the best of the sciences. For physics is not about the real world, it is about "abstractions" from the real world, and this is what makes it so scientific. It has all the proper attributes—the importance of exact measurement, the reduction of everything to mathematics, the carefully defined and precisely used terms, the pitilessly rigid trains of logical thought—that are commonly ascribed to everything that goes by the name of science. Other so-called sciences are scientific in so far as they approach the dignity of physics, and it would be only a slight exaggeration to say that physics *is* science, physics and nothing else. For physics shows, more often, more clearly and more successfully than any other branch of knowledge, the one operation that is truly scientific, and that is the framing of hypotheses to "explain," or render intelligible, the results of observation or experiment. The hypotheses are always in terms of "abstractions," which are, strictly speaking, unrealities, such as the perfect vacuum in which all bodies are supposed to fall equally quickly. Theoretical physics runs along merrily with these unreal abstractions, but its conclusions are checked, at every possible point, by experiments. The experiments have to agree with the theory as closely as possible, but since no measurements can be made without some slight inaccuracy, the agreement is never absolutely complete. "Nearly equal" is the same as "equal" to a physicist.

¶ 5 The best things in physics are fully as admirable as the scientists claim them to be, perhaps even more, in view of the scientists' habit of praising science for the wrong reasons. Humanists, the professional dishers-out of Shakespeare and other geniuses, claim that their specialty brings one in contact with "the finest that the human mind has produced." So does physics, for it would be hard to find, in the whole history of human thought, a grander conception than Newton's laws of motion and the theory of gravitation. This is an amazingly bold assumption, or rather pair of assumptions, that are now so much a part of all our thinking that it is difficult to realize their astonishing and striking character. It is first assumed that a moving body does not, as everyone would at first suppose, require a force to keep pushing it along, but on the contrary would go on moving for ever if it were not for some force *stopping* it. The second assumption is, on the face of it, even more preposterous; it is that any two objects, anywhere, are all the time "attracting" one another. Not the faintest suggestion is put forward as to how this mysterious "attraction" takes place, although it works at a distance, even a very great distance, with no sign of anything to account for it in the space between the two objects. Making these two wild and improbable-sounding assumptions, and a few sub-assumptions concerning the magnitude of the attractive force and of the effects of "force" on objects, the most amazing results come out. All the phenomena of astronomy, which had baffled the acutest minds since the dawn of history, the movement of the heavens, of the sun and the moon, the very complex movements of the planets, suddenly tumble together and become intelligible in terms of the one staggering assumption, this mysterious "attractive force." And not only the movements of the heavenly bodies, far more than that, the movements of earthly bodies too are seen to be subject to the same mathematically definable law, instead of being, as they were for all previous philosophers, mere unpredictable happen-so's. This is science on a grand scale. This is science worth knowing about.

Very few people who have been exposed to physics know ¶ 6
anything about gravitation in this sort of way. For instead of being explained as a wild, thrilling and gloriously successful intellectual adventure, it is taught just as one of the first things to be got through in "Introductory Physics I." The students are "given" the law, and since it comes fairly early in the course, before the work begins to get really tough, they are allowed to read several easy textbook pages which are devoted to praising Newton in extravagant terms, without, however, making it clear why he is deserving of praise, or giving any idea of how he discovered his famous law. Rapidly the course goes on to other things, for there is so much ground to be covered that it is difficult to take time out to explain why one should be bothering about physics at all.

¶ 7 Physics is full of magnificent theories—the true stuff of science. One of the finest is the wave theory of light; fine because in spite of being exceedingly indirect, it is amazingly successful in explaining what light actually does, in a big way and also in minute detail, with elaborate mathematical calculations. Light is supposed to consist of vibrations, or wave motion, in something or other, somewhat like waves on the surface of water, but moving very much more rapidly. The theory is particularly worth studying because it tells one about vibrations, what they will do and what they will not do. Now, every fortuneteller and dabbler in the psychic talks a blue streak about "vibrations," usually without having the faintest idea of what he is talking about. A little knowledge of the physics of light is therefore most useful in recognizing a crackpot for what he is (there are so many vibration phonies, they talk such utter nonsense, and they take in so many people). There ought to be special courses in "Wave Theory for People Who Want to Make Sense," or "Vibrations for Occultists." This would drive home an excellent reason for learning something about physics. But physics teachers don't seem to see it this way; to them, the reason for studying something about physics is to know something about physics—a narrow viewpoint.

¶ 8 The theory of light also gives a wonderful example of another of the great ideas of science, the "crucial experiment," or, as it used to be expressed with a fine dignity, in Latin, the *experimentum crucis.* A scientist has a theory, let us say, which accounts for something or other—the properties of light, the behaviour of falling drops of water or anything else. Another scientist has another theory, quite different, which will *also* account for exactly the same things. Which is right, or which is wrong? To settle the point, they work out all the possible consequences of the two theories, until they find a place where one theory says one thing, and the other something quite different. Then it is only necessary to do the appropriate experiment (and it will only do one thing, not the other), and this will allegedly "prove" one theory and "disprove" the other.

This is exactly what happened in the case of the theories of light. An older theory than the wave theory, attributed to the great Newton himself, was that light is not waves, but little "corpuscles," or tiny bits of something, which are shot out in straight lines by any bright object: when these corpuscles hit the eye, we "see." This theory also can explain many of the properties of light, although it is quite different from the wave theory. From about the beginning of the nineteenth century on, the wave theory became quite generally adopted, because it could explain very slickly and easily a number of things that had then been discovered, which would require considerable twisting and straining of the corpuscular theory. Later in the nineteenth century a very clear crucial experiment was done. It depended on measuring the velocity of light, and it worked like this: on the wave theory it was necessary to assume that light traveled more slowly in water than in air, but on the corpuscular theory light would be expected to travel *quicker* in water than in air. Measuring the velocity of light is not easy, but as soon as apparatus was available for doing it the crucial experiment was carried out, and it showed that light traveled slower in water than in air, and just that amount slower that the wave theory demanded. Scientists therefore concluded that the corpuscular theory was wrong, and that the wave theory was right, and this beautiful crucial experiment was regarded as one of the high spots of science. ¶ 9

But alas, although the corpuscular theory appeared to be completely dead, it did not stay dead. It became absolutely necessary to revive it. It was discovered that light has strange ways of behaving that can only be accounted for by assuming that it comes in little separate packets of something, which are now called "quanta," to get away from Newton's word "corpuscles." But then, there are also the phenomena that the wave theory is so successful in explaining, and, of course, the crucial fact that light travels slower in water than in air, which it was supposed the corpuscular theory couldn't possibly explain. It became necessary to devise a theory which has things both ways, combining the good features of ¶ 10 both of the earlier theories. "We teach quantum theory on Mondays, Wednesdays and Fridays, and wave theory on Tuesdays, Thursdays and Saturdays," said Sir William Bragg, and the great crucial experiment, which was supposed to have decided things once and for all, is played down. It shouldn't be played down, it ought to be played up, for one learns something from it about what physics actually is like. Physics is *not* a body of indisputable and immutable Truth; it is a body of well-supported probable opinion only, and its ideas may be exploded at any time. This ought to be more generally known, and should be widely publicized. Perhaps it would be hardly in human nature to expect physicists to do this for themselves, but somebody else ought to do it for them.

EXERCISES

I. Anthony Standen's "Science at Its Best" is a good example of what is sometimes called the "popularization" of science. But since the term "popularization" too often is used with the implication that scientific conceptions are somehow cheapened and injured by being explained at any other level than the strictly scientific, it might be better to say that this selection is an example of an explanation of a technical subject in terms that will be clear to the general or non-technical reader. It is evident that such tasks of explanation must be undertaken by persons who are competent—as Mr. Standen is—both as scientists and as writers; otherwise, the general public will either have some cheapened and distorted notion of what science really is or will live in complacent ignorance, with no notion of science at all. The problem of the writer who attempts such a task can best be put in the form of a question: How can a highly technical subject be discussed in terms that are non-technical or at least not too technical for general comprehension? No satisfactory answer, evidently, can be given to this puzzling question unless a method can be developed which will observe due respect for (1) the "truth" of science (i.e., its special kind of knowledge) and (2) the capacity of the reader, whose knowledge is "general" and not "special." In his organization of his composition, in his choice of words, and in the "tone" of his writing, the author must therefore constantly apply a principle of equilibrium. He must do justice to science, on the one hand; and on the other hand, he must interest and in-form his reader—cajoling him here and there, if necessary, but not at the expense of injuring the dignity of his subject, and above all taking care to link what it is assumed he does not yet know or understand with what he may be reasonably assumed already to know or understand. The procedure, accordingly, is first to set forth briefly the essential character of the science or scientific method to be explained; this first step necessarily involves definition and analysis. Next, to give illustrative examples—historic or contemporary, that clarify this essential character; these must be examples that may reasonably be expected to be familiar to the general reader. Then to proceed to less familiar, perhaps more complex examples that carry the reader into the more difficult technical aspects of the subject. Throughout this process of explanation, the writer takes care to distinguish what his subject really is from what it is not, and thus to combat and eliminate common misapprehensions.

II. At what points in the selection does Standen deal, directly or indirectly, with the common misapprehensions about science mentioned above? What are the implications of his title, "Science at Its Best"? Is his scale of valuations—"best," "fairly good," "mediocre," "downright bad"—a scale established by scientists themselves, or is Standen dealing here with some popular misconception? Does the word "best," in this connection, mean "morally best" or "most scientific"—or what? Point out the specific passages that support your answers to these questions.

III. Does Standen anywhere indict the average reader (or student) for neglect, stupidity, or blindness in failing to grasp the right conception of what physics is? Where does he put the blame for common misconceptions about physics? Explain—and either justify or criticize—the strategy that Standen uses in this apportionment of blame. In particular, discuss the effect of this strategy upon his prospective readers. Who are his prospective readers? Does he expect physicists and other scientists to read his essay and be influenced by it?

IV. Trace out carefully the steps by which Standen (1) classifies all sciences and (2) defines physics in relation to other sciences. This basic process of analysis and definition is carried through Pars. 1–4. It will be advisable for you to write out a straight-forward definition of physics in which you follow the *order* of explanation used by Standen, and to some extent his language; but you should omit from your definition whatever is not positively and strictly definition. By this means you should be able to disengage Standen's basic thought from those features of his discussion which represent his "strategy" or "method of attack." To what extent is Standen's discussion of misconceptions interwoven with his discussion of right conceptions about physics? Would it have been better for Standen to deal directly first with misconceptions and then, after disposing of them, to present right conceptions?

V. Trace out the steps by which Standen proceeds from the "known" to the "unknown," or from the "familiar" to the "less familiar" or "unfamiliar." Consider, in this connection, why Standen goes to Galileo and Aristotle for his first set of illustrations, to Newton for his next set, and to theories of light for his last group.

VI. Does Standen go too far in his attempt to ingratiate the average reader? Do you find anything in his general procedure, in his language, or in his "tone" that cheapens his explanation or does injury to the dignity and the truth of science? Is his manner anywhere too jocular, bantering, journalistic, or "popular"? Do you find any unevenness in his style? Does he, on the whole, observe satisfactorily the "principle of equilibrium" mentioned in I, above?

VII. Using Standen's type of approach, compose, for an assumed "general reader," an explanation of some technical subject. Suggested topics: What Television Really Is; The Difference Between Strategic and Tactical Use of Aircraft; The Functional Principle in Architecture; Color Photography —Its Uses and Abuses; What Is Grand Opera?; What Is "Due Process of Law"?; What Is Chemistry? (or Biology, or Sociology, or any other science or social science); Psychology Defined and Defended (as, for example, in reply to the "low rating" given to this science by Standen); or some religious ceremony or doctrine.

THE COVENANT*

by KONRAD Z. LORENZ

LESSON XI

At the dawn of the later stone age, there appears, as the first domestic animal, a small semi-domesticated dog, certainly descended from the golden jackal *(Canis aureus).* At this time, in north-west Europe, where skeletons of these dogs have been found, there were probably no more jackals, but there is every reason to believe that the turf-dog already lived as a true house-dog and that the lake-dwellers had brought it with them to the shores of the Baltic sea. ¶ 1

But how did stone-age man come by his dog? Very probably without intending it. Whole packs of jackals must have followed in the train of the wandering, hunting hordes of early stone-age man and surrounded his settlements just as the pariah dogs of the East do today, of whom no one knows exactly whether they are house-dogs run wild, or wild dogs that have taken the first step toward domestication. And our forefathers took just as few measures against these scavengers as the Oriental, in his happy-go-lucky way, does today. Indeed, the stone-age hunters, for whom the large beasts of prey were still a serious menace, must have found it quite agreeable to know that their camp was watched by a broad circle of jackals which, at the approach of a sabre-toothed tiger or a marauding cave-bear, gave tongue in the wildest tones. ¶ 2

Then, some time or other, to the function of the sentry was added that of a helper in the hunting field. Some time or other, the pack of jackals which used to follow the hunter in the hope of receiving the entrails of his prey, took to running before instead of behind the hunter; it began to track game and even to bring it to bay. It is very easy to imagine how these pre-historic dogs developed a new type of interest in the larger game animals. Originally, a jackal would show ¶ 3

* Reprinted by permission of the publisher, Thomas Y. Crowell Company, New York, and of Methuen and Co. Ltd., London, from *King Solomon's Ring: New Light on Animal Ways,* by Konrad Z. Lorenz. Copyright, 1952, by Thomas Y. Crowell Company.

no interest in the trail of a stag or wild horse, since by himself he could not hope to kill and eat it, but it is not too much to assume that, after having repeatedly received entrails or other refuse from that kind of beast, he might have found inducement to follow a trail which, by its scent, reminded him of a good meal. He might even, by a stroke of canine genius, have "conceived the idea" of calling the hunter's attention to the track. It is remarkable how quickly dogs realize when they can rely on the help of a strong friend. Even my rather cowardly French bulldog would, if accompanied by his friend, a huge Newfoundland, recklessly attack any dog he met. I am not, therefore, crediting the primitive jackal-dogs with too much intelligence when I surmise that, without being consciously trained by man, they learned to track and bring to bay large game animals.

¶4 To me it is a strangely appealing and even elevating thought that the age-old covenant between man and dog was "signed" voluntarily and without obligation by each of the contracting parties. All other domestic animals, like some slaves of ancient times, became house-servants only after having served a term of true imprisonment, all, that is, with the exception of the cat; for the cat is not really a domesticated animal and his chief charm lies in the fact that even today, he still walks by himself. Neither the dog nor the cat is a slave, but only the dog is a friend—granted, a submissive and servile friend. Very gradually, in the course of the centuries, it has become customary, in the "better families" of dogs, to choose, instead of another dog, a man as a leader of their pack. In many cases, this appears to have been the chief of a human tribe, and even dogs of today, particularly those of strong individual character, tend to consider the "paterfamilias" as their master. In huskies and other primitive breeds, a more complicated and less direct type of submission to man can often be observed. When many of these dogs are kept together, one of them stands out as leader, and the others are "faithful" and "respectful" only to him, and it is only the leader himself who is, in a true sense, his master's dog; the others are, strictly speaking, the leader's dogs. Reading between the lines, one can tell from Jack London's obviously true-to-life descriptions that in sledge-dog teams this type of relationship is the rule, and it is most probable that it also prevailed among the primitive jackal-dogs of the Stone Age. In modern dogs, however, it is interesting to note that most of them do not seem content with a dog as master and actively seek for a man as leading dog.

¶ 5 One of the most wonderful and puzzling phenomena is the choice of a master by a good dog. Quite suddenly, often within a few days, a bond is formed which is many times stronger than any tie that ever exists between us human beings. Wordsworth calls it:

> ". . . that strength of feeling, great
> Above all human estimate."

There is no faith which has never yet been broken, except that of a truly faithful dog. Of all dogs which I have hitherto known, the most faithful are those in whose veins flows, beside that of the golden jackal *(Canis aureus)* a considerable stream of wolf's blood. The northern wolf *(Canis lupus)* only figures in the ancestry of our present dog breeds through having been crossed with already domesticated Aureus dogs. Contrary to the wide-spread opinion that the wolf plays an essential role in the ancestry of the larger dog breeds, comparative research in behavior has revealed the fact that all European dogs, including the largest ones, such as Great Danes and wolfhounds, are pure Aureus and contain, at the most, a minute amount of wolf's blood. The purest wolf-dogs that exist are certain breeds of Arctic America, particularly the so-called Malemutes, huskies, etc. The Esquimaux dogs of Greenland also show but slight traces of Lapland Aureus characters, whereas the arctic breeds of the Old World, such as Lapland dogs, Russian lajkas, samoyedes, and chow-chows certainly have more Aureus in their constitution. Nevertheless the latter breeds derive their character from the Lupus side of their ancestry, and they all exhibit the high cheek-bones, the slanting eyes, and the slightly upward tilt of the nose which give its expression to the face of the wolf. On the other hand, the chow, in particular, bears unquestionably the stamp of his share of Aureus blood in the flaming red of his magnificent coat.

¶ 6 The "sealing of the bond," the final attachment of the dog to one master, is quite enigmatical. It takes place suddenly, within a few days, particularly in the case of puppies that come from a breeding kennel. The "susceptible period" for this most important occurrence in the whole of a dog's life is, in Aureus dogs, between eight and eighteen months, and in Lupus dogs, round about the sixth month.

¶ 7 The really single-hearted devotion of a dog to its master has two quite different sources. On the one side, it is nothing else than the submissive attachment which every wild dog shows toward his pack leader, and which is transferred, without any considerable alteration in character, by the domestic dog to a human being. To this is added, in the more highly domesticated dogs, quite another form of affection. Many of the characteristics in which domestic animals differ from their wild ancestral form arise by virtue of the fact that properties of body structure and behavior, which in the wild prototype are only marked in some transient stages of youth, are kept permanently by the domestic form. In dogs, short hair, curly tail, hanging ears, domed skulls, and the short muzzle of many domestic breeds are features of this type. In behavior, one of these juvenile characteristics which has become permanent in the domestic dog expresses itself in the peculiar form of its attachment. The ardent affection which wild canine youngsters show for their mother and which in these disappears completely after they have reached maturity is preserved as a permanent mental trait of all highly domesticated dogs. What originally was love for the mother is transformed into love for the human master.

¶ 8 Thus the pack loyalty, in itself unaltered but merely transferred to man, and the permanent child-like dependency resulting from domestication are two more or less independent springs of canine affection. One essential difference in the character of Lupus and Aureus dogs is attributable to the fact that these two springs flow with different strength in the two types. In the life of a wolf, the community of the pack plays a vastly more important role than in that of a jackal. While the latter is essentially a solitary hunter and confines himself to a limited territory, the wolf pack roams far and wide through the forests of the North as a sworn and very exclusive band which sticks together through thick and thin and whose members will defend each other to the very death. That the wolves of a pack will devour each other, as is frequently asserted, I have strong reason to doubt, since sledge-dogs will not do so at any price, even when at the point of starvation, and this social inhibition has certainly not been instilled into them by man.

The reticent exclusiveness and the mutual defence at any ¶ 9
price are properties of the wolf which influence favorably the character of all strongly wolf-blooded dog breeds and distinguish them to their advantage from Aureus dogs, which are mostly "hail-fellow-well-met" with every man and will follow anyone who holds the other end of the lead in his hand. A Lupus dog, on the contrary, who has once sworn allegiance to a certain man, is for ever a one-man dog, and no stranger can win from him so much as a single wag of his bushy tail. Nobody who has once possessed the one-man love of a Lupus dog will ever be content with one of pure Aureus blood. Unfortunately, this fine characteristic of the Lupus dog has against it various disadvantages which are indeed the immediate results of that loyalty. That a mature Lupus dog can never become *your* dog, is a matter of course. But worse, if he is already yours and you are forced to leave him, the animal becomes literally mentally unbalanced, obeys neither your wife nor children, sinks morally, in his grief, to the level of an ownerless street cur, loses his restraint from killing and, committing misdeed upon misdeed, ravages the surrounding district.

Besides this, a predominantly Lupus-blooded dog is, in ¶ 10

LESSON XI

Definition and Analysis in Combination...

spite of his boundless loyalty and affection, never quite sufficiently submissive. He is ready to die for you, but not to obey you; at least, I have never been able to extract implicit obedience from one of these dogs—perhaps a better dog trainer than I might be more successful. For this reason, it is seldom that you see, in a town, a chow without a lead and walking close beside his master. If you walk with a Lupus dog in the woods, you can never make him stay near you. All he will do is to keep in very loose contact with you and honor you with his companionship only now and then.

¶ 11 Not so the Aureus dog; in him, as a result of his age-old domestication, that infantile affection has persisted which makes him a manageable and tractable companion. Instead of the proud, manly loyalty of the Lupus dog which is far removed from obedience, the Aureus dog will grant you that servitude which, day and night, by the hour and by the minute, awaits your command and even your slightest wish. When you take him for a walk, an Aureus dog of a more highly domesticated breed will, without previous training, always run with you, keeping the same radius whether he runs before, behind, or beside you and adapting his speed to yours. He is naturally obedient, that is to say, he answers to his name not only when he wishes to and when you cajole him, but also because he knows that he *must* come. The harder you shout, the more surely he will come, whereas a Lupus dog, in this case, comes not at all but seeks to appease you from a distance with friendly gestures.

¶ 12 Opposed to these good and congenial properties of the Aureus dog are unfortunately some others which arise from the permanent infantility of these animals and are less agreeable for an owner. Since young dogs under a certain age are, for members of their own species, "taboo," that is, they must not under any circumstances be bitten, such big babies are often correspondingly trustful and importunate toward everybody. Like many spoilt human children who call every grown-up "uncle," they pester people and animals alike with overtures to play. If this youthful property persists, to any appreciable extent, in the adult domestic dog, there arises a very unpleasant canine character, or rather the lack of such a commodity. The worst part of it lies in the literally "dog-like" submission that these animals, who see in every man an "uncle," show toward anyone who treats them with the least sign of severity; the playful storm of affection is immediately transformed into a cringing state of humility. Everyone is acquainted with this kind of dog, which knows no happy medium between perpetual exasperating "jumping up," and fawningly turning upon its back, its paws waving in supplication. You shout, at the risk of offending your hostess, at the infuriating creature that is trampling all over your person and covering you from head to foot with hairs. Thereupon the dog falls beseechingly upon his back. You speak kindly to him, to conciliate your hostess, and—splash—quickly leaping up, the brute has licked you right across the face and now continues unremittingly to bestrew your trousers with hairs.

A dog of this kind, which is everybody's dog, is easily led ¶ 13
astray, since he trusts every stranger who speaks kindly to him. But a dog that you can get so easily—well, so far as I am concerned, you can keep him! Even the many alluring and beautifully proportioned breeds of gun-dog, whose "heads are hung with ears that sweep away the morning dew," are uncongenial to my taste in that most of them are ready to follow any man with a gun. Admittedly, their usefulness as gun-dogs is based on this general acceptance of anyone as master, and indeed, were this not so, one could never buy a ready-trained gun-dog or have one's dog schooled by a professional trainer. It is clear that a dog can only be trained by a man who commands his absolute obedience and trust. When you leave your dog with a trainer, you therefore imply, from the first, a breach of loyalty. The personal relationship between master and dog must necessarily be severely injured, even if the dog, on his return from the trainer, once more reverts to something of his former attachment to his owner.

¶ 14 Should one do the same thing with a Lupus-blooded dog, he would either learn nothing at all, and through stubborn shyness, if not by sheer aggressive ill-temper, drive his trainer to distraction, or, if one sent the dog early enough to the school, before his fidelity had found an object on which to rest unshakably, then, without doubt, the love of the animal would belong for good to his trainer. It is therefore out of the question to buy a Lupus dog as a fully-trained animal. Separated from the master of his choice, the dog would show no signs of ever having been trained. The Lupus dog either accepts one master, unconditionally and for all time, or, if he does not find one or if he loses him, he becomes as independent and self-sufficient as a cat and lives alongside the human being without ever developing any heart-felt connection with him.

EXERCISES

I. In Pars. 1–3, Lorenz explains—and to some extent defines—the common domesticated dog in terms of his origin. The dog is, according to Lorenz, a descendant of the golden jackal of remote primitive times. How much of this explanation is "conjectural"? How much rests upon evidence that can be subjected to logical and scientific tests? State in your own words the "hypothesis" upon the basis of which scientific evidence about the origin of the domesticated dog could be assembled, classified, and verified? To what extent is a zoologist like Lorenz able to test the validity of the hypothesis upon which he bases his investigations and conjectures? What advantages—as to verification of hypothesis—does a physicist enjoy, in comparison with a zoologist? (See Standen's "Science at Its Best," pp. 118–124.) Point out all words, phrases, or sentences in Lorenz's discussion (Pars. 1–3) that indicate his awareness of the conjectural features of his explanation. ("It is not too much to assume that" in Par. 3 is an example of the kind of phrase referred to.) Would Lorenz's discussion have been more impressive if he had *not* used such expressions of qualification and reservation? Would it have been honest?

II. Pars. 1–3 are a preliminary to the discussion of Lorenz's real subject —"the age-old covenant between man and dog"—which he takes up in Par. 4. Is "covenant" a technical and matter-of-fact scientific term? Or is it a metaphor which expresses, more aptly than a scientific term, the relationship between man and dog? Is there a technical scientific term for the relationship that Lorenz is discussing? What other terms does Lorenz use to express the meaning of "covenant"? (See especially Par. 6.) Examine Par. 4 to determine the extent to which Lorenz uses metaphorical rather than strictly technical terms. Is the explanation itself, regardless of questions of language, sufficiently clear, factual, logical, and scientific to be convincing? Why does Lorenz enclose certain terms in quotation marks? Would it be possible to write Par. 4 in completely technical terms?

III. By way of reinforcing and illustrating his points, Lorenz refers to certain literary accounts of the dog-and-master (or leader-and-pack) relationship. In Par. 4, the reference is to Jack London's novels, *The Call of the Wild* and *White Fang.* In Par. 5 Lorenz quotes from a poem by William Wordsworth. Is it "unscientific" of Lorenz to use such references? If the novels of Jack London and the poem by Wordsworth are to be considered "not scientific," are they then to be disregarded as "untrue"?

IV. In Par. 5, Lorenz develops a discussion of the "faithfulness" of dogs, especially dogs of the wolf strain. Distinguish, in this paragraph, the portions which are strictly matter-of-fact and those of a more figurative, literary nature. Why does Lorenz resort to figurative terms at some points and not at others? Does the word "faith," if used with reference to a dog, mean exactly what it means with reference to a human being?

V. Make note of any terms that, though they seem at first glance to be matter-of-fact, turn out on close examination to have some figurative content. For example, in Par. 8, "child-like dependency" carries a suggestion of a metaphorical correspondence between dog and human being. So, in the same paragraph, do the phrases "community of the pack" and "sworn and very exclusive band."

VI. Write a theme in which, after giving a definition in terms of origin, you explain the relationship between man and some domesticated animal or fowl. A theme of a similar type can be written regarding the origin and development of some staple food, fibre, type of building, utensil, weapon, or article of clothing.

LESSON XII

Refutation of Erroneous Views. Reductio ad Absurdum. Fallacies of Logic. Use of Abstract Example. Implied Definitions. Examination of Historical Evidence. Objective Terms Compared with Subjective or Biased Terms. The Strategy of Concessions. Hypothetical vs. Real Examples. Documentary Evidence. Annotation of Quoted Material.

THE RULE TO MIND ONE'S OWN BUSINESS *

by WILLIAM GRAHAM SUMNER

¶ 1 The passion for dealing with social questions is one of the marks of our time. Every man gets some experience of, and makes some observations on social affairs. Except matters of health, probably none have such general interest as matters of society. Except matters of health, none are so much afflicted by dogmatism and crude speculation as those which appertain to society. The amateurs in social science always ask: What shall we do? What shall we do with Neighbor A? What shall we do for Neighbor B? What shall we make Neighbor A do for Neighbor B? It is a fine thing to be planning and discussing broad and general theories of wide application. The amateurs always plan to use the individual for some constructive and inferential social purpose, or to use the society for some constructive and inferential individual purpose. For A to sit down and think, What shall I do? is commonplace; but to think what B ought to do is interesting, romantic, moral, self-flattering, and public-spirited all at once. It satisfies a great number of human weaknesses at once. To go on and plan what a whole class of people ought to do is to feel one's self a power on earth, to win a public

* From *What Social Classes Owe to Each Other,* by William Graham Sumner, Harper & Brothers, 1883.

position, to clothe one's self in dignity. Hence we have an unlimited supply of reformers, philanthropists, humanitarians, and would-be managers-in-general of society.

¶ 2 Every man and woman in society has one big duty. That is, to take care of his or her own self. This is a social duty. For, fortunately, the matter stands so that the duty of making the best of one's self individually is not a separate thing from the duty of filling one's place in society, but the two are one, and the latter is accomplished when the former is done. The common notion, however, seems to be that one has a duty to society, as a special and separate thing, and that this duty consists in considering and deciding what other people ought to do. Now, the man who can do anything for or about anybody else than himself is fit to be head of a family; and when he becomes head of a family he has duties to his wife and his children, in addition to the former big duty. Then, again, any man who can take care of himself and his family is in a very exceptional position, if he does not find in his immediate surroundings people who need his care and have some sort of a personal claim upon him. If, now, he is able to fulfil all this, and to take care of anybody outside his family and his dependents, he must have a surplus of energy, wisdom, and moral virtue beyond what he needs for his own business. No man has this; for a family is a charge which is capable of infinite development, and no man could suffice to the full measure of duty for which a family may draw upon him. Neither can a man give to society so advantageous an employment of his services, whatever they are, in any other way as by spending them on his family. Upon this, however, I will not insist. I recur to the observation that a man who proposes to take care of other people must have himself and his family taken care of, after some sort of a fashion, and must have an as yet unexhausted store of energy.

¶ 3 The danger of minding other people's business is twofold. First, there is the danger that a man may leave his own business unattended to; and, second, there is the danger of an impertinent interference with another's affairs. The "friends of humanity" almost always run into both dangers. I am one of humanity, and I do not want any volunteer friends. I regard friendship as mutual, and I want to have my say about it. I suppose that other components of humanity feel in the same way about it. If so, they must regard any one who assumes the *rôle* of a friend of humanity as impertinent. The reference of the friend of humanity back to his own business is obviously the next step.

¶4 Yet we are constantly annoyed, and the legislatures are kept constantly busy, by the people who have made up their minds that it is wise and conducive to happiness to live in a certain way, and who want to compel everybody else to live in their way. Some people have decided to spend Sunday in a certain way, and they want laws passed to make other people spend Sunday in the same way. Some people have resolved to be teetotalers, and they want a law passed to make everybody else a teetotaler. Some people have resolved to eschew luxury, and they want taxes laid to make others eschew luxury. The taxing power is especially something after which the reformer's finger always itches. Sometimes there is an element of self-interest in the proposed reformation, as when a publisher wanted a duty imposed on books, to keep Americans from reading books which would unsettle their Americanism; and when artists wanted a tax laid on pictures, to save Americans from buying bad paintings.

¶5 I make no reference here to the giving and taking of counsel and aid between man and man: of that I shall say something in the last chapter. The very sacredness of the relation in which two men stand to one another when one of them rescues the other from vice separates that relation from any connection with the work of the social busybody, the professional philanthropist, and the empirical legislator.

¶6 The amateur social doctors are like the amateur physicians—they always begin with the question of *remedies,* and they go at this without any diagnosis or any knowledge of the anatomy or physiology of society. They never have any doubt of the efficacy of their remedies. They never take account of any ulterior effects which may be apprehended from the remedy itself. It generally troubles them not a whit that their remedy implies a complete reconstruction of society, or even a reconstitution of human nature. Against all such social quackery the obvious injunction to the quacks is, to mind their own business.

¶ 7 The social doctors enjoy the satisfaction of feeling themselves to be more moral or more enlightened than their fellow-man. They are able to see what other men ought to do when the other men do not see it. An examination of the work of the social doctors, however, shows that they are only more ignorant and more presumptuous than other people. We have a great many social difficulties and hardships to contend with. Poverty, pain, disease, and misfortune surround our existence. We fight against them all the time. The individual is a center of hopes, affections, desires, and sufferings. When he dies, life changes its form, but does not cease. That means that the person—the center of all the hopes, affections, etc.—after struggling as long as he can, is sure to succumb at last. We would, therefore, as far as the hardships of the human lot are concerned, go on struggling to the best of our ability against them but for the social doctors, and we would endure what we could not cure. But we have inherited a vast number of social ills which never came from Nature. They are the complicated products of all the tinkering, muddling, and blundering of social doctors in the past. These products of social quackery are now buttressed by habit, fashion, prejudice, platitudinarian thinking, and new quackery in political economy and social science. It is a fact worth noticing, just when there seems to be a revival of faith in legislative agencies, that our States are generally providing against the experienced evils of over-legislation by ordering that the Legislature shall sit only every other year. During the hard times, when Congress had a real chance to make or mar the public welfare, the final adjournment of that body was hailed year after year with cries of relief from a great anxiety. The greatest reforms which

LESSON XII

Refutation of Erroneous Views...

could now be accomplished would consist in undoing the work of statesmen in the past, and the greatest difficulty in the way of reform is to find out how to undo their work without injury to what is natural and sound. All this mischief has been done by men who sat down to consider the problem (as I heard an apprentice of theirs once express it), What kind of a society do we want to make? When they had settled this question *a priori* to their satisfaction, they set to work to make their ideal society, and to-day we suffer the consequences. Human society tries hard to adapt itself to any conditions in which it finds itself, and we have been warped and distorted until we have got used to it, as the foot adapts itself to any conditions in which it finds itself, and we have been warped and distorted until we have got used to it, as the foot adapts itself to an ill-made boot. Next, we have come to think that that is the right way for things to be; and it is true that a change to a sound and normal condition would for a time hurt us, as a man whose foot has been distorted would suffer if he tried to wear a well-shaped boot. Finally, we have produced a lot of economists and social philosophers who have invented sophisms for fitting our thinking to the distorted facts.

¶ 8 Society, therefore, does not need any care or supervision. If we can acquire a science of society, based on observation of phenomena and study of forces, we may hope to gain some ground slowly toward the elimination of old errors and the re-establishment of a sound and natural social order. Whatever we gain that way will be by growth, never in the world by any reconstruction of society on the plan of some enthusiastic social architect. The latter is only repeating the old error over again, and postponing all our chances of real improvement. Society needs first of all to be freed from these meddlers—that is, to be let alone.

EXERCISES

I. What generalization does Sumner make in Par. 1? Is it completely stated in any one of the first three sentences of the paragraph? What is the topic and what is the topic sentence (if any) of the paragraph? How does Sumner support the generalization mentioned above? In his references to Neighbor A and Neighbor B is Sumner following the method used by Santayana in his "Origin of Tyranny"? Why does Sumner use the term "Neighbor A" rather than some more concrete term like "wealthy industrialist" or "idle rich man" or "Rockefeller"? Why does he say "Neighbor B" instead of giving the name of some known or identifiable individual or referring to "the poor of the county," the "unemployed miners," "the downtrodden masses," and the like? In the sentence, "For A to sit down and think . . . ." is Sumner referring to the same classes or individuals as in his references to "Neighbor A," "Neighbor B," above? Look up *reductio ad absurdum* in the dictionary. Is Sumner using the method of argument indicated by this term?

II. What is the effect in Sen. 1, Par. 1, of the word "passion" as compared with some relatively colorless word like "tendency"? Is this an intended effect? In using the word "passion" does Sumner "beg the question"—that is, assume something as true that has not been proved? Is he guilty of the logical fallacy known as *argumentum ad hominem?* Or does the argument of the paragraph, as it develops, support Sumner's contention that the tendency of his time to deal with social questions was indeed a "passion"? Examine carefully the contrast that Sumner makes in his predications regarding A's thinking (1) "What shall I do?" and (2) "what B ought to do." To what extent is Sumner making an analysis of the process of "rationalization" by which "reformers" justify their procedure?

III. Examine Par. 1 in relation to the whole composition—that is, as the beginning of a discussion of a ticklish subject. Does Sumner go to any trouble to avoid "hurting the feelings" of various good, well-meaning people who may be "reformers, philanthropists, humanitarians, etc."? Does he apologize in advance for the pain he is about to inflict, or adopt some affectation of modesty? Or is he interested in speaking the truth bluntly, no matter whose feelings may be hurt? In this connection, examine carefully all the distinctions and qualifications that Sumner makes as he develops his discussion. For example, he does not say (Par. 1) that "social scientists" always ask "What shall we do?" but that "the *amateurs* in social science" ask this question. Note all other instances in which similar qualifications or distinctions are made.

IV. The strategy of Sumner's composition in essence is this: first, assert a strong negative, directed against errors that should be condemned, but, second, follow the negative by an equally strong affirmative that sets forth the principle to which Sumner would have people adhere. Discuss Sumner's use of this strategy. Does he allow social science any role in the remedying of social evils?

V. In Par. 2, Sumner refers to the "individual" and to "society" without defining either term. His statements may nevertheless imply certain definitions. Write out the definitions of "individual" and "society" that seem to you latent in Sumner's discussion.

VI. In Par. 3, what does Sumner mean by the phrase, "an impertinent interference with another's affairs"? Why does he enclose "friends of humanity" in quotation marks? Why does he speak in the first person at this point? Do you consider it impertinent for a person to insist on being your friend when you do not want to be befriended by that person? Do you have a right to wish *not* to be befriended?

VII. Are the examples given in Par. 4 good examples of "impertinent interference"? Does Sumner anywhere indicate where the line is to be drawn between "impertinent" and "pertinent" interference?

VIII. Give the meaning of the following words or phrases as it applies in the context where the words or phrases appear: *dogmatism, crude speculation, constructive and inferential social purpose, philanthropists, humanitarians* (Par. 1); *teetotalers, eschew luxury* (Par. 4); *empirical legislator* (Par. 5); *social quackery* (Par. 6); *tinkering, buttressed, platitudinarian thinking, apprentice, a priori, sophisms* (Par. 7). On the whole, is Sumner's language difficult? Academic? Pedantic? Plain and straight-forward?

IX. Sumner's "The Rule to Mind One's Own Business" was published in 1883. Write a review of the selection in which you consider how applicable Sumner's argument is under present conditions.

IS CIVILIZATION A UNITY? *

by ARNOLD J. TOYNBEE

The second argument against the comparability of our twenty-one civilizations is the contrary of the first. It is that there are not twenty-one distinct representatives of such a species of society but only one civilization—our own. ¶ 1

This thesis of the unity of civilization is a misconception into which modern Western historians have been led by the influence of their social environment. The misleading feature is the fact that, in modern times, our own Western Civilization has cast the net of its economic system all round the world, and this economic unification on a Western basis has been followed by a political unification on the same basis which has gone almost as far; for though the conquests of Western armies and governments have been neither as extensive nor as thorough as the conquests of Western manufactures and technicians, it is nevertheless a fact that all the states of the contemporary world form part of a single political system of Western origin. ¶ 2

These are striking facts, but to regard them as evidence of the unity of civilization is a superficial view. While the economic and political maps have now been Westernized, the cultural map remains substantially what it was before our Western Society started on its career of economic and political conquest. On the cultural plane, for those who have eyes to see, the lineaments of the four living non-Western civilizations are still clear. But many have not such eyes; and their outlook is illustrated in the use of the English word "natives" and of equivalent words in other Western languages. ¶ 3

When we Westerners call people "natives" we implicitly take the cultural colour out of our perception of them. We see them as wild animals infesting the country in which we happen to come across them, as part of the local flora and ¶ 4

* From *A Study of History*, by Arnold J. Toynbee: abridgment by D. C. Somervell.

fauna and not as men of like passions with ourselves. So long as we think of them as "natives" we may exterminate them or, as is more likely to-day, domesticate them and honestly (perhaps not altogether mistakenly) believe that we are improving the breed, but we do not begin to understand them.

¶ 5 But apart from illusions due to the world-wide success of the Western Civilization in the material sphere, the misconception of the "unity of history"—involving the assumption that there is only one river of civilization, our own, and that all others are either tributary to it or else lost in the desert sands—may be traced to three roots: the egocentric illusion, the illusion of "the unchanging East," and the illusion of progress as a movement that proceeds in a straight line.

¶ 6 As for the egocentric illusion, it is natural enough, and all that need be said is that we Westerners have not been its only victims. The Jews suffered from the illusion that they were not *a* but *the* "chosen people." What we call "natives" they called "gentiles," and the Greeks called "barbarians." But the finest flower of egocentricity is perhaps the missive presented in A.D. 1793 by the philosophic emperor of China, Ch'ien Lung, to a British envoy for delivery to his master, King George III:

> "You, O King, live beyond the confines of many seas; nevertheless, impelled by your humble desire to partake of the benefits of our civilization, you have despatched a mission respectfully bearing your memorial . . . . I have perused your memorial; the earnest terms in which it is couched reveal a respectful humility on your part which is highly praiseworthy . . . .
>
> "As to your entreaty to send one of your nationals to be accredited to my Celestial Court and to be in control of your country's trade with China, this request is contrary to all usage of my Dynasty and cannot possibly be entertained . . . If you assert that your reverence for Our Celestial Dynasty fills you with a desire to acquire our civilization, our ceremonies and code of laws differ so completely from your own that, even if your envoy were able to acquire the rudiments of our civilization, you could not possibly transplant our manners and customs to your alien soil. Therefore, however adept the envoy might become, nothing would be gained thereby.
>
> "Swaying the wide world, I have but one aim in view, namely, to maintain a perfect governance and to fulfil the duties of the state. Strange and costly objects do not interest me. If I have commanded that the tribute

offerings sent by you, O King, are to be accepted, this was solely in consideration for the spirit which prompted you to despatch them from afar. Our Dynasty's majestic virtue has penetrated into every country under Heaven, and kings of all nations have offered their costly tribute by land and sea. As your ambassador can see for himself, we possess all things. I set no value on objects strange or ingenious, and have no use for your country's manufactures."

In the course of the century following the composition of this dispatch the pride of Ch'ien Lung's countrymen suffered a series of falls. It is the proverbial fate of pride. ¶ 7

The illusion of "the unchanging East" is so obviously a popular illusion without foundation in serious study that a search for its causes has no great interest or importance. Perhaps it is due to the fact that "the East," which in this context means anything from Egypt to China, was at one time far ahead of the West and now seems to be far behind; *ergo,* while we have been moving it must have stood still. More particularly we must remember that for the average Westerner the only familiar chapter of the ancient history of "the East" used to be that contained in the narratives of the Old Testament. When modern Western travellers observed, with mingled astonishment and delight, that the life lived to-day on the Transjordanian border of the Arabian desert corresponded, point by point, with the description of the lives of the patriarchs in the Book of Genesis, the unchanging character of the East seemed proved. But what such travellers encountered was not "the unchanging East" but the unchanging Arabian Steppe. On the Steppe the physical environment is so hard a taskmaster to human beings that their ability to adapt themselves is confined within very narrow limits. It imposes upon all human beings in all ages who have the hardihood to be its inhabitants a rigid and unvarying way of life. As proof of an "unchanging East" such evidence is puerile. There are, for example, in the Western World Alpine valleys untouched by modern tourist invasion whose inhabitants live just as their predecessors must have lived in the days of Abraham. It would be as reasonable to deduce from these an argument for an "unchanging West." ¶ 8

¶ 9 The illusion of progress as something which proceeds in a straight line is an example of that tendency to over-simplification which the human mind displays in all its activities. In their "periodizations" our historians dispose their periods in a single series end to end, like the sections of a bamboo stem between joint and joint or the sections of the patent extensible handle on the end of which an up-to-date modern chimney-sweep pokes his brush up the flue. On the brush-handle which our modern historians have inherited there were originally two joints only—"ancient" and "modern," roughly though not exactly corresponding to the Old Testament and the New Testament and to the dual back-to-back reckoning of dates B.C. and A.D. This dichotomy of historical time is a relic of the outlook of the internal proletariat of the Hellenic Society, which expressed its sense of alienation from the Hellenic dominant minority by making an absolute antithesis between the old Hellenic dispensation and that of the Christian Church, and thereby succumbed to the egocentric illusion (much more excusable in them, with their limited knowledge, than in us) of treating the transition from one of our twenty-one societies to another as the turning-point of all human history.[1]

LESSON XII

Refutation of Erroneous Views...

¶ 10 As time has gone on, our historians have found it convenient to extend their telescopic brush-handle by adding a third section, which they have called "medieval" because they have inserted it between the other two. But, while the division between "ancient" and "modern" stands for the break between Hellenic and Western history, the division between "medieval" and "modern" only stands for the transition between one chapter of Western history and another. The formula "ancient + medieval + modern" is wrong; it should run "Hellenic + Western (medieval + modern)" Yet even this will not do, for, if we honour one chapter-division

[1]In the same way the founders of the French Revolutionary Republic, imagining that they were starting a new epoch of history and that all that lay behind them was a "back number," started a new Year I on the 21st September, 1792; the common sense and conservatism of Napoleon dropped the scheme twelve years later, but for those twelve years it survives to incommode the student with its Fructidors and Thermidors.

of Western history with a separate "period," why refuse the same honour to the others? There is no warrant for laying greater stress on a division round about 1475 than for one round about 1075, and there is ample reason for supposing that we have recently passed into a new chapter whose beginnings may be placed round about 1875. So we have:

Western I ("Dark Ages"), 675–1075.
Western II ("Middle Ages"), 1075–1475.
Western III ("Modern"), 1475–1875.
Western IV ("Post-Modern"?), 1875–?

But we have strayed from the point, which is that an equation of Hellenic and Western history with History itself —"ancient and modern," if you like—is mere parochialism and impertinence. It is as though a geographer were to produce a book entitled *World Geography* which proved on inspection to be all about the Mediterranean Basin and Europe. ¶ 11

EXERCISES

I. Toynbee, in *A Study of History,* wishes to make a comparative study of "twenty-one civilizations." He must therefore dispose of the argument, advanced by "modern Western historians," that there is "only one civilization—our own," before he presents his own study. Thus, like William Graham Sumner in "The Rule to Mind One's Own Business," Toynbee must attack a wrong view. His discussion here is largely a destructive analysis of this wrong view. In his method of attacking the wrong view, however, Toynbee differs considerably from Sumner. Some of the points of difference are suggested in the questions below.

A. How do Toynbee's indications of the nature and causes of the wrong view differ from Sumner's descriptive labels—that is, "misconception," "misleading feature," "superficial view," as compared with Sumner's "passion for dealing with social questions," "social doctors," and the like?

B. Is Toynbee more non-partisan and objective in his tone and approach?

C. Does he make any concessions to his opponents? Is it good strategy to make concessions when one is undertaking a destructive analysis? Does Toynbee concede anything that will weaken his own argument?

D. Does Toynbee present hypothetical examples or real examples? How does he compare with Sumner in this respect? Is Toynbee more concrete and specific than Sumner? Is the difference in the two methods due partly to the fact that Toynbee is arguing as a historian and Sumner from a philosophical point of view?

E. Do you discover any differences not covered in the above questions?

II. In Par. 5, what implied distinction is Toynbee making between economic and political history, on the one hand, and cultural history, on the other hand? Which kind of history is Toynbee writing? The words "and their outlook is illustrated" introduce an extended illustration (Pars. 3 and 4) in which Toynbee is explaining a certain kind of cultural blindness. Is he referring merely to the "blindness" of economic and political historians, or of Western historians and of Westerners in general? Does his illustration refer to known facts? Is it pertinent and helpful? Would Toynbee and the economic and political historians agree on a definition of what civilization is? On the basis of Pars. 2, 3, and 4, construct (1) a definition of civilization that Toynbee would accept and (2) the definition of civilization that Toynbee attributes to the economic and political historians.

III. Beginning with Par. 5, Toynbee makes a more sweeping analysis of the causes of Western misconceptions as to the "unity of history." Show the extent to which this analysis deals with (1) errors common to all humankind; (2) errors peculiar to the West. What does Toynbee gain by broadening his field of analysis at this point?

Is Toynbee's analysis a "formal" analysis, in the strict sense, or an "informal" analysis? (In formal analysis, one consistent principle of classification or division must be followed, and the analysis must be logically complete—that is, nothing must be left unaccounted for; in informal analysis, the treatment is selective, only the most significant classes or divisions being considered.) Is Toynbee in Par. 5 analyzing illusions in general or only those that cause misconceptions as to the nature of human history?

IV. Make a study of Toynbee's use of figurative language. Since we expect a historian to be precise (not vague), factual (not fanciful), and objective (not opinionated or partisan), the question arises whether we should also expect him to use language as "dry" and "colorless" as the language of physical science is supposed to be. You can begin to study this general question by observing Toynbee's actual practice.

A. In Par. 2, would "has *extended* its economic system" be preferable to "*cast the net* of its economic system"? In this same sentence the word "conquests" is used twice, once in a literal, matter-of-fact sense, then in a figurative sense. Would it be easy to find a good matter-of-fact substitute for "conquests" in its metaphorical use?

B. In Par. 3, the phrase "superficial view" may be simply a matter-of-fact term. Show how the influence of "view," taken metaphorically, is so far extended that it develops into an elaborate figure of speech which determines the pattern of composition of Par. 3 and, in part, of Par. 4. Show how the following terms fit into this extended figure of speech: "cultural map," "cultural plane," "those who have eyes to see," "lineaments," "clear," "have not such eyes," "outlook" (Par. 3); "cultural colour," "we see them" (Par. 4).

C. In Pars. 6, 7, and 8, figurative language is less prominent. Is the lack of figurative language in these paragraphs due to the fact that Toynbee is citing actual historical evidence to support his points rather than engaging in critical interpretation?

D. In Par. 9, Toynbee uses the "bamboo stem" and "brush-handle" figures to preface his more matter-of-fact discussion of the periods of history. Why does he here again resort to an extended figure?

V. Give the derivation and meaning of the following words: *egocentric* (Par. 5); *dichotomy* (Par. 9); *proletariat* (Par. 9); *parochialism* (Par. 11).

VI. Write a theme in which, preserving a non-partisan tone, you refute a popular error by analyzing the cause or causes of the error. Suggested topics: misconceptions about your native town, city, state, or region; or about some historical character, political controversy, or historical event with which you are acquainted; or about some work of art that you have studied (poem, play, novel, musical composition).

AUDIENCE AND AUTHORSHIP AS MIRRORED IN THE BALLADS *

by LOUISE POUND

LESSON XII

Refutation of Erroneous Views...

¶ 1 Special emphasis is often placed upon the social solidarity of the period from which the popular ballads emerged. Professor F. J. Child had in mind the English and Scottish ballads when he wrote, "The condition of society in which a truly national or popular poetry appears explains the character of such poetry. It is a condition in which the people are not divided by political organizations and book culture into markedly distinct classes, in which, consequently there is such community of ideas and feelings that the whole people form one individual."[1] Said Professor Henry Beers, "We have to do here with the folk-song, the *traditional* ballad, product of the people at a time when the people was homogeneous and the separation between lettered and unlettered classes had not yet taken place."[2] "This homogeneous character of the ballad-making folk, by the way, is enough to explain the high rank of most personages in the ballads—princes, knights, and so on," said Professor Gummere.[3] Elsewhere he remarked more specifically, "Those high-born people who figure in traditional ballads—Childe Waters, Lady Maisry, and the rest—do not require us to assume composition in aristocratic circles; for the lower classes of the people in the ballad days had no separate literature, and a ballad of the folk belonged to the community as a whole. The same habit of thought, the same standard of action, rules alike the noble and his meanest retainer."

¶ 2 The unmistakable fact is that, judging from the ballads

[1] Article "Ballads" in *Johnson's Cyclopaedia.*

[2] *English Romanticism in the Eighteenth Century,* p. 272.

[3] *Old English Ballads,* Introd., p. xxvii; "Ballads" in *A Library of the World's Best Literature,* vol. III, p. 1307. To these citations may be added the opinion of Professor G. L. Kittredge, who believes that the ballads "belonged, in the first instance, to the whole people, at a time when there were no formal divisions of literate and illiterate; when the intellectual interests of all were substantially identical, from the king to the peasant." Introduction to *English and Scottish Popular Ballads,* p. xii.

themselves, they were composed primarily for the delectation of the upper classes. The difficulty with the view set forth in the various quotations just cited is that the conditions which they assume do not fit anywhere, at any stage, in the chronology of society. The generalization is not made of primitive peoples, among whom, contrary to the usual view of literary historians, composition is not characteristically "communal" but individual,[4] but it would be far truer of primitive than of medieval society. Even for the pre-Norman period, one cannot think of the thrall or serf creating song of the same type as the court scop or the noble. If Gurth in *Ivanhoe* sang songs, they would not be of the same character as those of Richard Coeur-de-Lion. There *was* no period when "in a common atmosphere of ignorance, so far as book-lore is concerned, one habit of thought and one standard of action animate every member from prince to ploughboy." Try to imagine Jack Straw's "menye" ruled by the same habit of thought as Chaucer's Squire, or Froissart's Jacquerie by the same standard of action as Froissart himself. Chaucer knows his contemporary society too well to place the same quality of matter in the mouths of his higher and his lower characters. The interests and the tastes of the medieval nobility and the medieval peasantry were no more identical than were their occupations or their costumes or their destinies in general.

Songs of the adventures of the nobly-born, of the deeds of the men of noble houses, were not addressed primarily to throngs of the rural variety, nor were they evolved by such throngs—not even the songs of Robin Hood, for whom the ballads claim noble descent, or whom some of them picture as an outlawed noble. In our earliest reference to him he is placed alongside Randolph, Earl of Chester.[5] The very ¶ 3

[4] Compare the views of anthropologists. The institution of the *bard* appears in all the earliest Indo-European literatures. There must have been (one would conjecture) *ur*-Aryan bards. If so, there is here a strong argument for high-born literary tradition.

[5] *Piers Plowman,* B text:

> "I cannot perfectly my paternoster, as the priest it singeth,
> But I can rhymes of Robin Hood and Randolph, Earl of Chester."

Whether these "rhymes" were or were not ballads, or ballads of the Child type, it is impossible to determine.

LESSON XII

Refutation of Erroneous Views...

formula of introduction, used in the *Geste,* "Lyth and listen, *gentlemen,*" suggests that his adventures originally entertained the higher not the lower classes. *Robin Hood Newly Revived* calls upon "gentlemen . . . in this bower" to listen. Robin is as "courteous" as a knight errant. "So curteyse an outlawe as he was one" was never found, says the *Geste,* and he is as devoted to "our lady" as the most chivalrous knight.[6] But most of the ballads have much more of the aristocratic in them than do the ballads of Robin Hood. Where we have the genuine improvisations of the unlettered, they deal always with themselves, or with happenings of near interest, in their own region, or involving their own circle, not with the interests and adventures and experiences of a widely severed class—the governing class.[7] If the peasant throngs of the Middle Ages improvised songs we can imagine pretty well the crude character of their improvisations, and their themes. They did not concern the love affairs of the nobly-born, and knightly doings in hall and bower. Nor did they concern the exploits of nobles. It is known that the great houses of medieval England and Scotland kept their own hereditary family bards, who composed pieces to be recited or sung, not for existence in written form, and their themes were the feats of their clan or of the noble houses with which they were connected. Professor Firth is probably right[8] when he thinks he detects fragments remaining of several cycles—a cycle about the Percys, as the first ballad of Chevy Chase, about the Stanleys, as *The Rose of England,* and about the Howards, as *Flodden Field* and *Sir Andrew Barton.* Such a mode of composition would account, too, for the vitality of these pieces, as well as for their quality. If the men-at-arms of the Borderers made their own songs to celebrate their

[6] In any case, it will hardly do to speak of the Robin Hood cycle as "confined to humble tradition and the interest of a class" (Gummere, *The Popular Ballad,* 271). And alongside the Robin Hood ballads, telling of archery, we should recall Ascham's *Toxophilus,* celebrating archery, in its decay, for the upper classes, in prose.

[7] See pp. 153–161.

[8] C. H. Firth, *The Ballad History of the Reigns of the Later Tudors,* Transactions of the Royal Historical Society, 3d Series, Vol. III, London, 1909.

deeds, as Professor Gummere thinks,[9] their "communal" songs would have had little chance of preservation beside the popular songs, for oral destination, of the bards employed for that purpose, repeated by them on notable occasions and becoming traditional.

¶ 4 The social atmosphere of the ballads is the atmosphere of the upper classes. Certainly no peasant audience or authorship is mirrored in them.[10] The picture we get from them is a picture of the life of chivalry, not of the doings of the common people; such as we have, for example, from genuinely "communal" ranch or lumberman or cowboy or fisherman or negro songs today. And the same composers who made heroic and historical narratives for their masculine hearers might well have made romantic and other pieces, on familiar or novel themes, for the delectation of their nobly-born women hearers, or of mixed audiences. Such songs were short, or fairly short, of a type suited for oral recital or for singing or memorizing. The English and Scottish ballads seem to have affiliations with classical narratives, medieval romances, scriptural matter, and lives of saints. There are also many plots which, as Professor Ker points out,[11] could have existed only as ballad plots; it is as ballads that they seem to have been created, and it is as ballads that they are memorable. Some of them might have been utilized occasionally as dance songs; but if so, this was not typical, and it was not an essential of their composition.

[9] *The Cambridge History of English Literature,* II, Ch. XVII, p. 453; also *The Popular Ballad,* p. 250.

[10] The earliest reference to *The Fair Flower of Northumberland* mentions it as sung before the *King* and *Queen.* According to Thomas Deloney (Reprint by R. Sievers, *Palaestra,* XXV, 1904, *Historie of Jno. Winchcomb,* p. 195), to whom we owe our earliest text, maidens "in dulcet manner chanted out this song, two of them singing the ditty and all the rest bearing the burden." Seven versions of the ballad have survived in all, but that given by Deloney is the only one that is early. It is also unquestionably the best version. Ophelia's songs in *Hamlet* are of ballad quality, another evidence of the aristocratic currency and acceptability of ballads in the age of Elizabeth. The popularity of Danish ballads in the highest circles is well known, and when they were first printed it was through the favor of the Queen.

[11] *On the History of the Ballads: 1100–1500, Proceedings of the British Academy,* Vol. IV.

¶ 5 The lowly, as over against the aristocrats, hardly play any part in the English and Scottish ballads; and the ballads which do show non-aristocratic characters are those which would be least missed, if eliminated. One mentions a hostler. Thomas Potts is a serving-man, in the seventeenth century ballad of that name, but he weds a lord's daughter, and is himself ennobled. The Kitchie Boy, who is the hero of another, also weds a lady of noble birth, in a ballad which is a late adaptation of *King Horn.* Lamkin in the ballad of that name is a mason. Add Richie Story, who marries a footman, although herself an aristocrat, and the list is about exhausted. All are late pieces. The ballads, in due time, like fiction and the drama, were subjected to democratization of characters. Later British balladry stays no longer by the nobly-born for its heroes and heroines. Among medieval types of literature the ballad of the Child type was a type which lasted well, but it too finally yielded to later melodies and styles, with other characters and plots. The personages and the stories houses of medieval England and Scotland kept their own "people" did not improvise them, for the songs which the people do improvise, when they can be certainly determined, do not incline to be narratives, and they reflect the immediate horizons of their makers and the limitations of their expression. Folk-throngs cannot produce real narratives, even today, nor do primitive throngs. There is no instance recorded where a collaborating folk-throng or a primitive throng, for that matter, has produced a memorable song-story. Crude songs, at most pieces of tales rather than tales, are the best they can create. The power to convey a complete story comes late, not at the beginning of lyric art.

EXERCISES

I. Louise Pound's "Audience and Authorship as Mirrored in the Ballads" offers a sound example of a composition based upon research and thoroughly documented in a form standard among scholars. Observe that all quotations and other references to source material are accompanied by citations contained in footnotes, which are numbered consecutively.

The composition is also an excellent example of the procedure followed when a researchist wishes to disprove—or at least to question—some theory or opinion advanced by persons of respected authority.

The question at issue is whether the traditional ballads contained in such a work as Francis J. Child's *English and Scottish Popular Ballads* (or in Sargent and Kittredge's abridged edition of this work, referred to in Note 3) were composed *for* the people of England and Scotland as a whole, with no preference as to "class," or whether, on the contrary, they were composed for the courtly and aristocratic class, and so eventually drifted into the possession of common folk. Miss Pound argues for the latter view.

Her discussion also covers, to some extent, the allied question of whether—as various authorities once held—the ballads of tradition originated more or less spontaneously, by a process of "communal composition," among common folk of a "primitive" type. Miss Pound holds that the character of the ballads themselves offers strong evidence against such a view of their origin.

II. Answer the following questions concerning the arrangement and method used by Miss Pound:

A. What is the purpose of the various quotations used in Par. 1? Observe the form used in the annotations that accompany these quotations. Does this form correspond with the form recommended or required by your instructor? If it does not, in what way would you revise Miss Pound's footnotes? Is there a standard form for *all* researchists, no matter what their field of inquiry may be?

B. What is Louise Pound referring to when she says (Par. 2): "The generalization is not made of primitive peoples"? Was the pre-Norman period of English history "primitive"? What is the relevance, in this connection, of the references to Gurth, *Ivanhoe,* Richard Coeur-de-Lion, Jack Straw's "menye," Chaucer's Squire, Froissart's Jacquerie?

C. What does Louise Pound mean by saying ". . . but it would be far truer of primitive than of medieval society"? Is Miss Pound mixing *two* points of discussion in Par. 2? Or does the paragraph clearly make *one* point to which her contrast between primitive and medieval society is related? Where else does Miss Pound take up the question of the *kind* of thing composed under "primitive" conditions? Is the subject of Par. 2 the contrast between medieval and "primitive" society? Or is Miss Pound here principally concerned with arguing that "The interests and the tastes of the medieval nobility and the medieval peasantry were no more identical than were their occupations . . ."?

D. What is the nature of the evidence presented by Louise Pound in Pars. 3 and 4? Does it sustain her general argument? Why does she not quote more extensively from the ballads themselves? Does *your own* knowledge of traditional ballads bear out Miss Pound's statement (Par. 4) that "The social atmosphere of the ballads is the atmosphere of the upper classes"? Refer to ballads in your anthology of literature or, for more extensive study, to the Sargent and Kittredge edition mentioned above.

E. To your knowledge, are there "genuinely 'communal' " elements in American ranch, lumberman, cowboy, fisherman, or Negro songs? (See Par. 4.) Are the American ballads that you know full-scale ballads of the medieval type, or do they illustrate the view advanced by Miss Pound in Par. 5, in the passage beginning, "Folk-throngs cannot produce real narratives, even today . . ."?

F. What distinctions does Miss Pound make in Par. 5?

III. For what purposes other than mere authentication can footnotes be used? Examine Miss Pound's footnotes with this question in mind.

LESSON XIII

Technical Subject Discussed in Literary Terms.
Metaphor and Truth. Metaphorical and Literal Meaning.
Overstatement for Effect. Ambiguity.

GOING TO THE LEAF OF THINGS *

by DONALD CULROSS PEATTIE

What we love, when on a summer day we step into the coolness of a wood, is that its boughs close up behind us. We are escaped, into another room of life. The wood does not live as we live, restless and running, panting after flesh, and even in sleep tossing with fears. It is aloof from thoughts and instincts; it responds, but only to the sun and wind, the rock and the stream—never, though you shout yourself hoarse, to propaganda, temptation, reproach, or promises. You cannot mount a rock and preach to a tree how it shall attain the kingdom of heaven. It is already closer to it, up there, than you will grow to be. And you cannot make it see the light, since in the tree's sense you are blind. You have nothing to bring it, for all the forest is self-sufficient; if you burn it, cut, hack through it with a blade, it angrily repairs the swathe with thorns and weeds and fierce suckers. Later there are good green leaves again, toiling, adjusting, breathing—forgetting you. ¶ 1

For this green living is the world's primal industry; yet it makes no roar. Waving its banners, it marches across the earth and the ages, without dust around its columns. I do not hold that all of that life is pretty; it is not, in purpose, sprung for us, and moves under no compulsion to please. If ¶ 2

*Reprinted by permission of the publishers, G. P. Putnam's Sons, from *Flowering Earth,* by Donald Culross Peattie. Copyright, 1939.

you ever fought with thistles, or tried to pull up a cattail's matted rootstocks, you will know how plants cling to their own lives and defy you. The pond-scums gather in the cistern, frothing and buoyed with their own gases; the storm waves fling at your feet upon the beach the limp sea-lettuce wrenched from its submarine hold—reminder that there too, where the light is filtered and refracted, there is life still to intercept and net and by it proliferate. Inland from the shore I look and see the coastal ranges clothed in chaparral—dense shrubbery and scrubbery, close-fisted, intricately branched, suffocating the rash rambler in the noon heat with its pungency. Beyond, on the deserts, under a fierce sky, between the harsh lunar ranges of unweathered rock, life still, somehow, fights its way through the year, with thorn and succulent cell and indomitable root.

¶3 Between such embattled life and the Forest of Arden, with its ancient beeches and enchanter's night-shade, there is no great biologic difference. Each lives by the cool and cleanly and most commendable virtue of being green. And though that is not biological language, it is the whole story in two words. So that we ought not to speak of getting at the root of a matter, but of going back to the leaf of things. The orator who knows the way to the country's salvation and does not know that the breath of life he draws was blown into his nostrils by green leaves, had better spare his breath. And before anyone builds a new state upon the industrial proletariat, he will be wisely cautioned to discover that the source of all wealth is the peasantry of grass.

¶4 The reason for these assertions—which I do not make for metaphorical effect but maintain quite literally—is that the green leaf pigment, called chlorophyll, is the one link between the sun and life; it is the conduit of perpetual energy to our own frail organisms.

¶5 For inert and inorganic elements—water and carbon dioxide of the air, the same that we breathe out as a waste—chlorophyll can synthesize with the energy of sunlight. Every day, every hour of all the ages, as each continent and, equally important, each ocean rolls into sunlight, chlorophyll ceaselessly creates. Not figuratively, but literally, in the grand First Chapter Genesis style. One instant there are a gas and water, as lifeless as the core of earth or the chill of space; and the next they are become living tissue—mortal yet genitive, progenitive, resilient with all the dewy adaptability of flesh, ever changing in order to stabilize some unchanging ideal of form. Life, in short, synthesized, plant-synthesized, light-synthesized. Botanists say photosynthesized. So that the post-Biblical synthesis of life is already a fact. Only when man has done as much, may he call himself the equal of a weed.

¶ 6 Plant life sustains the living world; more precisely, chlorophyll does so, and where, in the vegetable kingdom, there is not chlorophyll or something closely like it, then that plant or cell is a parasite—no better, in vital economy, than a mere animal or man. Blood, bone and sinew, all flesh is grass. Grass to mutton, mutton to wool, wool to the coat on my back—it runs like one of those cumulative nursery rhymes, the wealth and diversity of our material life accumulating from the primal fact of chlorophyll's activity. The roof of my house, the snapping logs upon the hearth, the desk where I write, are my imports from the plant kingdom. But the whole of modern civilization is based upon a whirlwind spending of the plant wealth long ago and very slowly accumulated. For, fundamentally, and away back, coal and oil, gasoline and illuminating gas had green origins too. With the exception of a small amount of water power, a still smaller of wind and tidal mills, the vast machinery of our complex living is driven only by these stores of plant energy.

¶ 7 We, then, the animals, consume those stores in our restless living. Serenely the plants amass them. They turn light's active energy to food, which is potential energy stored for their own benefit. Only if the daisy is browsed by the cow, the maple leaf sucked of its juices by an insect, will that green leaf become of our kind. So we get the song of a bird at dawn, the speed in the hoofs of the fleeing deer, the noble thought in the philosopher's mind. So Plato's Republic was builded on leeks and cabbages.

¶ 8 *Technical Subject Discussed in Literary Terms . . .*

Animal life lives always in the red; the favorable balance is written on the other side of life's page, and it is written in chlorophyll. All else obeys the thermodynamic law that energy runs forever down hill, is lost and degraded. In economic language, this is the law of diminishing returns, and it is obeyed by the cooling stars as by man and all the animals. They float down its Lethe stream. Only chlorophyll fights up against the current. It is the stuff in life that rebels at death, that has never surrendered to entropy, final icy stagnation. It is the mere cobweb on which we are all suspended over the abyss.

EXERCISES

I. Although Donald Culross Peattie is a scientist, he states his subject and develops much of his discussion in literary rather than in scientific terms. We ought not to speak, he says (Par. 3) "of getting at the root of a matter, but of going back to the leaf of things." Mr. Peattie concedes that such language "is not biological language," and thus seems to imply that some defense or explanation of his use of non-biological language might be in order. In Par. 4, however, he insists that he is making his assertions "not for metaphorical effect" but quite literally. Again, in Par. 5, he says that chlorophyll creates "Not figuratively, but literally, in the grand First Chapter Genesis style."

A. Since the assertions of Pars. 1, 2, and 3 are obviously more "metaphorical" than technical, more "literary" than scientific—at least in language—it is important to decide (1) why Peattie prefers metaphorical language in these paragraphs and (2) why he insists that his assertions are to be taken "quite literally."

Does Peattie mean *literally* that the wood (Par. 1) is "aloof" in a human sense? That a tree (Par. 1) is closer to the kingdom of heaven "than you will grow to be"? That green leaves (last sentence of Par. 1) can "forget"? That the green wood (Par. 2) waves banners and marches? That chaparral is "close-fisted" (Par. 2)? That the grass (Par. 3) is a "peasantry"?

Is Peattie's matter-of-fact statement (Par. 4) that chlorophyll "is the one link between the sun and life" a sufficient reason for taking the position that trees, grass, and other green things *literally* are capable of the human feelings and acts ascribed to them?

Or is Peattie making these very strong statements because mere scientific terms would not sufficiently impress upon a reader the truth that he wishes to convey? By his use of the word "literally" does Peattie, as scientist, concede that "metaphorical," "figurative," "poetical," "mythical," "religious" terms can convey the "truth" of scientific discoveries more adequately than pure scientific language? Or is there an implication that such non-scientific language may better *persuade* men to accept scientific truth? Or does he use such terms only because he is writing for the general reader and not for a group of biologists?

B. What portions of the discussion are *less* metaphorical, *more* scientific and technical, than the paragraphs just referred to? Does Peattie's use of metaphor in some parts of his discussion weaken or invalidate the more strictly factual parts? Or does such partially literary treatment serve to emphasize and clarify his broad assertion—which we will assume is scientific—that chlorophyll "is the one link between the sun and life"?

C. In Par. 5, Peattie says: "Every day, every hour of all the ages . . . chlorophyll ceaselessly creates." Is this an overstatement, made for rhetorical effect? Or is it merely a "strong" form of statement of a general scientific truth? Would Peattie's position be logically or rhetorically firmer if he had inserted some reservation like "so far as we yet know"? Compare the procedure of Lorenz, in "The Covenant" (pp. 127–134). Is a general scientific truth worth anything, as truth, if it is subject to reservations? Find other statements which, like the one quoted, may be taken as "strongly worded" expressions of general scientific truth. How do such statements compare with more completely figurative and exaggerated statements such as the following: "So Plato's Republic was builded on leeks and cabbages"? (Par. 7). Find other statements of the latter sort.

II. Is our situation, as to economic and industrial resources, so dangerous or critical as to justify an intense degree of concern such as is apparent in Peattie's discussion? Discuss the present application of the last two sentences of Par. 3.

III. Explain the meaning and discuss the appropriateness and effectiveness of the following sentences or passages:

A. "For this green living is the world's primal industry . . . without dust around its columns." (Par. 2, first two sentences)

LESSON XIII

Technical Subject Discussed in Literary Terms . . .

B. "Between such embattled life and the Forest of Arden . . . no great biologic difference." (Sen. 1, Par. 3)

C. "Only when man has done as much, may he call himself the equal of a weed." (Par. 5, last sentence)

D. "The roof of my house . . . my imports from the plant kingdom." (Par. 6)

E. "They float down its Lethe stream . . . suspended over the abyss." (Par. 8, last four sentences)

IV. In Par. 5, Peattie speaks of chlorophyll as "creating" . . . "in the grand First Chapter Genesis style." No doubt he is referring specifically to Genesis I, 11, which is as follows in the King James translation: "And God said, let the earth bring forth grass, the herb yielding seed and the fruit tree yielding fruit after his kind, whose seed is in itself, upon the earth: and it was so." Is Peattie using the word *create* in the same sense as it was used in Genesis? ("In the beginning, God created the heavens and earth.") Discuss the correspondence and differences of meaning involved in Peattie's succession of terms—*Genesis, genitive, progenitive.* What does he mean by "the post-Biblical synthesis of life"?

V. Make a list of all terms that are purely scientific and technical. *Photosynthesized* (Par. 5) is such a term. Do these terms have no metaphorical meaning at all? No connotation, but only denotation? Compare terms like *photosynthesized* with obviously metaphorical, non-scientific expressions like "succulent cell and indomitable root" (Par. 2); "resilient with all the dewy adaptability of flesh" (Par. 5); "all flesh is grass" (Par. 6).

VI. Suggestions for theme topics:

Beauty and Her T-Bone Steak
Yes, We All Wear Grass Skirts—If You Insist on Being Scientific
My Breakfast Table and the Economic System
The Twinkling of an Eye—As a Physicist Thinks of Eyes
The Twinkling of an Eye—According to a Psychologist
The Twinkling of an Eye—According to a Poet
High Fidelity Sound Reproduction
The Truth about Radar
The Opera Singer's Diaphragm and Art

PART FIVE

VARIED PATTERNS OF PROSE: NARRATION AND DESCRIPTION, FACTUAL AND FICTIONAL

The changing wisdom of successive generations discards ideas, questions facts, demolishes theories. But the artist appeals to that part of our being which is not dependent on wisdom: to that in us which is a gift and not an acquisition—and, therefore, more permanently enduring. He speaks to our capacity for delight and wonder, to the sense of mystery surrounding our lives; to our sense of pity, and beauty, and pain; to the latent feeling of fellowship with all creation—and to the subtle but invincible conviction of solidarity that knits together the loneliness of innumerable hearts, to the solidarity in dreams, in joy, in sorrow, in aspirations, in illusions, in hope, in fear, which binds men to each other, which binds together all humanity—the dead to the living and the living to the unborn.

—Joseph Conrad, Preface to *The Nigger of the Narcissus.* Reprinted by permission of J. M. Dent & Sons, Ltd., publishers.

LESSON XIV

Three Types of Reminiscent Narrative.
Interior Monologue.
Use of Present and Past Tense in Narrative.
Dialogue. Paradox and Reversal of Action.
Resolution of Incongruities. Foreshadowing.
Comment by Author.
Repetition, Parallelism, Climax, Anticlimax.

OVER THE ATLANTIC—FLYING BLIND*

by CHARLES A. LINDBERGH

As I fly through the body of night, haze lessens, and I discover that I'm among the cloud mountains themselves—great shadowy forms on every side, dwarfing my plane, dwarfing earthly mountains with their magnitude, awesome in their weird, fantastic shapes. Huge pillars push upward thousands of feet above the common mass. Black valleys and chasms open below me to unfathomed depth. ¶ 1

There's no possibility of flying above those mountains. They look higher than any clouds I ever saw before. How have I come into their midst without knowing they were there? I must have followed a great valley, blinded by the mist. Or did these sky giants draw aside to entice me among them, and close in again now that they have me hopelessly entrapped? Well, if I can't follow the valleys, I'll have to challenge the mountains themselves. Flying through an occasional thunderhead will be less tiring than spending hours on end down in the writhing body of the storm. A few minutes of blind flying followed by relaxation under a star-filled sky is nothing much to dread. It may even be a welcome ¶ 2

*Reprinted from *The Spirit of St. Louis,* by Charles A. Lindbergh; used by permission of the publishers, Charles Scribner's Sons. Copyright, 1953, by Charles Scribner's Sons.

change, sharpen my dull senses, break up the monotony of routine flight.

¶ 3 Then I'll hold my course, stay above the stratus layer of the storm, and tunnel through the thunderheads that rise directly on my route.

¶ 4 A pillar of cloud blocks out the stars ahead, spilling over on top like a huge mushroom in the sky. I tighten my belt, push the nose down a bit, and adjust the stabilizer for level flight. In the seconds that intervene while I approach, I make the mental and physical preparation for blind flying.

¶ 5 The body must be informed sternly that the mind will take complete control. The senses must be drafted and lined up in strictest discipline, while logic replaces instinct as commander. If the body feels a wing dropping, and the mind says it is not (because the turn indicator's ball and needle are still centered), the muscles must obey the mind's decision no matter how wrong it seems to them. If the eyes imagine the flicker of a star below where they think the horizon ought to be, if the ears report the engine's tempo too slow for level flight, if the nerves say the seat back's pressure is increasing (as it does in a climb), the hands and the feet must still be loyal to the orders of the mind.

¶ 6 It's a terrific strain on the mind also when it turns from long-proven bodily instincts to the cold, mechanical impartiality of needles moving over dials. For countless centuries, it's been accustomed to relying on the senses. They can keep the body upright on the darkest night. They're trained to catch a stumble in an instant. Deprived of sight, they can still hold a blind man's balance. Why, then, should they be so impotent in an airplane?

¶ 7 The mind must operate as mechanically as the gyroscope which guides it. The muscles must move as unfeelingly as gears. If the senses get excited and out of control, the plane will follow them, and that can be fatal. If the senses break ranks while everything is going right, it may be impossible, with the plane falling dizzily and needles running wild, to bring them back into line, reinstruct them, and force them to gain control while everything is going wrong. It would be like rallying a panicked army under the fire of an advancing enemy. Like an army under fire, blind flying requires absolute discipline. That must be fully understood before it starts. LESSON XIV

Wings quiver as I enter the cloud. Air roughens until it ¶ 8
jerks the *Spirit of St. Louis* about as though real demons were pulling at fuselage and wings. No stars are overhead now to help, no clouds are below. Everything is uniform blackness, except for the exhaust's flash on passing mist and the glowing dials in my cockpit, so different from all other lights. What lies outside doesn't matter. My world and my life are compressed within these fabric walls.

Flying blind is difficult enough in smooth air. In this swirl- ¶ 9
ing cloud, it calls for all the concentration I can muster. The turn and bank indicators, the air speed, the altimeter, and the compass, all those phosphorescent lines and dots in front of me, must be kept in proper place. When a single one strays off, the rest go chasing after it like so many sheep, and have to be caught quickly and carefully herded back into position again. . . .

It's cold up here at—I glance at the altimeter—10,500 feet ¶ 10
—*cold*—good Lord, there *are* things to be considered outside the cockpit! How could I forget! I jerk off a leather mitten and thrust my arm out the window. My palm is covered with stinging pinpricks. I pull the flashlight from my pocket and throw its beam onto a strut. The entering edge is irregular and shiny—*ice!* And as far out into the darkness as the beam penetrates, the night is filled with countless, horizontal, threadlike streaks. The venturi tubes may clog at any moment.

I've got to turn around, get back into clear air—quickly! ¶ 11
But in so doing those instrument needles mustn't move too far or too fast. Mind, not body, must control the turn. My bodily senses want to whip the *Spirit of St. Louis* into a bank and dive it out of the thunderhead, back into open sky:

¶ 12 "Kick rudder hard—no time to lose—the turn indicator's icing up right now."

¶ 13 But the mind retorts, "Steady, steady. It's easy enough to get into a steep bank, but more difficult to get out of one and on your course again. If you turn too fast, you'll lose more time than you save; the plane may get entirely out of control."

¶ 14 "If the turn indicator ices up, it'll get out of control any-way. There's no time—only a few seconds—quick—quick—harder rudder—kick it . . ."

¶ 15 "Don't do anything of the sort. I've thought all this out carefully and know just what's best to do. You remember, you are to obey my orders!"

¶ 16 "Yes, yes—but just a little faster, then—just a little . . . ."

¶ 17 "No, no faster; turn just the right amount. You're to do exactly what I say; no more, no less!"

¶ 18 "Just a little!"

¶ 19 "No, none!"

¶ 20 I keep pressing rudder cautiously until the turn indicator's needle creeps a quarter-inch to the left. I push the stick over just enough to hold the proper bank—ball high—low—center again—slow and steady movements—mustn't let jerks from the turbulence throw me off . . . . The air speed drops ten miles an hour . . . . The altimeter shows a hundred foot descent . . . .

¶ 21 "Turn faster! You see the air speed's dropping. It's ice doing that! Quick, or it'll be too late!"

¶ 22 "No, it's not ice—at least not very likely. It's probably just the normal slowing down in a bank."

¶ 23 "But the altimeter's dropping too! It's ice, I tell you!"

¶ 24 I open the throttle another 50 revolutions. I don't dare push the stick forward very much to gain speed. The *Spirit of St. Louis* is too close to the top of the main cloud layer. There were less than a thousand feet to spare when I entered the thunderhead. That endless stratus layer is probably full of ice too. If I drop down into it, I may never see the stars again.

The altimeter needle falls 200 feet . . . . 300 feet . . . . I ¶ 25
push the throttle wide open . . . . I *must* stay above that vast
layer of cloud at the thunderhead's base . . . . The bank indicator shows a skid—ball to right of center—a blast of air
strikes my cheek—Ease up on the rudder . . . . The air speed
rises to 100 miles an hour . . . . The pitch indicator points
nose down . . . . Stick back slightly . . . .

I ought to be turned around now—Center the turn indi- ¶ 26
cator—level out the plane—flashlight onto the liquid compass. (It's no time to trust the earth-inductor; it will be
working backward anyhow, on a back-track heading.) No,
not yet—about 30 degrees more to go—the card's swinging
too much to read accurately.

I bank again and glance at the altimeter—10,300 feet. ¶ 27
Good—it's gone up a little. I throw my flashlight onto the
wing strut. Ice is thicker!

The earth-inductor needle begins moving backward, jump- ¶ 28
ing erratically . . . . Level out wings . . . . About the right
heading this time. Now, if the turn indicator doesn't ice up
for a few minutes more . . . . I put my hand out the window
again . . . . the pinpricks are still there.

Steady the plane. Make the compass card stop swinging ¶ 29
. . . . but the air's too rough . . . . Is the turn indicator getting sluggish—icing? . . . . It seems to move back and forth
more slowly . . . . Everything depends on its working till I
get outside this cloud . . . . Just two or three more
minutes . . . .

My eyes sense a change in the blackness of my cockpit. I ¶ 30
look out through the window. Can those be the same stars?
Is this the same sky? How bright! How clear! What safety
I have reached! Bright, clear, safe? But this is the same hazy
air I left, the same fraction of an earthly hour. I've simply
been existing in a different frame of space and time. Values
are relative, dependent on one's circumstance. They change
from frame to frame, and as one travels back and forth between them. Here I've found security where I left danger,
flying over a major storm, above a frigid northern ocean.

Here's something I never saw before—the brilliant light of a black night.

¶ 31 I was in the thunderhead for ten minutes at most; but it's one of those incidents that can't be measured by minutes. Such periods stand out like islands in a sea of time. It's not the limitless vista of experience, not hours or years that are most important. It's the islands, no matter how small. They impress the senses as they draw the eye at sea. Against them, years roll in and break, as waves upon a coast.

EXERCISES

I. *The Spirit of St. Louis*—the book in which General Lindbergh gives his own complete account of the planning and execution of the first non-stop airplane flight from America to Europe—is written almost entirely in the *present* tense instead of in the *past* tense which is the normal tense of narrative. Use of present tense for a narrative of such a length is most unusual. For this unique book, however, it may be defended. General Lindbergh's narrative follows the pattern of a "log" or "diary" of events from day to day and, during the transatlantic passage itself, from hour to hour. Since the narrative contains not only the jottings of technical data that would be normal in a pilot's log, but also the full dramatic context of Lindbergh's experience, it becomes an exploitation at a high literary level of the *form* of a log for purposes that go far beyond mere keeping of a record. In a functional sense, it is therefore appropriate that General Lindbergh's narrative be written in present tense. It may be further argued that the present tense gives an effect of immediacy, even of great urgency, that belongs to this unique experience, since almost every moment of the thirty-three hours of transatlantic flight is truly a moment of tension or crisis. The peculiarly solitary and abstract nature of the pilot's task, which forces him into isolated communion with his own thoughts, may also justify the representation of the long flight as an extended monologue—a conversation that the lone pilot has with himself from moment to moment. (See the questions asked under Section IV, p. 62, regarding Langewiesche's "An Air View of the United States.")

A. If the above reasons for use of the present tense do not seem convincing to you, what reasons would you give for preferring past tense?

B. Test your views of this stylistic issue by changing the verbs in some portion of the narrative from present tense to the appropriate tense for indicating past time. How does the revised version compare in effectiveness with the original?

II. The episode here presented from *The Spirit of St. Louis* is an account of a highly dramatic incident in General Lindbergh's famous flight. At night, in mid-passage, the young pilot, already buffeted by a storm, is faced by "cloud mountains" and decides to go through them—flying blind—rather than "follow the valleys." Pars. 1–3 state this situation in vivid form and give the pilot's decision. The key statement of this section—contrasting sharply with the scene within the thunderhead itself—is, "A few moments of blind flying . . . is nothing much to dread" (Par. 2). What contrast do you feel *within* the preliminary section itself? Does it prepare you, dramatically, for the lone pilot's actual struggle while engulfed in the thunderhead?

III. What is the function of Par. 4?

IV. In Pars. 5, 6, and 7, the process of blind flying is described in cool, almost abstract terms. This section is strongly *impersonal* rather than *personal.* Why? Does the author express any particular pride about his own skill in blind flying? Or does he present blind flying as an objective problem that can be solved if certain conditions are met? What are those conditions? Exactly what must be the relationship, as General Lindbergh states it, between mind and body during blind flying?

V. Pars. 8 and 9 might well have the subtitle "Entering the Cloud." To what extent are these paragraphs abstract and impersonal? Or concrete and personal? Does Par. 9 *unnecessarily* repeat any of the subject matter of Pars. 5, 6, and 7?

VI. Pars. 10–29 constitute the main portion of the episode for which the preceding paragraphs have been a preparation. The subtitle here might be "The Struggle Within the Cloud." Action begins in earnest. The narrative is tensely personal and concrete. Almost immediately it takes the form of "dialogue," and although the speakers are not labelled, they clearly are "Body" and "Mind." Earlier General Lindbergh has said that in blind flying "Body" must be completely under the discipline of "Mind." The "bodily instincts" (which act through the senses) are no longer to be trusted completely. Yet the senses must still operate sufficiently for the pilot to see his indicator dials and, by touch and sight, to control rudder and stick. The "dialogue," then, is a dramatized representation of the reports, false or true, that "Body" makes to "Mind," and of the judgment and discipline that "Mind" exercises in giving its orders.

Make a "plot," by paragraphs, of the false and true reports that "Body" makes and of "Mind's" answers and orders.

At what point does this dramatized action reach its crisis?

VII. What does General Lindbergh mean by the phrase (Par. 30), "existing in a different frame of space and time"? When he says that "values are relative," does he refer to any and all values or only to certain specific "values" inherent in a pilot's task? Interpret his statement (Par. 31): "It's not the limitless vista of experience . . . . It's the islands, no matter how small."

Does General Lindbergh's rendering of "The Struggle Within the Cloud" convey the effect of "existing in a different frame of space and time"? Is this an effect peculiar to flight in an airplane—especially to blind flying?

Is it appropriate, or not, that in Par. 31 General Lindbergh should return to the more abstract and general tone of the earlier part of the composition?

VIII. Reviewing the composition as a whole, ask yourself whether the dramatic conflict depicted is as simple as it may have seemed on first reading. Is there more than one conflict? Are "Body" and "Mind" adequate terms for the conflicting forces? What was it that enabled the pilot resolutely to choose between false and true reports of "Body" and to keep "Body" in its place as an obedient servant? Would an intellectually *correct* judgment of "Mind" have sufficed? Questions like these have been asked in one form or another throughout human history. It is interesting to reflect that, in putting into dialogue form the conflict of "Body" and "Mind," General Lindbergh parallels to a noticeable extent the dialogues or debates between Body and Soul that run through European literature of the Middle Ages and the Renaissance. (For a seventeenth-century example, see Andrew Marvell's "A Dialogue Between the Soul and Body.") Similar dialogues, in which personified qualities appear as characters, are found in Bunyan's prose allegory, *The Pilgrim's Progress.* Before you give final answers to the questions asked above, you would do well to read other portions, if not all, of Lindbergh's *The Spirit of St. Louis.* Note especially the passages (like that on pages 389–390) in which, during extreme crisis, the young pilot feels that "presences" are with him in the airplane and asks himself, "Am I now more man or spirit? . . . What strange connection exists between us?"

THE EIGHTY-SEVEN MINUTE CHAPEL TALK *

by JESSE STUART

In the spring following the publication of *Man With a* ¶ 1
Bull-Tongue Plow, I received a letter from H. L. Donovan, President of Eastern State Teachers College, who asked me to come and speak at college chapel. He said he was sorry that twenty-five dollars was all the honorarium he could offer me. When I received this letter I called my Superintendent, and read the letter to him over the telephone.

"By all means take it," he advised me. "Don't miss an op- ¶ 2
portunity like that. I'm proud to have a teacher in my school system who is asked to speak before a college assembly."

I hired Rank Meadows to take me in his car. It was ap- ¶ 3
proximately 120 miles to Eastern State College. I gave him all that I was to get for my talk to take me there and bring me back. We left long before daylight and arrived at Eastern early in the morning. I met President H. L. Donovan, who was a very friendly college president. I told him I had never before spoken to a college group and that I wasn't sure that I could do it.

"You take it easy," he advised me. "I'll go up on the plat- ¶ 4
form with you myself. You rest in your room until about ten o'clock. Be at the chapel by ten-fifteen. We'll start promptly at ten-thirty. You know," he then said to me, "you've written a fine book, and I want you to get up there and tell them about it and how you did it. Tell them how you got it published and a little bit about your background."

It would have been much easier for me if I hadn't stopped ¶ 5
at the bulletin board before I went into the college chapel. Here I stood before a little notice on the bulletin board which read: "Jesse Stuart, farm boy and schoolteacher from Greenwood County, will read some of his farm rhymes." Some husky football player stood beside me and read the

*Reprinted from *The Thread That Runs So True,* by Jesse Stuart; copyright, 1949, by Curtis Publishing Company, 1949, by Charles Scribner's Sons; used by permission of the publishers.

bulletin same time I did. "Hell," he said, turning to me, "if Eastern can't furnish us with a better chapel program than this, I'm not going, are you?"

¶ 6 "Hell, yes, I'm going," I said. "I have to go. I want to see what this is all about."

¶ 7 This Eastern student, who thought I was a student also, and I walked into the chapel together.

¶ 8 "We'd better grab a seat," he said, as the chapel started filling up.

¶ 9 Just then President Donovan walked over to me.

¶ 10 "Are you ready?" he asked.

¶ 11 "Much as I'll ever be," I answered, while the fellow I met at the bulletin board looked strangely at me.

¶ 12 I followed President Donovan onto the stage, where I faced a sea of approximately 1,700 faces.

¶ 13 "Take it easy," President Donovan whispered during chapel preliminaries. "I'm going to make my introductory remarks short so we can give you the full thirty minutes."

¶ 14 President Donovan didn't take more than three minutes to introduce me. He told the Eastern pupils this was my first time to appear before a college group, that I was a native of the state, a farmer and schoolteacher, and that he had asked me to tell them something about my background and how I wrote *Man With a Bull-Tongue Plow,* a book, he suspected, judging from the size, was a lifetime's work. After I had talked to President Donovan, I had outlined my talk on the back of an envelope. I was ready to start talking soon as he was through with his introduction.

¶ 15 The first thing I told was my reception at the bulletin board. There was a roar of applause. From this time on, everything I said, though it was serious to me, was funny to them. In that sea of faces before me, I never saw a serious face. I told of my schooling, grades, high school, and college, and of my teaching. I told them of the education my parents had. I told them how we had lived, renting farm after farm until we finally managed to buy fifty acres. I told them the truth; yet they laughed. Perhaps not any other speaker had talked to them as frankly as I had. I told them I had written *Man With a Bull-Tongue Plow* mostly on leaves, while I farmed on my father's farm and while I was Superintendent of Greenwood County Schools. When I told them it had taken me lacking one day of eleven months to write it, that I wrote it for pleasure and recreation while I farmed and was County School Superintendent, they laughed as I had never heard people laugh before. They bent over in their seats and laughed and wiped their eyes with handkerchiefs at the serious, truthful talk I was trying to give them. Often I had to stand on the platform and wait many seconds for the laughter to subside before I could go on. When the bell rang for the chapel to end, the shouts went up: "More! More!"

¶ 16 "Go on," Dr. Donovan signalled me when I looked toward him. He was laughing.

¶ 17 Classes were postponed and bells rang until I had spoken eighty-seven minutes! And the laughter was stronger at the end than it was at the beginning. The applause seemed endless. There was not a serious face among the faculty members. Dr. Donovan laughed as heartily as his students. At the end of this program, pupils and teachers came forward. I was hot, and wet with perspiration. I met pupil and teacher until Dr. Donovan made it possible for me to leave the stage. Scarcely a person left the chapel until Dr. Donovan took me through a side door. Somebody had ripped the farm rhymes announcement from the bulletin board for a souvenir.

EXERCISES

I. In this deceptively simple account of a personal experience Jesse Stuart composes in a pattern that might be termed *reversal of action.* The "tables are turned," as we commonly say, so that the victim becomes the victor, the supposedly weak person turns out to be the really strong one, the ugly duckling is revealed to be a swan. So it goes in many a folk tale, but the general pattern is capable of subtle and highly interesting variations.

The "reversal" of action—or of fortune—can be used, however, only in a situation that in some way involves a paradox—a seeming contradiction that contains a truth. In "The Eighty-seven Minute Chapel Talk" the invitation to speak at chapel came to Jesse Stuart for routine reasons, or plausible reasons, but not for the "right" reasons, not for reasons based on "right" assumptions. The assumptions of all parties concerned were in fact "wrong" in one sense; but in the end turn out to be "right" in ways that nobody concerned would have expected. The paradox of the situation is partly in the fact that the polite formulas of invitation, introduction, and glowing praise, which all dignitaries recite endlessly but hardly ever believe in, turn out to be stunningly true.

II. The "forward" phase of the action extends from Par. 1 through Par. 14. In this phase Mr. Stuart skilfully prepares for the reversal that is to follow in the "backward" movement of the action. Phase 1 contains a series of false assumptions concerning Jesse Stuart as chapel speaker. The narrative does not state that they are false assumptions, but the reader makes the inference well enough. The large underlying assumption—which is perfectly natural and conventional—is that chapel talks in general are dull and commonplace. Little can be expected of chapel speakers—and less, perhaps, of an inexperienced chapel speaker. Therefore the honorarium is small, and only a limited portion of the chapel hour is allowed to the speaker. On the basis of the usual assumptions, President Donovan, the Superintendent, and finally the football player commit themselves to positions that turn out to be ridiculous. Meanwhile, the speaker himself, Jesse Stuart, is making his own wrong assumption. His wrong assumption is that the audience of college students will "take seriously" his completely truthful talk.

The *turning point* of the action comes in the first two sentences of Par. 15. After this, the action is reversed. Every assumption made in Phase 1 topples as the audience begins to laugh, and the action runs "backward." The component parts of the "backward" movement—Phase 2—are balanced precisely—and with a delightful and just degree of humorous incongruity—against the component parts of Phase 1. We have a neat and telling example of "poetic justice"—or the "sport" that Shakespeare makes Hamlet refer to, of seeing the engineer "hoist with his own petard."

III. Draw up a "plot" or "scheme" to show by graphic means all the items of Phase 1 that are balanced—and humorously contradicted—by corresponding parts of Phase 2. Such a "plot" may be drawn up in parallel columns.

IV. Make a study of the process of inference through which you, as reader, are able to grasp the assumptions that the participants make at various stages of the action. What inferences can be made, for example, from the size of honorarium offered? From the Superintendent's telephone conversation with Jesse Stuart? Explore the full extent of such inferences. How do you explain the fact that, though the narrative makes use of a rich framework of inference, the language is simple and economical to the point of spareness?

MY GRANDMOTHER'S HONEYMOON *

by MARY ELLEN CHASE

LESSON XIV

¶ 1 *Three Types of Reminiscent Narrative . . .*

Few brides have had so eventful a honeymoon as my grandmother. This statement cannot, I feel sure, be termed sweeping even though it is curtailed neither by time nor by place.

¶ 2 She was married in the Congregational Church in Blue Hill on the 16th of July in the year 1849, two years and three months after my grandfather had fallen in love with her in the selfsame spot, but on a more sombre occasion. She was twenty-two years old, and my grandfather was twenty-six. She wore the first silk dress she had ever worn in all her life. It was of pearl gray taffeta striped in rose, made by her own hands in the modish, double skirt style with ample hoops and bishop's sleeves and with bows of rose velvet closing the basque and encircling the tiny waist. The neck and cuffs were finished with hemstitched ruffles in finest cambric. Although she secretly longed for one of the new, more stylish hats, which set well upon the head and featured not only broad streamers at the sides and rosettes above the ears, but a plume falling jauntily over the crown at the left, she acceded to my grandfather's sole request and wore a gray silk poke bonnet with a wreath of pink roses beneath the brim. She carried his gift, an ivory-handled pink silk parasol, which he had brought her from France and which attracted much attention by virtue of its convenient hinge, enabling one to adjust it at any angle against the sun.

¶ 3 In her spare hours from midwifery and seamstressing she had made her trousseau, allowing no fingers save her own to aid in its elaborate fashioning. Her underwear and night clothes were her especial pride. She had six of each article—six nightdresses and six frilled night-caps; six of every sort of petticoat then modestly worn; six pairs of drawers, their long legs trimmed with rows of fine tucks and edged with yards upon yards of Van Dyke crochet; six chemises. These last-named were formed with tiny cap sleeves, marvellously shirred and bordered with hemstitched ruffles. They were the pride of her entire outfit, having been made from sheer and expensive linen, for the purchase of which her parents had not been slow to criticize her. As children we were well-grounded in the details of my grandmother's trousseau. Indeed, to her dying day she never ceased to mourn its tragic loss, seemingly counting her own life but small compensation for those wondrously wrought chemises of fair (and expensive) linen floating through the blue-green depths of the South Atlantic.

My grandfather in July, 1849, was the proud master and ¶4
owner of a barque of fifteen hundred tons burden. He christened her *The Bride.* Chartered by a New York firm, she was to carry on her maiden voyage flour to Bermuda and, as a more precious freight, my grandmother, the one trunk which held all her wedding clothes, and the romantic hopes and plans of her and her husband. For this was to be no ordinary honeymoon. To my grandfather's travelled eyes Bermuda was just around the corner from Blue Hill. Picking up a mixed cargo there for England, they were to proceed across the Atlantic to Liverpool, thence to Cadiz, thence, after some weeks of Spanish life, through the Straits and across the Mediterranean and the Red Sea into the Indian Ocean toward Calcutta, thence up the Chinese coast to Shanghai. There they might linger, my grandfather spending some months in the coast-carrying trade, my grandmother remaining in the Shanghai home of some American merchants and seeing a bit of Oriental life. Then, if all things had gone well, they would continue their journeyings and their livelihood by proceeding across the Pacific laden with rice for California where the gold rush was on. And to terminate what was quite likely to be a two years' voyage with coast trading here and there, they would load up with gold ore and round the Horn for New York and home.

My grandmother, as she hemstitched the ruffles for her ¶5

chemises, was probably quite unable to assimilate any of these forecastings. She had come from farming, not from seafaring stock; and Bangor, Maine, had been her *terminus ad quem.* But her personality at seventy was sufficiently intense and buoyant to suggest under what excitement she must have whipped and shirred at twenty.

¶ 6 They sailed from New York on the first day of August, 1849, after a fortnight of unparalleled adventurings. There was the purchase in a bewildering store of a brown fur muff and tippet, the former oblong and inclined to flatness, with dangling brown tassels at either end, the latter cut after the new Parisian shawl shape with pointed ends and rich satin clasps; there were introductions to obsequious and interested merchants, one of whom proffered a case of jellies and fruits to enliven the daily fare of *The Bride* by providing repasts more befitting a honeymoon; there was the startling and unforgettable taste of a delicacy quite unknown to her, ice cream, the sudden and unexpected coldness of which she never forgot; there was the exciting boarding of the ship, the acquaintance with her new and narrow quarters, the tidy, compact arrangement of her new possessions.

¶ 7 After four days at sea there occurred that colossal event, to which so many hours of my childhood were blissfully dedicated. Somewhere off Hatteras *The Bride* encountered a fearful gale. It rose suddenly without sufficient warning. At five one morning my grandmother was aroused in her berth by the appearance of my grandfather armed with a pair of his own woollen stockings and a sailor's peajacket and trousers. She would best get into these, he said, as he scented trouble. My grandmother told us how she was sitting filled with fear on the edge of her berth drawing on a woollen stocking when the ship capsized, how she completed her strange costuming at a stranger angle!

¶ 8 She was carried on the deck, now careening perilously above the engulfing waters, and lashed to a mast. There she remained for thirty-six black hours while the wind tore away the rigging and mountainous seas tore away her clothing.

She told us of confusion unutterable, the screams of the sailors, the snapping and creaking of the ship, the cursing and the prayers. She told us of the frightful, suffocating impact of multitudinous waves, smiting the breath from her body, of intolerable suffering from hunger and cold and the more intolerable anguish, as the hours went on, from chafed and smarting flesh. We knew that the deafness which saddened sixty years of her life began with those monstrous seas as they washed over her head. Long before a British barque bore down upon them, fears of death had given place to ardent desire for it.

The British ship lay to in the semi-darkness, not daring to ¶ 9
launch her boats even though the storm had abated. And then came that stupendous climax which in our minds always ranked our grandmother with those favoured ones of Scriptural record, with the daughter of Jairus, with Tabitha, and with Simon Peter's wife's mother. For according to her own asseveration she was saved by a miracle! A meteor fell, and by its light enabled the British captain to launch his boats and to take off the shipwrecked officers and crew.

As a child, I always saw this act of God as a gigantic ball ¶ 10
of fire somewhat resembling my mother's wash-tub, suspended in mid-air above my grandfather's dismantled and ruined vessel; in fact, I was conscious of a bitter disappointment when, at a more mature age, I learned it was but a strange glow in the sky and over the waters. But my grandmother's telling of it, whatever impression she intended to convey, left nothing to be desired. Neither did her account of those events which followed hard upon their tardy saving. Stripped of all their earthly possessions, even to their clothing, they were taken on board the British ship which, fortunately for those days, carried a doctor. My grandmother was too ill to witness from her hospitable decks the final destruction of *The Bride,* which was swallowed by the sea in less than an hour after their rescue. But before they reached St. Georges, she was again ready to live.

I feel sure that her instinct for drama triumphed over even ¶ 11 her complete and ruthless poverty as, helped by my grandfather and the British captain, she ascended the white steps of the leading St. Georges hotel. She was completely clad in sailor's clothing even to shoes. On the topmost step, to her dire, and, I dare say, *delighted* embarrassment, one of her white woollen stockings escaped from its improvised garter and fell below the leg of her trousers. The news of her misfortune swept through the city, and she was almost immediately inundated with clothing of every description. Unfortunately, however, the Bermuda ladies were moved beyond the practical thought of consultation and comparison. For the first articles sent to minister to her necessities were a comical and lavish succession of thirteen white silk bonnets!

¶ 12 Within two months of the day of their wedding my grandparents were once more at home. But not for long. Insurance plus native resiliency procured another ship, the *Eliza Ann Chase,* in which they again set forth with yet another stock of wedding chemises. My grandmother, like many another woman of her generation who had chosen to marry a sailor, chose also to stay by him whatever the cost. Now fate changed her tactics and was kind. For twelve years my grandmother sailed, in comparative safety, only remaining at home during the months preceding the birth of her children. She read and sewed on the quarter deck in the sun of many foreign harbours; she lingered in foreign cities; she looked alike upon Moorish mosques and Gothic cathedrals; she tempered her Puritan inheritance with amiable and welcome leaven.

¶ 13 One cannot ask a better legacy than such a life affords, both to itself and to those who are reared upon its long effects. The breadth and depth of experience of my grandmother's seafaring years, grafted as they were upon a childhood and a youth of hardship and its attendant discipline, were bound to bear rich fruit. Nor was her lot unique in her generation or in her environment. It fell to other coast women of equally simple background and nurture and worked its gracious way with them also. It gave to their descendants more than can easily be estimated or measured. Maine in the heyday of sailing ships was yet a young State, separated only in 1820 from Massachusetts, its mother. By such fortunes as those of my grandmother she stamped her coast towns and villages with an indelible character, which is yet traceable, and thus established early her own personality.

In the great white houses of Searsport and Damariscotta, ¶ 14
Belfast and Wiscasset, Bucksport and Blue Hill, there still lingers something of that *venustas,* that *sales* and *urbanitas* extolled by Catullus—the enlightened heritage of those days when provincial minds met the larger, outer world across the seas. Such a possession will remain invincible armour against the new prosperity of the coast as long as such an inheritance is nurtured and cherished.

When I went to college in 1904, my grandmother, then ¶ 15
nearing eighty, presented me, not without due formality, with one of the chemises of her second trousseau. Perhaps she gave it as a curious rather than as a useful article. I may say, however, that I wore it with pride, the hemstitched ruffles of its capped sleeves forming no insuperable obstacle to swiss muslin evening gowns of twenty-five years ago!

EXERCISES

I. Much of the interest of "My Grandmother's Honeymoon"— viewed as prose composition—derives from Mary Ellen Chase's skilful management of the series of astounding contrasts that marked the eventful honeymoon of her grandmother. The bride, a farm girl skilled in "midwifery and seamstressing," takes an elaborate trousseau—including six chemises—on her honeymoon voyage, which is to be a two-year trip around the world; but presently the ship is caught in a storm off Cape Hatteras, and she must spend thirty-six hours lashed to the mast. Finally she is rescued by a "miracle," but she loses all feminine articles of clothing whatsoever.

A. Trace the pattern of contrasts as Mary Ellen Chase develops that pattern in the composition as a whole. Make a "scheme" or "plot" in your notebook to indicate this pattern; or else make appropriate markings in the text. Distinguish between contrasts that are *explicitly stated* and those that are *implied* or unobtrusively indicated. Would "incongruities" be a better term than "contrasts"?

B. Does Mary Ellen Chase "point up" the contrasts or incongruities by definitely calling the reader's attention to them as they appear in the narrative? Or does she, instead, refrain from intrusive comment, make the incongruities the substance itself of the narrative, and so let them speak for themselves?

C. Thinking in terms of the pattern of contrasts, determine the function in the composition as a whole of Pars. 2 and 3. Why does Miss Chase give, at considerable length, the specific details of her grandmother's trousseau? Would the reason be that Miss Chase, as a woman author, cannot resist the temptation to discuss clothing? Is she simply using—and faithfully reporting—her grandmother's attitude in this matter? Or is Miss Chase as a discerning and accomplished artist (considerations of gender being ignored as irrelevant) intent mainly on emphasizing a point that has great human and thematic importance in her narrative? Explain the function in the narrative of the sentence (Par. 3): "Indeed, to her dying day she never ceased to mourn its tragic loss, seemingly counting her own life but small compensation for those wondrously wrought chemises of fair (and expensive) linen floating through the blue-green depths of the South Atlantic."

D. Is the sentence just quoted "planted" in this paragraph in order to *foreshadow* what is to come? Is there any connection between this sentence and Par. 15?

E. In what way is the rhetorical pattern of this same sentence affected by the general pattern of incongruity or contrast in the composition? Are the phrases, "its tragic loss" and "but small compensation," seriously meant?

F. In similar fashion trace the pattern of studied incongruity used in the following sentences:

1. "My grandmother told us . . . how she completed her strange costuming at a stranger angle!" (Par. 7)
2. "As a child, I always saw . . . but a strange glow in the sky and over the waters." (Par. 10)
3. "For the first articles sent . . . succession of thirteen white silk bonnets!" (Par. 11)
4. "Insurance plus native resiliency . . . stock of wedding chemises." (Par. 12)

In the above sentences, what use does the author make of repetition, parallel structure, anticlimax?

II. Explain the reference to "those favoured ones of Scriptural record" in Par. 9. Are there specific reasons why such a reference is appropriate in this narrative?

III. The title of the autobiographical work from which this selection is taken is *A Goodly Heritage.* What relationship to the general title has the sentence (Par. 12) "she tempered her Puritan inheritance with amiable and welcome leaven."? How do Pars. 13 and 14 illustrate the application of this general title to the specific experience related? What is the meaning of the following sentence (Par. 14): "Such a possession will remain invincible armour against the new prosperity of the coast as long as such an inheritance is nurtured and cherished"?

IV. Write a theme in which you relate how some "goodly heritage"—pertaining to family or to a local, state, or national tradition—played a part in some interesting and possibly critical event. You may choose as subject some incident with which you are already well acquainted in family, local, state, or national tradition. Or you may choose a character and incident from history. In the latter instance, you may need to consult authoritative sources. For example, the conduct of Pliny the Elder during the eruption of Vesuvius exemplifies an aspect of the Roman character in general, but for the Elder Pliny as an individual a specific feature of character is summed up in his nephew's statement: "What he had begun through love of knowledge, he carried out in the spirit of a hero." *(Quod studioso animo incohaverat, obit maximo).* (See the *Letters of Pliny,* VI, 16 and 20.) Similarly, *The Autobiography of Benjamin Franklin* might offer an opportunity for a narrative study of some aspect of Franklin's "goodly heritage."

LESSON XV

Diction: Ambiguity and Multiple Meanings.
Metaphorical and Non-Metaphorical Images.
Meaning of Words in Relation to Context.
Fine Writing and Realism.
Euphemisms: for Grandiose Effects; for Humorous Effects.
Use of Slang, Cant, Colloquial Words. Figures of Speech.

INVENTORY OF THE MAN-MOUNTAIN'S POCKETS *

by JONATHAN SWIFT

¶ 1 He [the Emperor of the Lilliputians] desired I would not take it ill, if he gave orders to certain proper officers to search me; for probably I might carry about me several weapons, which must needs be dangerous things, if they answered the bulk of so prodigious a person. I said, his Majesty should be satisfied, for I was ready to strip myself, and turn up my pockets before him. This I delivered part in words, and part in signs. He replied, that by the laws of the kingdom I must be searched by two of his officers; that he knew this could not be done without my consent and assistance; that he had so good an opinion of my generosity and justice, as to trust their persons in my hands: that whatever they took from me should be returned when I left the country, or paid for at the rate which I would set upon them. I took up the two officers in my hands, put them first into my coat-pockets, and then into every other pocket about me, except my two fobs, and another secret pocket I had no mind should be searched, wherein I had some little necessaries that were of no consequence to any but myself. In one of my fobs there was a silver watch, and in the other a small quantity of gold in a purse. These gentlemen, having pen and ink, and paper about them, made an exact inventory of every thing they

* From "A Voyage to Lilliput," *Gulliver's Travels*, by Jonathan Swift.

saw; and when they had done, desired I would set them down, that they might deliver it to the Emperor. This inventory I afterwards translated into English, and is word for word as follows.

Imprimis, In the right coat-pocket of the Great Man- ¶ 2
Mountain (for so I interpret the words *Quinbus Flestrin)* after the strictest search, we found only one great piece of coarse cloth, large enough to be a foot-cloth for your Majesty's chief room of state. In the left pocket we saw a huge silver chest, with a cover of the same metal, which we the searchers were not able to lift. We desired it should be opened, and one of us stepping into it, found himself up to the mid leg in a sort of dust, some part whereof flying up to our faces, set us both a sneezing for several times together. In his right waistcoat-pocket we found a prodigious bundle of white thin substances, folded one over another, about the bigness of three men, tied with a strong cable, and marked with black figures; which we humbly conceive to be writings, every letter almost half as large as the palm of our hands. In the left there was a sort of engine, from the back of which were extended twenty long poles, resembling the palisados before your Majesty's court; wherewith we conjecture the Man-Mountain combs his head, for we did not always trouble him with questions, because we found it a great difficulty to make him understand us. In the large pocket on the right side of his middle cover (so I translate the word *ranfu-lo,* by which they meant my breeches) we saw a hollow pillar of iron, about the length of a man, fastened to a strong piece of timber, larger than the pillar; and upon one side of the pillar were huge pieces of iron sticking out, cut into strange figures, which we know not what to make of. In the left pocket, another engine of the same kind. In the smaller pocket on the right side, were several round flat pieces of white and red metal, of different bulk; some of the white, which seemed to be silver, were so large and heavy, that my comrade and I could hardly lift them. In the left pocket were two black pillars irregularly shaped; we could

not, without difficulty, reach the top of them as we stood at the bottom of his pocket. One of them was covered, and seemed all of a piece: but at the upper end of the other, there appeared a white round substance, about twice the bigness of our heads. Within each of these was enclosed a prodigious plate of steel; which, by our orders, we obliged him to show us, because we apprehended they might be dangerous engines. He took them out of their cases, and told us, that in his own country his practice was to shave his beard with one of these, and to cut his meat with the other. There were two pockets which we could not enter: these he called his fobs; they were two large slits cut into the top of his middle cover, but squeezed close by the pressure of his belly. Out of the right fob hung a great silver chain, with a wonderful kind of engine at the bottom. We directed him to draw out whatever was fastened to that chain; which appeared to be a globe, half silver, and half of some transparent metal: for on the transparent side we saw certain strange figures circularly drawn, and thought we could touch them, till we found our fingers stopped by that lucid substance. He put this engine to our ears, which made an incessant noise like that of a watermill and we conjecture it is either some unknown animal or the god that he worships: but we are more inclined to the latter opinion, because he assured us (if we understood him right, for he expressed himself very imperfectly), that he seldom did anything without consulting it. He called it his oracle, and said it pointed out the time for every action of his life. From the left fob he took out a net almost enough for a fisherman, but contrived to open and shut like a purse, and served him for the same use: we found therein several massy pieces of yellow metal, which, if they be real gold, must be of immense value.

¶ 3 Having thus, in obedience to your Majesty's commands, diligently searched all his pockets, we observed a girdle about his waist made of the hide of some prodigious animal; from which, on the left side, hung a sword of the length of five men; and on the right, a bag or pouch divided into two cells, each cell being capable of holding three of your Majesty's subjects. In one of these cells were several globes or balls of a most ponderous metal, about the bigness of our heads, and required a strong hand to lift them: the other cell contained a heap of certain black grains, but of not great bulk or weight, for we could hold above fifty of them in the palms of our hands.

¶ 4 This is an exact inventory of what we found about the body of the Man-Mountain, who used us with great civility, and due respect to your Majesty's commission. Signed and sealed on the fourth day of the eighty-ninth moon of your Majesty's auspicious reign.

CLEFREN FRELOCK, MARSI FRELOCK

EXERCISES

I. The prose of Jonathan Swift is plain and simple. At first reading it may seem to have no features of sufficient richness or complexity to warrant a close study. Dr. Samuel Johnson said of Swift: "He always understands himself, and his reader always understands him; the peruser of Swift wants little previous knowledge; it will be sufficient that he is acquainted with common words and common things." On the other hand, a modern critic, Robert B. Heilman, in his "Introduction" to *Gulliver's Travels* (Modern Library College Edition), writes as follows: "In form it fuses at least three types: realistic fiction, the fantastic voyage, and utopian romance. As to style: the author insists upon 'the simplest manner and style' but constantly has recourse to irony, symbolism, and ambiguity."

The problem of the student of Swift is, then, to discover just how so "simple" a style can contain "irony, symbolism, and ambiguity."

II. Consider first the function of *perspective* or *point of view* in giving a double meaning to simple and familiar words. In the opening passages of the *Travels,* Lemuel Gulliver is established as a rather average sort of Englishman from Nottinghamshire who has attended Cambridge University, then studied medicine, and gone to sea as "surgeon to the *Swallow*" and subsequently on other British ships. Shipwrecked off Van Diemen's Land, he manages to reach an island inhabited by the Lilliputians, who are like human beings in every respect except that they are of minute size. In "The Voyage to Lilliput" Gulliver therefore becomes a giant among the Lilliputians, and we have two scales of value pertaining to size: the scale applied by Gulliver as a normal human being; and the scale of the Lilliputians, who in addition to being excessively small are ignorant of the world to which Gulliver belongs. Every word relating to size can therefore be matter-of-fact if it refers to *actual* size and at the same time ironic or ambiguous in so far as it sets off one scale of size-values against the other. Other implied meanings enter according to the degree to which Gulliver or the Lilliputians make inferences as to attitude, conduct, purposes, and the like.

A. Examine all words or phrases referring to size in order to see (1) whether Swift consistently maintains two different scales of dimension—one for Gulliver, another for the Lilliputians—and (2) the extent to which such words or phrases have more than one meaning in the context where they occur. For example, the adjective *prodigious* in the phrase, "the bulk of so prodigious a person" (Sen. 1, Par. 1), means "extraordinary," "out of the course of nature," "monstrous" from the Lilliputian point of view, but to Gulliver—and to us—it has no such actual meaning. Gulliver's size is "prodigious" to us only in a *figurative* sense—as we are able, somewhat indulgently, to imagine and tolerate this entirely natural "mistake" of the Lilliputians.

B. The expressions listed below represent "judgments" that, because of the double perspective described, may carry some ambiguity of meaning. In each instance note whether the expressions have (1) only one purely matter-of-fact meaning; (2) more than one meaning; (3) a meaning short of absolute truth.

1. "some little necessaries that were of no consequence to any but myself" (Par. 1)
2. "made an exact inventory of every thing they saw" (Par. 1)
3. "one great piece of coarse cloth" (Par. 2)
4. "which, if they be real gold, must be of immense value" (Par. 2)
5. "This is an exact inventory" (Par. 4)

III. To what extent are the Lilliputians' descriptions of the objects in Gulliver's pockets inexact or inadequate because of their lack of knowledge of the "world" of Gulliver (i.e., the British or western civilization with its manners, morals, economic and utilitarian arrangements, beliefs, etc.)? To what extent are the descriptions inadequate because they are, from the Lilliputian point of view, precisely matter-of-fact and logical? Look up the dictionary definitions of *handkerchief* (note the Lilliputian reference to *foot-cloth), snuff-box, snuff, journal, comb, pistol,* and *watch* and compare these definitions with the descriptions given by the Lilliputians. Do you see any resemblance?

Study particularly the sentences describing Gulliver's watch. Does Swift mean to use the Lilliputians' description—"innocent" and "naive" as it seems—as a standard of judgment by which Gulliver (or men in general) could be brought to realize the limitations of their own strictly logical judgments? Could the inventory be taken as a parody of a commercial inventory or of some scientific procedure? How exact can any inventory be?

IV. Herbert Read has observed *(English Prose Style,* pp. 26–27) that Swift avoids metaphor but nevertheless cultivates a style that has sharp, clear images. Does your study of Swift support this view? Even though the images themselves are not metaphorical, can the entire selection (or even "The Voyage to Lilliput" as a whole) be thought of as metaphorical in the broad sense?

V. In view of the preceding study, compose a statement dealing with the influence of a context upon the meanings of words that appear in the context. For this purpose, compare the diction of Defoe in "The Balance Sheet of Robinson Crusoe" (pp. 10–13) with the diction of Swift.

A BACKWOODS POLITICAL RALLY *

by CAROLINE M. KIRKLAND

LESSON XV

Diction: Ambiguity and Multiple Meanings . . .

¶ 1 The prairie-land passed, our road was log-causeway; a long straight track through a dead swamp—and in this all horrors are expressed, all mud-holes, all thumps, all impossibility of turning out. This was a pretty place to meet a political convention! a new kind of locomotive of immeasurable power, not very easily managed except by adepts.

¶ 2 It was a formidable apparition certainly; and we were fain to shrink into infinitesimal nothingness, and to find a place for our outer wheels on the sloping ends of the corduroy, even at the risk of a souse into a sea of black mud; for there was a deep ditch on either side. The chance that even our sober steeds would endure the clatter of drums and fifes, cymbals and triangles—noisy orators and still noisier singers—was a small one; but there was no retreat, and we remained perched on our "bad eminence," until the whole procession had passed.

¶ 3 There were perhaps thirty vehicles, of which the smallest were large wagons, with four horses each. There were gaily painted barges—"canoes," I ought to say, in the spirit of the day—mounted on wheels, and containing crowds of people; every man and every horse bearing a banner, inscribed either with high-sounding patriotism on a large scale, or with electioneering squibs on a very small one. There were rectangular countenances, drawn evidently with the aid of compass and square, and haloed round with snow-white fleece—accredited representatives of the much-disfigured father of our country; then again, faces wherein a very long drooping nose was surmounted by a pair of eyes that seemed to be running into one—awful travesties of the popular candidate. There were golden eagles spreading their gorgeous wings amid the stars, on fields of silk as blue as their own heaven, and rac-

* From *A New Home, or Life in the Clearings,* by Caroline M. Kirkland. Edited by John Nerber. G. P. Putnam's Sons. Copyright, 1953, by John Nerber. (Original editions: *A New Home,* 1839; *Forest Life,* 1842. This selection first appeared in *Forest Life.*)

coons enough (in effigy) to have fed the whole national eyry, if golden eagles could eat.

A huge ball was rolled along, with great appearance of effort, by several men, and these actors, by their shouted watchwords and their various significant decorations, gave us to understand that the said ball typified the interests of their favorite. A miniature log-cabin, the very ditto of those by the roadside, mounted on a platform spacious enough to carry much of the out-door arrangements of a settler's primitive establishment, was drawn by a long string of oxen, the tips of whose horns streamed with flags and knots of gay ribbon. The emblems which met the eye every moment embraced all degrees of ingenuity and absurdity, and the costume of those who exhibited them was almost equally various. ¶ 4 LESSON XV

There was an Indian, in blue and red paint and a feather petticoat, bearing a banner with the inscription, "Our best brave"; here an impersonation of Liberty, strait-laced and anxious, in pink ribbons and black prunello boots. Now a car from which an orator was setting forth in no inelegant terms the pretensions of the idol; and anon another bearing his image, in the act of presenting a horse to a minister. Under the influence of omnipotent corduroy, the minister, first tottering like Mr. Stiggins, abominably knocked down his benefactor, and the horse sympathetically tumbled on them both and completed the pyramid. ¶ 5

Such trifling disasters passed unfelt and almost unnoticed in the enthusiasm of the hour. Beneath all the little oddities which are almost inseparable from the getting up of a popular show on so large a scale with rather incongruous materials, there was evidently an undercurrent of warm feeling and genuine interest which makes every thing respectable; and however one might feel disposed to laugh at some particulars of the exhibition, there was an impressiveness about the whole which made one sensible of "the majesty of the people." For my own part I confess that this immense moving mass of life with its alternations of warlike music, ani- ¶ 6 mated declamation, and sweet chorus of female voices, caused the blood to tingle in my veins and my heart to overflow at my eyes. Sympathy has wondrous power, and, after waiting till the whole grotesque train had passed, we drove to the end of the corduroy, and then turned about, and, with a host of other gazers, followed the multitude.

Diction: Ambiguity and Multiple Meanings...

¶ 7 The place of destination was a grove whose sylvan beauty never could be surpassed, even in Michigan, which is all groves. It was at no great distance from the road, but it was in all the wildness of nature, and looked as if the axe had never yet profaned its hallowed aisles. Here, in the midst of primeval solitude and silence, a great stage had been hastily erected, and, facing it, a wide amphitheatre of rough benches —the whole roofed in by noble oaks and maples, with "unpierced shade."

¶ 8 Rapidly, and with a silence and regularity which bespoke thorough drilling, did the immense assemblage dispose itself appropriately over the broad area—the orators and officials taking their places upon the platform, where the banners were planted and arranged in very effective drapery—the ladies on the front seats next to the music, and the common world on the remaining benches.

¶ 9 The Marseillois was now performed—with verses by a native poet of course—and the entire company joined in the chorus which imparted a stentorian energy to their "most sweet voices." A marshal now announced that a clergyman present would "make a prayer," and the multitude stood, with heads uncovered, and in a throbbing silence, till it was finished. Then the band played and the ladies sang "Hail Columbia," and again the leafy canopy quivered to the excitement of the hour. Then came the speeches, blazing with patriotism, and touching, in their wide scope, on every disputed and disputable point in politics. And here I was much amused with the discreet timing of the cheers, which was performed by a young gentleman furnished with a flag which he waved most graciously, bowing at every shout, as if to thank the "good friends, kind friends, sweet friends," who took his hints in such good part.

The "sentiments" were drank at intervals, in very innocent liquids; so that if there was truth in the rapture of the hour, it was not wine that brought it out. Everybody *seemed* to feel, to the heart's core, all the privileges, advantages, rights, grievances, and hopes, on which the chosen orators harangued so warmly and I doubt not that vows were made that day which told afterwards for good or evil, in opinion and action. ¶ 10

EXERCISES

I. Caroline Kirkland's account of an old-time political rally in the backwoods of Michigan contains humorous and realistic details, clearly and often vividly treated. Here and there the diction of the prose is itself humorous and realistic, but at other points the author uses an over-refined, somewhat affected diction which might be called *euphemistic.* A *euphemism* is "a word or phrase that is less expressive or direct but considered less distasteful, less offensive than another" *(Webster's New World Dictionary).* In other terms, a euphemism signifies a tendency to use language too grand for the occasion—"fine writing" where plainer language might serve.

For example, the first sentence of Par. 2 sets the over-pretentious literary phrase "fain to shrink into infinitesimal nothingness" in close juxtaposition to the plain and familiar "at the risk of a souse into a sea of mud." Caroline Kirkland is prone to mix outmoded literary terms like "fain," "sylvan beauty," "leafy canopy" with passages of prose that are straightforward, sufficiently sharp and unpretentious, and often striking. It is as if the author feels that so vulgar and inelegant a spectacle as a backwoods political rally, even though it greatly attracts her interest and some honest admiration, is not to be discussed in public by such a person as Mrs. Kirkland unless the narration of the event is touched up by occasional insertions of "polite" language. These insertions amount to disclaimers or apologies; they put Mrs. Kirkland at a safe distance from the somewhat embarrassing object she has encountered.

II. Select those words, phrases, or passages that seem to you euphemistic. Are all such words, phrases, or passages *clearly* euphemistic, in the sense that they are "too fine for the occasion"? Or are there instances in which *verbosity* would be a more accurately descriptive term? Revise selected sentences or passages by substituting plain terms for euphemistic terms, or by using spare and economical language where Caroline Kirkland has been verbose. Do your revisions constitute a definite improvement of the original text?

III. Select passages which you would commend for clarity, felicitousness, direct vividness, humor, or other qualities. Give your reasons for commending such passages.

IV. Does Caroline Kirkland use such terms as "sylvan grove" and "leafy canopy" for the reason suggested in I, above? Does she think that "leafy canopy" is more decorous, elegant, tasteful, or romantic than—say—"oak leaves"? Does she in any instance use euphemisms to create a humorous effect? Is she trying to give the rough surroundings and rougher people some air of exaltation which she feels really belongs to them? Or does her use of high-sounding words derive from some feeling of condescension on her part? If you find evidence of such condescension, cite the passages where it occurs. But before reaching a decision on such issues you should remind yourself that Caroline Kirkland—whatever her prose style—chose to live on the Michigan frontier and to endure the hardships of cabin life and of corduroy roads—or worse. Should she, as a cultured woman writing about life in the backwoods, have tried to develop a "backwoodsy" style of writing, such as you may find in some other representations of frontier life? How far should one take the rule of Chaucer—derived ultimately from Plato—that "the word must be cousin to the deed"?

V. Examine the writings of some of Caroline Kirkland's contemporaries in order to determine where there was a current style for her to use for a model and whether any of her contemporaries were similarly guilty of "euphemisms." See, for example, such novels of James Fenimore Cooper as *The Deerslayer* and *The Last of the Mohicans;* or William Gilmore Simms' *The Partisan, Mellichampe,* or *Woodcraft;* or Augustus Baldwin Longstreet's *Georgia Scenes;* or *The Autobiography of David Crockett.*

VI. Write an account of some public occasion that you have witnessed, or of some surprising encounter you have had with a crowd. Use the style that you deem "proper to the occasion."

FUN AND GAMES ITALIENNE *

by RED SMITH

Trouble with most Americans, they don't take their games ¶ 1
seriously enough. In this respect we are a backward people, lagging far behind other nations. By way of illustration, here is an item from "The Times" of London, not that upstart sheet on 43d St.:

"Palermo—Prince Raimondo Lanza di Trabia, disguised ¶ 2
as one of his own footmen, slipped through a ring of police guarding his castle near here early today and fought a sword duel with a neighboring baron over a football dispute.

"In the duel, forbidden by law in Italy, the prince was ¶ 3
wounded twice in the right arm and had to give up. His opponent, Baron Salvatore Alu, was untouched.

"The two men have alternated in recent years as presi- ¶ 4
dent of the Palermo football club. The supporters of each blame the other for the fact that Palermo is near the bottom of the first division of Italy's football league."

This illustrates how provincial is the widespread notion ¶ 5
that a passionate enthusiasm for sports is a peculiarly American characteristic. Actually, by comparison with the nationals of other lands, the American at play is a model of decorum whose temperament borders on the phlegmatic.

For example, if Mr. George Edward Arcaro happens to ¶ 6
get beat a dirty nose on a 3-to-5 choice at Aqueduct or Jamaica, some of the more raffish element among his following may lift up their voices and address him as follows: "Boo!" When a favorite is beaten or disqualified at a French race course, it is well within the capacity of the crowd to burn down the grandstand.

A style of literary composition highly favored by baseball ¶ 7
writers is a story beginning: "A riot was narrowly averted at Ebbets Field last night . . . ." or "A near-riot occurred in the Polo Grounds when . . . ." In most cases further reading

*From *The New York Herald Tribune,* September 4, 1953. Copyright, 1954, New York Herald Tribune, Inc. Reprinted by permission.

discloses that Jackie Robinson had cocked a snoot at Eddie Stanky, or Leo Durocher had stated that in his considered opinion Mr. August Donatelli, estimable umpire and charming fellow though he is, had inadvertently and excusably erred in a decision.

¶ 8 Ask yourself how many times you have witnessed an uprising in a ballpark that could be described accurately as a riot or even a near-riot. Once in a long while a scuffle breaks out between players, but these are generally short-lived, and the physical damage inflicted in most baseball fist fights wouldn't wake a sleeping infant. On the rare occasions when items of glassware or decadent vegetation are thrown from the stands, the incident is viewed as a national scandal.

¶ 9 In the Mexico bull ring, the matador figures he has lost his grip if, having dispatched some weary porterhouse, he is not showered with the hats and sometimes the shoes of males in the audience and the ladies do not fling their corsages, furs, jewels, and pale white torsos at his feet.

¶ 10 There is much room for improvement here, and in spite of Mr. Tennyson's warning that one good custom can corrupt the world, the feeling is that Italian customs could be transplanted advantageously.

¶ 11 Take the case of the New York Giants, who occupy a position more or less comparable to that of the Palermo football club. That is, the Giants are near the bottom of the first division of the National League, if you are counting from the cellar up.

¶ 12 Who's responsible for this situation—Durocher, the manager, or Horace Stoneham, the president? Let 'em decide the issue on the field of honor—i.e., under the rightfield stands—jousting with pool cues at sunrise. If a choice of weapons were allowed, Durocher might prefer a pair of dice at ten paces, betting his balding scalp against Horace's right eye.

¶ 13 Or consider the possibilities which may develop in Brooklyn within the near future. The Borough Beyond the Bridge has been the scene of baseball strife since June 19, 1846.

The Dodgers have participated in six World Series without gaining the championship, and they are about to enter their seventh with, it is universally agreed, the strongest team ever spawned in Flatbush.

The master architect of this team is Charley Dressen, and Brooklyn worships every hair on his busy little head. Yet if the Dodgers should fall again before the might of the Yankees, would there be a single voice raised in Brooklyn to stay O'Malley's sword hand? And O'Malley wouldn't have to sneak through police lines disguised as a footman named Babe Hamberger. He'd be rushed to the dueling ground in a squad car. ¶ 14

It is always a mistake to feel that our way is the only way and that we couldn't profit by foreign example. The Palermo football players can't win for losing, so the club president gets carved like a Christmas turkey. When a team flops over here, it's the players who get cut, right up to the limit of 25 per cent. ¶ 15

EXERCISES

I. "Fun and Games Italienne" may well be studied in close comparison with "A Backwoods Political Rally." Here again the diction is of a very mixed character—even more mixed than in the prose of Caroline Kirkland. The diction of Red Smith, able and popular sports writer, contains some slang expressions ("lost his grip," Par. 9); colloquialisms ("Trouble with most Americans, they don't . . ." Par. 1); cant expressions belonging to sports ("get beat a dirty nose," Par. 6); and the regular matter-of-fact diction of standard journalism (Pars. 2, 3, 4). But Red Smith's "column" is far less slangy, colloquial, and journalistic than sports columns are commonly supposed to be. The effect of the column depends very largely upon Red Smith's artful use of inflated, euphemistic expressions which are *intended* to be absurdly inappropriate and yet by that absurd inappropriateness to emphasize a paradoxical truth. Or else, if not euphemistic, the expressions are deliberate exaggerations that carry a similar effect. The tone of the column is ironic. The column is in fact a kind of "joke" written in a style of pretended seriousness—just as certain kinds of "jokes" are told with a "dead-pan" expression on the teller's face. Thus the kind of phrase that would have seemed "elegant" or "decorous" to Caroline

Kirkland and that she might have wished to be taken seriously, is here *not* taken seriously—or not too seriously. Whatever serious purpose Red Smith has is disguised by the mock-serious tone of his discourse. The reader is at liberty to decide for himself "how to take" the discussion. There may be some question as to who is the butt of the joke—Italian sports-lovers, American sports-lovers, or possibly the advocates of "one world." The column has its own peculiar and intended ambiguity. It affords another lesson in the ways by which words take on double meanings or shifts of meaning according to the context in which they are used.

II. Make a list of euphemisms which Caroline Kirkland might have considered elegant, decorous, or artistic, but which Red Smith uses with ironic effect. The second sentence of Par. 7 contains a cluster of such euphemisms: "Leo Durocher had stated that in his considered opinion Mr. August Donatelli, estimable umpire and charming fellow though he is, had inadvertently and excusably erred in a decision."

A. What brings about the ironic effect in passages like that quoted above? Is it that the polite euphemisms are set in jangling contrast with some slang phrase like "cocked a snoot"? Does the reader carry in mind, as he reads the polite euphemisms, what Leo Durocher really did say, in all probability, on such an occasion?

B. In some instances Red Smith's language is evidently intended as a parody of the language of learned persons, politicians, literary men, or others who may take themselves too seriously. Who is being parodied in the following passages? How do you know, from the context, that a parody is intended?

1. In this respect we are a backward people, lagging far behind other nations." (Par. 1)
2. "Actually, by comparison with the nationals of other lands, the American at play is a model of decorum whose temperament borders on the phlegmatic." (Par. 5)
3. "It is always a mistake to feel that our way is the only way and that we couldn't profit by foreign example." (Par. 15)

III. Account for the *anticlimax* occurring in Sen. 1, Par. 6: "For example, if Mr. George Edward Arcaro . . . ." In general, does Red Smith show a preference for sentence constructions that develop an anticlimax? Or does he, on the whole, tend toward a climactic structure? Is there a good reason why, in this particular column, one would be preferable to the other?

IV. Find examples of the following figures of speech: hyperbole, litotes, synecdoche, paronomasia (play on words, pun).

COONROD HIGGINBOTTOM *

by GEORGE W. BAGBY

LESSON XV

His name, for the most part, is Jeems—Jeems Jimmison. Sometimes it is a rather homely name, as, for example, Larkin Peasley. Occasionally it is a pretty and even a romantic name, as for instance, Conrad, or, to speak properly, Coonrod—Coonrod Higginbottom. ¶ 1

Being a married man, it is incumbent on Coonrod to settle down in life; and to this end he selects, with unerring accuracy, a piece of the poorest "hennest" grass-land in his native county. The traveler enters this domain through a rickety "big-gate," partly upheld by mighty posts, which remind him of the druidical remains of Stonehenge. The road leads apparently nowhere, through thickets of old-field pine and scrub-oak. Here and there is an opening in the woods, with a lonely crank-sided tobacco-house in the midst, looking as if it were waiting resignedly for the end of the world to come. He hears the crows cawing, the woodpeckers tapping, and the log-cocks drumming, but sees no human being. Far away the roosters are crowing, and perhaps the scream of the peacock is heard. Slowly sailing, white-billed buzzards eye him from on high and make him nervous. Over the trees, he can't tell where exactly, come the voices of the ploughers—"Gee," "Wo-haw," "Git up." . . . ¶ 2

. . . The native Virginian, with a Powhatan pipe in his mouth and a silver spectacle-case in his hand, awaits you, and asks you to "light" and "come in" in the same breath. While a negro boy is running up from the "new ground" to take your horse, a mulatto girl is flying, with a pail on her head, to the spring for fresh water and a jug of milk. Two or three little negroes are chasing the chickens whose necks are soon to be twisted or chopped off with an axe at the woodpile; ham is being sliced, eggs are frying in the frying-pan, a hoe-cake is on the fire, another head of cabbage is ¶ 3

*From "Bacon and Greens" in *The Old Virginia Gentleman and Other Sketches,* by George W. Bagby. Copyright, 1943, by Ellen M. Bagby. Reprinted by permission of the publisher, The Dietz Press, Inc.

thrown into the pot, somebody is sheeting the bed upstairs, and (before your leggings are off) the case-bottle is at your elbow, and the native Virginian has taken possession of you, as if you were the Prodigal Son or the last number of the Richmond *Enquirer.*

* * * * *

Diction: Ambiguity and Multiple Meanings...

¶ 4 We will not stop to describe his old weather-boarded, often wainscoted house, with its queer old furniture and its old family portraits, which indicate for Jeems Jimmison or his wife a better origin than his name would lead you to expect. One peculiarity, though, must not go unmentioned. No matter how small this house is, it is never full. There is always room for one more in it; and, on special occasions, such as a wedding or a Christmas frolic, the number of feather beds, straw beds, shuck beds, pallets, and shakedowns which this old house produces is literally incredible. To feed and lodge, if need be, the entire state is not a point of honor with Coonrod, but a matter of course—no other idea ever entered his head. What is called "hospitality" by other folks is with him so much a part of his nature that he has no name for it (unless he keeps an "Entertainment"), and he never uses the word. How he managed, on a worn-out estate, to repeat, as it were, the miracle of the loaves and the fishes is a mystery which must be charged, I fear, to the "barbarism of slavery," for the art of feeding and lodging everybody seems already to be passing away.

¶ 5 Nor can we stop to describe the good wife of the native Virginian, with her check apron, key-basket, and knitting sheath—the pattern of domestic virtue; a matron, compared with whom the Roman matron, so famed, is as inferior as paganism is to the religion of our Savior; the hardest-worked slave on the estate—toiling, as she does, from year to year and year after year, for every human being, black and white, male and female, young and old, on the plantation, and yet a Christian gentlewoman, refined, tender, pure—almost too good and pure for earth. Think what she has done for Virginia! Think too, that under the new order of things, she also may be passing away. Of all the sad things which press upon us in these troubled days, there is none so sad as this; no, not one. For without the Virginia matron there is no longer any Virginia; and without Virginia, what, to Virginians, is this world? Let us hasten away from the thought.

¶ 6 In like manner, we must hasten away from Larkin's sons and daughters; the former brave and wild—destined to run much their father's course; the latter unaccountably pretty, spirited, and cultivated. If it be a matter of wonder how Mrs. Coonrod manages to get up such marvelous breakfasts and dinners out of her dingy, dirt-floored kitchen, still more wonderful are the girls whom she raises in her "shakledy" old house, ten miles from anywhere, and entirely out of the world. We cannot spare the time to praise the boys and girls—the noble products of a social system which mankind has united to put down—for the native Virginian, as we now find him, is almost entirely alone, his family being scattered far and wide—all married and thriving, except one "black sheep," who has taken to drink, to fiddling, and to shrouding everybody in the neighborhood who dies.

¶ 7 In person, the old man is above the medium height, "dark-complected," spare built and generally long and lean in the lower limbs,—and that's the reason he rides a horse so well. His voice is loud, owing to a habit he has of conversing familiarly with the hands in the field about a mile and a half off. His vision is wonderfully acute—partly from long practice with the rifle, and partly from the custom of inspecting his neighbors' vehicles at incredible distances. If he live on the side of the road, you will see him on Sunday eyeing a cloud of dust on the remote horizon. "Jeems," he will say to his son; "Jeems, ain't that old Peter Foster's carry-all?" "Yes," says Jeems, without a moment's hesitation; "and I'll be dad-shim'd if that off mule has been shod yit." . . . He says "thar" and "whar," "upstars" and "down in the parster," talks about "keepin' a appintment," not next year, but "another year," when he expects to raise "a fine chance uv curcumbers" in the "gearden," and a "tollibly far crap o' tubbarker." If he is a tidewater man, he does not say "chance," but "charnce," and, instead of saying the "har" of the head, he says "heyar." If he eats cornfield peas much, he becomes a virulent Virginian, and caps the climax of bad English by some such expression as "me and him was a-gwine a-fishin'." This he does, not for the lack of knowledge, but partly because he loves to talk as unlike a Yankee as possible, partly because he "don' keer" particularly about his language or anything else, except his political and religious opinions, and mainly because he is entirely satisfied (as, indeed, all Virginians are) that the English is spoken in its purity nowhere on this earth but in Virginia. "Tharfo' " he "kin affode" to talk "jest" as he "blame chooses."

¶ 8 His individuality, his independence and indifference to matters on which other people set great store, is shown, not only in his pronunciation, but in his dress—you see it in the tie of his cravat, the cut of his coat, the fit of his waistcoat, the set of his pantaloons, the roaching of his hair, and the color of his pocket-handkerchief—a red bandanna with yellow spots. But the whole character of the man is fully told only when you come to open his "secretary." There you will find his bonds, accounts, receipts, and even his will, jabbed into pigeon-holes or lying about loose in the midst of a museum of powder-horns, shot-gourds, turkey-yelpers, flints, screws, pop-corn, old horseshoes, and watermelon seed.

¶ 9 How such a man, with such a "secretary," can succeed in life, and how, above all, he and the like of him contrived to play the part which they have played in the history of this country, is something to be accounted for only on the bacon-and-greens principle.

EXERCISES

I. Dr. George W. Bagby's "Coonrod Higginbottom" is a humorous portrait of a typical rural Virginian of the nineteenth century. The period referred to is pre-Civil War. The sketch was originally a part of a lecture entitled "Bacon and Greens," in which Bagby humorously attributed the characteristics of the native Virginian to his habit of partaking copiously of bacon and greens. "The native Virginian," he wrote, "is different from all other folks whatsoever, and the difference between him and other folks is precisely the difference between his bacon and greens and other folks' bacon and greens." Although Bagby was viewed by many of his contemporaries as primarily a humorist, Thomas Nelson Page described him as "a Virginian realist" . . . "the first to picture Virginia as she was"—in contrast to preceding writers who had unduly idealized or romanticized plantation life.

A. Bearing in mind the questions asked (See Exercises, pp. 195–196) regarding the language and methods used by Caroline Kirkland, determine how adequately the language and method used in "Coonrod Higginbottom" solves the problem of the vocabulary and style that ought to be used in treating rural, "backwoodsy," or other special or "regional" material. In this connection you may also wish to refer to the selection from David Crockett (pp. 268–270).

B. To what degree does Bagby use deliberate exaggeration in order to secure a humorous effect? Can you determine from the context of this selection how much underlying seriousness there is in Bagby's portrait? In what respects is he a "realist"? How does Bagby compare, in language, method, and humor, with Red Smith?

II. Read appropriate portions of some authoritative work on American pronunciation and dialect: for example, H. L. Mencken, *The American Language;* Cleanth Brooks, *The Relation of the Alabama-Georgia Dialects to the Provincial Dialects of Great Britain;* or, in Thomas Pyle's *Words and Ways of American English,* such chapters as Chapter 3, "Some Characteristics of American English and Their Backgrounds," and Chapter 10, "American Pronunciation." After such study, determine which pronunciations or dialectal expressions used by Bagby are peculiar to Virginia only, and which may be found in other Southern states, or in New England, or the Middle States, or elsewhere. Craigie's *Dictionary of American English* may also be used in this study.

LESSON XVI

Travel Sketches. Impressions Created Through Sensory Images.
Point of View. Variety of Sentence Structure. Change of Pace.
Method of Fiction Used in Factual Narrative.
References to Time, Place, Historical Background.
Grammatical-Rhetorical Study of Sentence Patterns.

MORNING IN MEXICO*

by D. H. LAWRENCE

¶ 1 One says Mexico: one means, after all, one little town away South in the Republic: and in this little town, one rather crumbly adobe house built around two sides of a garden patio: and of this house, one spot on the deep, shady verandah facing inwards to the trees, where there are an onyx table and three rocking-chairs and one little wooden chair, a pot with carnations, and a person with a pen. We talk so grandly, in capital letters, about Morning in Mexico. All it amounts to is one little individual looking at a bit of sky and trees, then looking down at the page of his exercise book.

¶ 2 It is a pity we don't always remember this. When books come out with grand titles, like *The Future of America* or *The European Situation,* it's a pity we don't immediately visualize a thin or a fat person, in a chair or in bed, dictating to a bob-haired stenographer or making little marks on paper with a fountain pen.

¶ 3 Still, it is morning, and it is Mexico. The sun shines. But then, during the winter, it always shines. It is pleasant to sit out of doors and write, just fresh enough, and just warm

*Reprinted from *Mornings In Mexico,* by D. H. Lawrence, by permission of Alfred A. Knopf, Inc. Copyright, 1927, by Alfred A. Knopf, Inc.

enough. But then it is Christmas next week, so it ought to be just right.

¶4 There is a little smell of carnations, because they are the nearest thing. And there is a resinous smell of ocote wood, and a smell of coffee, and a faint smell of leaves, and of Morning, and even of Mexico. Because when all is said and done, Mexico has a faint, physical scent of her own, as each human being has . . . .

LESSON XVI

¶5 And cocks are still crowing. The little mill where the natives have their corn ground is puffing rather languidly. And because some women are talking in the entrance-way, the two tame parrots in the trees have started to whistle.

¶6 The parrots, even when I don't listen to them, have an extraordinary effect on me. They make my diaphragm convulse with little laughs, almost mechanically. They are a quite commonplace pair of green birds, with bits of bluey red, and round, disillusioned eyes, and heavy, overhanging noses. But they listen intently. And they reproduce. The pair whistle now like Rosalino, who is sweeping the patio with a twig broom; and yet it is so unlike him, to be whistling full vent, when any of us is around, that one looks at him to see. And the moment one sees him, with his black head bent rather drooping and hidden as he sweeps, one laughs.

¶7 The parrots whistle exactly like Rosalino, only a little more so. And this little-more-so is extremely, sardonically funny. With their sad old long-jowled faces and their flat disillusioned eyes, they reproduce Rosalino and a little-more-so without moving a muscle. And Rosalino, sweeping the patio with his twig broom, scraping the tittering leaves into little heaps, covers himself more and more with the cloud of his own obscurity. He doesn't rebel. He is powerless. Up goes the wild, sliding Indian whistle into the morning, very powerful, with an immense energy seeming to drive behind it. And always, always a little more than lifelike.

¶8 Then they break off into a cackling chatter, and one knows they are shifting their clumsy legs, perhaps hanging on with their beaks and clutching with their cold, slow claws, to climb to a higher bough, like rather raggedy green buds climbing to the sun. And suddenly, the penetrating, demonish mocking voices:

¶ 9 "Perro! Oh, Perro! Perr-rro! Oh, Perr-rro! Perro!"

¶ 10 They are imitating somebody calling the dog. *Perro* means dog. But that any creature should be able to pour such a suave, prussic-acid sarcasm over the voice of a human being calling a dog, is incredible. One's diaphragm chuckles involuntarily. And one thinks: *Is it possible?* Is it possible that we are so absolutely, so innocently, so *ab ovo* ridiculous?

¶ 11 And not only is it possible, it is patent. We cover our heads in confusion.

¶ 12 Now they are yapping like a dog: exactly like Corasmin. Corasmin is a little fat, curly white dog who was lying in the sun a minute ago, and has now come into the verandah shade, walking with slow resignation, to lie against the wall near by my chair. "Yap-yap-yap! Wouf! Wouf! Yapyapyap-yap!!" go the parrots, exactly like Corasmin when some stranger comes into the zaguán.* Corasmin and a little-more-so.

¶ 13 With a grin on my face I look down at Corasmin. And with a silent, abashed resignation in his yellow eyes, Corasmin looks up at me, with a touch of reproach. His little white nose is sharp, and under his eyes there are dark marks, as under the eyes of one who has known much trouble. All day he does nothing but walk resignedly out of the sun, when the sun gets too hot, and out of the shade, when the shade gets too cool. And bite ineffectually in the region of his fleas.

¶ 14 Poor old Corasmin: he is only about six, but resigned, unspeakably resigned. Only not humble. He does not kiss the rod. He rises in spirit above it, letting his body lie.

¶ 15 "Perro! Oh, Perr-rro! Perr-rro! Perr-rr-rro!!" shriek the parrots, with that strange penetrating antediluvian malevolence that seems to make even the trees prick their ears. It is a sound that penetrates one straight at the diaphragm, be-

**Zaguán* means "entrance hall, vestibule."

longing to the ages before brains were invented. And Corasmin pushes his sharp little nose into his bushy tail, closes his eyes because I am grinning, feigns to sleep; and then, in an orgasm of self-consciousness, starts up to bite in the region of his fleas.

"Perr-rro! Perr-rro!" And then a restrained, withheld sort ¶ 16
of yapping. The fiendish rolling of the Spanish "r," malevo- LESSON XVI
lence rippling out of all the vanished, spiteful aeons. And following it, the small, little-curly-dog sort of yapping. They can make their voices so devilishly small and futile, like a little curly dog. And follow it up with the ringing malevolence that swoops up the ladders of the sunbeams right to the stars, rolling the Spanish "r."

Corasmin slowly walks away from the verandah, his head ¶ 17
drooped, and flings himself down in the sun. No! He gets up again, in an agony of self control, and scratches the earth loose a little, to soften his lie. Then flings himself down again.

Invictus! The still-unconquered Corasmin! The sad little ¶ 18
white curly pendulum oscillating ever slower between the shadow and the sun.

> In the fell clutch of circumstance
> I have not winced nor cried aloud,
> Under the bludgeonings of chance
> My head is bloody, but unbowed.

But that is human bombast, and a little too ridiculous ¶ 19
even for Corasmin. Poor old Corasmin's clear yellow eyes! He is going to be master of his own soul, under all the vitriol those parrots pour over him. But he's not going to throw out his chest in a real lust of self-pity. That belongs to the next cycle of evolution.

I wait for the day when the parrots will start throwing ¶ 20
English at us, in the pit of our stomachs. They cock their heads and listen to our gabble. But so far they haven't got it. It puzzles them. Castilian, and Corasmin, and Rosalino come more natural.

EXERCISES

I. An important feature of D. H. Lawrence's "Morning in Mexico" is the simplicity and economy of the means used by the author to convey an "impression" or a series of impressions of the scene. Lawrence depends heavily upon images that are consistently "sensational"—that is, physical and sensory rather than mental. Or, to put it another way, the "mental" impression that we derive of this morning in Mexico comes from the physical images that Lawrence presents. Like Jonathan Swift in "Inventory of the Man-Mountain's Pockets," Lawrence on the whole avoids metaphor, but he does so for a different reason. On principle, Lawrence distrusts "intellectual" processes. He is a rebel against urban civilization and its over-refinement. To him, sense-impressions are "truer" than interpretations based on logical judgments because sense-impressions lie closer to the secret of life itself, to the real vitality which modern man's highly developed intellectualism has obscured and to some extent perverted. In Par. 15 Lawrence writes: "It is a sound that penetrates one straight at the diaphragm, belonging to the ages before brains were invented." Yet since Lawrence after all has a brain and is a highly civilized man, he must arrange the images derived from sense-impressions in a pattern with a "meaning" to which he can give intellectual adherence and for which he hopes to win our intellectual support. The "meaning" of "Morning in Mexico" seems to be that the parrot-cries, if properly "heard," penetrate the mask of our over-fine, our too arrogant human pretensions. Along with Rosalino the mozo and Corasmin the dog we are a little embarrassed to discover that a parrot can rebuke our vanity. The complicated aspects of this parrot-perspective on humanity are developed in Lawrence's rather joking account of "evolution" which, in Lawrence's book, follows the sketch given here. The parrot is "in another dimension," Lawrence says. Realization of that "other dimension" reminds us that we should look closely at our own "dimension."

II. Read the selection with the special purpose of studying the use of words that appeal to the senses—especially words that constitute "sensational" images without being metaphorical.

In particular, study Lawrence's ability to suggest the "extraordinary effect" of the parrot-whistle and the parrot-talk by (1) showing how the writer-narrator, Rosalino, and Corasmin react physically; (2) by *describing* the sound itself; (3) by reproducing the sound.

Note all instances in which Lawrence diverges from purely physical images and uses, instead, images that are both physical and metaphorical.

For example, in Par. 6, the parrots are described as having "round, disillusioned eyes, and heavy, overhanging noses." Does Lawrence have any special reason for describing the eyes of the parrots as "disillusioned"? Explain other such metaphors in terms of an "effect" that Lawrence wishes to create.

Why does Lawrence say that the parrots "whistle exactly like Rosalino, *only a little more so*"? Trace out every use of the "exactly like—only a little more so" theme. Why is it repeated at various points?

III. What point of view is used in the narrative? How is this point of view established? Is it consistently maintained? Could "Morning in Mexico" be classified as a travel sketch, like Rebecca West's "Home by Gruda"? How would you characterize the difference in interests and fundamental convictions of the two writers? How do these differences affect their choice of subject, choice of details, prose style?

IV. What is the function of the quotation (Par. 18) from Henley's "Invictus"? Does Lawrence use this quotation to make fun of Corasmin? Or of those who take Henley's poem too seriously? Is a rebuke to sentimentalists intended?

V. Pars. 3, 4, and 5 constitute a section of the narrative that describes "morning" in terms of physical sensations leading up to the point (Sen. 3, Par. 5) where the parrots begin to whistle. How many of the sentences in this section begin with *and* or *but?* To what extent are the sentences compound in structure? To what extent does Lawrence use pairs of words or phrases in coördinate construction? Is the structure of the sentences so devised as to conform to the "mood" or "theme" developed in this section of the narrative?

VI. Study the variations of sentence structure employed in Pars. 6 and 7. This section may be said to have a certain "rhythmic pattern"—although of course it is not, like poetry, in meter and rhyme. To what extent does the rhythmic pattern depend upon echoes and repetitions deliberately carried from sentence to sentence? What "change of pace" can you discover? ("Change of pace" may be defined as variation of sentence structure for the purpose of avoiding mechanical or monotonous effects.)

VII. Sen. 1, Par. 8 is artfully arranged to imitate, in its pattern, the movement of climbing parrots. Analyze the rhetorical-grammatical pattern to show how Lawrence obtains this effect.

VIII. Choose three other sentences that seem to you especially well adapted in structure and diction to the impression that they seek to create. Analyze these sentences as you analyzed the sentence referred to above. Then compose sentences of your own in which you follow the pattern of Lawrence's sentences.

IX. What use does Lawrence make of onomatopoeia?

HOME BY GRUDA*

by REBECCA WEST

Our chauffeur was the son of a Swabian, which is to say a German belonging to one of those families which were settled by Maria Theresa on the lands round the Danube between Budapest and Belgrade, because they had gone out of cultivation during the Turkish occupation and had to be recolonized. His father had come to Dubrovnik before he was born, and he can never have known any other people but Slavs, yet quite obviously Slavs struck him as odd and given to carrying on about life to an excessive degree. He himself, particularly when he spoke in English, attempted to correct the balance by under-statement. Hence, when we approached the village of Gruda, on our way from Dubrovnik to Kotor, he turned his head and said, "Nice people." He meant, it proved, that the men and women of this district were undistinguishable in appearance from gods and goddesses. This was one of those strange pockets one finds scattered here and there at vast intervals in the universe, where beauty is the common lot. ¶ 1

"But why," the chauffeur was asking himself, "make a fuss about that?" He put the question to himself with a kind of stolid passion, when we passed through the village again on our way home to Dubrovnik, and a group of three young girls, lovely as primroses in a wood, came towards us, laughing and stretching out their hands and crying out, "Pennies, pennies," as if they were not only begging but were ridiculing the ideas of beggary and benevolence alike. Since we were on the return journey we knew we had time to waste, and hammered on the glass and made the chauffeur stop. He slowed up under protest. "They will beg," he said. "Why not?" said my husband. They were, indeed, most prettily prepared to do so, for each of them carried a little bouquet of flowers for an excuse. ¶ 2

* From *Black Lamb and Grey Falcon,* by Rebecca West. Copyright 1940, 1941, by Rebecca West. Reprinted by permission of The Viking Press, Inc., New York.

¶3 "Pennies, pennies!" they cried, laughing, while we stared at them and adored them. This was no case of a racial tendency imposing itself on the mass, each germ-cell had made an individual effort at beauty. One was black, one was chestnut, one was ash-blonde; they were alike only in their golden skins, their fine eyebrows, their full yet neat mouths, the straightness of their bodies within their heavy black woollen gowns. "Have you any pennies, my dear? I have none," said my husband, full of charitable concern. "Not one," I answered, and I turned to the chauffeur. "Give me three tenpenny pieces," I said. "Three tenpenny pieces!" he exclaimed very slowly. "But you must not give them three tenpenny pieces. Three tenpenny pieces! It is very wrong. They should not beg at all. Begging is disgraceful. And even if it were excusable, three tenpenny pieces is far too much."

¶4 There was much to be said for his point of view. Indeed, he was entirely right and we were wrong. But they were so beautiful, and in spite of their beauty they would be poor all their lives long, and that is an injustice I never can bear. It is the flat violation of a promise. Women are told from the day they are born that they must be beautiful, and if they are ugly everything is withheld from them, and the reason scarcely disguised. It follows therefore that women who are beautiful should want for nothing. "Please, I would like to give it to them," I besought the chauffeur, "just three tenpenny pieces; it's not much for us English with the exchange as it is."

¶5 He did not answer me at once. His nature, which was so profoundly respectful of all social institutions, made him hate to refuse anything to an employer. At last he said, "I have only one tenpenny piece on me." As I took it we both knew that we both knew that he lied. Glumly he started the engine again, while the lovely girls stood and laughed and waved good-bye to us, a light rain falling on them, the wet road shining at their feet, the creamy foam of the tamarisk on the bank behind them lighter in the dusk than it is in the day, but the yellow broom darker. "I wonder how old those girls were," said my husband, a few miles further on. "Let's ask the chauffeur. Since he's a native he ought to know." The chauffeur answered, "They were perhaps fifteen or sixteen. And if they are encouraged to be impudent when they are so young, what will they be like when they are old?"

EXERCISES

I. "Home by Gruda" is Rebecca West's own title for the chapter of *Black Lamb and Grey Falcon* from which this sketch is excerpted. The sketch is a fine example of how the literary methods of fiction can be adapted to use in a narrative of actual experience. The sketch is a traveler's report of an incident, and is therefore matter-of-fact in content. In itself, too, it is a fairly trivial incident. The chauffeur, the three girl beggars, the immediate surroundings are perhaps items of no great importance. Nevertheless Rebecca West contrives to turn a report of a minor encounter into a work of art in miniature, and weaves into it a bit of history, a sense of place, a glimpse of clashing, different personalities and races, and a slight but unmistakable suggestion of tragedy waiting on the edge of gaiety.

II. The pattern of the sketch is woven out of three main strands: the "stolid passion" of the Swabian chauffeur; the beggar girls "lovely as primroses in a wood"; and the attitude of the English travelers. Work out the pattern of the narrative in terms of the inter-action of these three elements. The following questions may help:

A. Observe that Rebecca West does not begin the sketch, as an ordinary travel narrative might begin, with a direct reference to place and time, but with a characterization of the Swabian chauffeur and a parenthetical historical explanation of his presence ("which is to say a German belonging to . . . ."). Miss West gives the course of the journey itself in a subordinate clause, unobtrusively placed in the middle of the paragraph ("when we approached the village of Gruda"). Nowhere in the five paragraphs does she emphasize the journey itself—from Dubrovnik to Kotor, by way of Gruda, and return. Where, then, does the emphasis fall?

B. Study closely the inter-relationship between the chauffeur's "understatement" ("nice people," Par. 1), the contrasting "overstatement" of the English travelers ("the men and women were undistinguishable . . . from gods and goddesses"), and the appearance and actions of the three beggar girls. Does the "nice people—gods and goddesses" contrast establish a thematic contrast which is followed throughout? Indicate the recurrences and variations of this thematic contrast, in so far as it plays a part in the narrative.

C. The paragraphs of narrative prose do not follow the principles of organization of the paragraphs of expository and argumentative prose. Do the paragraphs have "topics"? Are they "stages" or "phases" of the action that is being dramatically related? Devise titles that indicate the developing pattern of the incident and the reason for the paragraph divisions. Why does not Rebecca West set off the various quoted speeches in separate paragraphs according to the conventional rule?

D. Are the English travelers too sentimental or extravagant in their attitude toward the beggar girls? Do you find any confirmation in the sketch as a whole of the statement: "This was one of those strange pockets . . . where beauty is the common lot." (Par. 1)? If there is such confirmation, is it set forth in matter-of-fact detail? In descriptive passages containing figures of speech? Is the attitude of the chauffeur a kind of confirmation? What is the importance of the following passage: "laughing and stretching out their hands and crying out, 'Pennies, pennies,' as if they were not only begging but were ridiculing the ideas of beggary and benevolence alike" (Par. 2)?

E. Do the incongruities of the situation (goddesses begging, the commonsense of the chauffeur, the idealism of the travelers) suggest an incongruous mingling of national-racial elements in the local situation? Does the gift of pennies symbolize good-will? The futility of gifts? The quixotic folly of tourists? Is Rebecca West being "ironical" in her treatment of the incident? Look up *irony* in the dictionaries available to you.

III. The effectiveness of the sketch depends to a large degree upon the restrained use of *hyperbole.* Identify all hyperbolical statements. If hyperbolical statements are to be considered, as the dictionary says, "statements exaggerated fancifully, as for effect," try to decide whether the effectiveness in this instance depends (1) merely on "fanciful" exaggerations or (2) on the use of such exaggerations in a matter-of-fact context that supports them and makes them seem less fanciful than they would seem in a romance or tall tale. Are there any examples of *litotes?*

IV. Study Rebecca West's use of "loose" sentence structure—particularly of loose sentences in which independent clauses are linked by *and, but, or, yet.* Sen. 2, Par. 1 is such a sentence: "His father had come . . . , and he can never have known . . . , yet . . . Slavs struck him as odd . . . ." Find other instances of this type of sentence structure. Does Rebecca West use it to excess? Are the sentences that precede and follow such sentences of the A . . . and B . . . yet C . . . pattern?

V. Write a theme in which you use some minor incident—a roadside encounter, a street-corner meeting, a waiting-room scene, a stop at some historic spot—to symbolize the human and social elements of a larger situation. If you wish, try using Rebecca West's pattern—understatement balanced by overstatement.

LESSON XVII

Image and Idea in Fiction.
Relationship of Point of View to Choice of Words.
Adjectives and Adjectival Constructions.
Synecdoche and Other Figures of Speech.
Mental and Physical Images. Dual Pattern.
Participial and Gerundive Phrases. Historical Correctness.

MEETING IN SOURABAYA*

by JOSEPH CONRAD

¶ 1 One evening Heyst was driven to desperation by the rasped, squeaked, scraped snatches of tunes pursuing him even to his hard couch, with a mattress as thin as a pancake and a diaphanous mosquito net. He descended among the trees, where the soft glow of Japanese lanterns picked out parts of their great rugged trunks, here and there, in the great mass of darkness under the lofty foliage. More lanterns, of the shape of cylindrical concertinas, hanging in a row from a slack string, decorated the doorway of what Schomberg called grandiloquently "my concert-hall." In his desperate mood Heyst ascended three steps, lifted a calico curtain, and went in.

¶ 2 The uproar in that small, barn-like structure, built of imported pine boards, and raised clear of the ground, was simply stunning. An instrumental uproar, screaming, grunting, whining, sobbing, scraping, squeaking some kind of lively air; while a grand piano, operated upon by a bony, red-faced woman with bad-tempered nostrils, rained hard notes like hail through the tempest of fiddles. The small platform was filled with white muslin dresses and crimson sashes slanting from shoulders provided with bare arms, which sawed

* Reprinted from *Victory*, by Joseph Conrad, by permission of J. M. Dent & Sons, Ltd., London.

away without respite. Zangiacomo conducted. He wore a white mess-jacket, a black dress waistcoat, and white trousers. His longish, tousled hair and his great beard were purple-black. He was horrible. The heat was terrific. There were perhaps thirty people having drinks at several little tables. Heyst, quite overcome by the volume of noise, dropped into a chair. In the quick time of that music, in the varied, piercing clamour of the strings, in the movements of the bare arms, in the low dresses, the coarse faces, the stony eyes of the executants, there was a suggestion of brutality—something cruel, sensual, and repulsive.

"This is awful!" Heyst murmured to himself. ¶ 3

But there is an unholy fascination in systematic noise. He ¶ 4
did not flee it incontinently, as one might have expected him to do. He remained, astonished at himself for remaining, since nothing could have been more repulsive to his tastes, more painful to his senses, and, so to speak, more contrary to his genius, than this rude exhibition of vigour. The Zangiacomo band was not making music; it was simply murdering silence with a vulgar ferocious energy. One felt as if witnessing a deed of violence; and that impression was so strong that it seemed marvellous to see the people sitting so quietly on their chairs, drinking so calmly out of their glasses, and giving no signs of distress, anger, or fear. Heyst averted his gaze from the unnatural spectacle of their indifference.

When the piece of music came to an end, the relief was so ¶ 5
great that he felt slightly dizzy, as if a chasm of silence had yawned at his feet. When he raised his eyes, the audience, most perversely, was exhibiting signs of animation and interest in their faces, and the women in white muslin dresses were coming down in pairs from the platform into the body of Schomberg's "concert-hall." They dispersed themselves all over the place. The male creature with the hooked nose and purple-black beard disappeared somewhere. This was the interval during which, as the astute Schomberg had stipulated, the members of the orchestra were encouraged to favour the members of the audience with their company—

that is, such members as seemed inclined to fraternize with the arts in a familiar and generous manner; the symbol of familiarity and generosity consisting in offers of refreshment.

¶ 6 The procedure struck Heyst as highly incorrect. However, the impropriety of Schomberg's ingenious scheme was defeated by the circumstances that most of the women were no longer young, and that none of them had ever been beautiful. Their more or less worn cheeks were slightly rouged; but apart from that fact, which might have been simply a matter of routine, they did not seem to take the success of the scheme unduly to heart. The impulse to fraternize with the arts being obviously weak in the audience, some of the musicians sat down listlessly at unoccupied tables, while others went on perambulating the central passage arm in arm, glad enough, no doubt, to stretch their legs while resting their arms. Their crimson sashes gave a factitious touch of gaiety to the smoky atmosphere of the concert-hall; and Heyst felt a sudden pity for these beings, exploited, hopeless, devoid of charm and grace, whose fate of cheerless dependence invested their coarse and joyless features with a touch of pathos.

¶ 7 Heyst was temperamentally sympathetic. To have them passing and repassing close to his little table was painful to him. He was preparing to rise and go out when he noticed that two white muslin dresses and crimson sashes had not yet left the platform. One of these dresses concealed the raw-boned frame of the woman with the bad-tempered curve to her nostrils. She was no less a personage than Mrs. Zangiacomo. She had left the piano, and, with her back to the hall, was preparing the parts for the second half of the concert, with a brusque, impatient action of her ugly elbows. This task done, she turned, and, perceiving the other white muslin dress motionless on a chair in the second row, she strode towards it between the music-stands with an aggressive and masterful gait. On the lap of that dress there lay, unclasped and idle, a pair of small hands, not very white, attached to well-formed arms. The next detail Heyst was led to observe was the arrangement of the hair—two thick brown tresses rolled round an attractively shaped head.

"A girl, by Jove!" he exclaimed mentally. ¶ 8

It was evident that she was a girl. It was evident in the ¶ 9
outline of the shoulders, in the slender white bust springing LESSON XVII
up, barred slantwise by the crimson sash, from the bell-shaped spread of muslin skirt hiding the chair on which she sat averted a little from the body of the hall. Her feet, in low white shoes, were crossed prettily.

She had captured Heyst's awakened faculty of observation; ¶ 10
he had the sensation of a new experience. That was because his faculty of observation had never before been captured by any feminine creature in that marked and exclusive fashion. He looked at her anxiously, as no man ever looks at another man; and he positively forgot where he was. He had lost touch with his surroundings. The big woman, advancing, concealed the girl from his sight for a moment. She bent over the seated youthful figure, in passing it very close, as if to drop a word into its ear. Her lips did certainly move. But what sort of word could it have been to make the girl jump up so swiftly? Heyst, at his table, was surprised into a sympathetic start. He glanced quickly round. Nobody was looking towards the platform; and when his eyes swept back there again, the girl, with the big woman treading at her heels, was coming down the three steps from the platform to the floor of the hall. There she paused, stumbled one pace forward, and stood still again, while the other—the escort, the dragon, the coarse big woman of the piano—passed her roughly, and, marching truculently down the centre aisle between the chairs and tables, went out to rejoin the hook-nosed Zangiacomo somewhere outside. During her extraordinary transit, as if everything in the hall were dirt under her feet, her scornful eyes met the upward glance of Heyst, who looked away at once towards the girl. She had not moved. Her arms hung down; her eyelids were lowered.

Heyst laid down his half-smoked cigar and compressed ¶ 11
his lips. Then he got up. It was the same sort of impulse

which years ago had made him cross the sandy street of the abominable town of Delli in the island of Timor and accost Morrison, practically a stranger to him then, a man in trouble, expressively harassed, dejected, lonely.

¶ 12 It was the same impulse. But he did not recognize it. He was not thinking of Morrison then. It may be said that, for the first time since the abandonment of the Samburan coal mine, he had completely forgotten the late Morrison. It is true that to a certain extent he had forgotten also where he was. Thus, unchecked by any sort of self-consciousness, Heyst walked up the central passage.

¶ 13 Several of the women, by this time, had found anchorage here and there among the occupied tables. They talked to the men, leaning on their elbows, and suggesting funnily—if it hadn't been for the crimson sashes—in their white dresses an assembly of middle-aged brides with free and easy manners and hoarse voices. The murmuring noise of conversations carried on with some spirit filled Schomberg's concert-room. Nobody remarked Heyst's movements; for indeed he was not the only man on his legs there. He had been confronting the girl for some time before she became aware of his presence. She was looking down, very still, without colour, without glances, without voice, without movement. It was only when Heyst addressed her in his courteous tone that she raised her eyes.

¶ 14 "Excuse me," he said in English, "but that horrible female has done something to you. She has pinched you, hasn't she? I am sure she pinched you just now, when she stood by your chair."

¶ 15 The girl received this overture with the wide, motionless stare of profound astonishment. Heyst, vexed with himself, suspected that she did not understand what he said. One could not tell what nationality these women were, except that they were of all sorts. But she was astonished almost more by the near presence of the man himself, by this largely bald head, by the white brow, the sunburnt cheeks, the long, horizontal moustaches of crinkly bronze hair, by the kindly expression of the man's blue eyes looking into her own. He saw the stony amazement in hers give way to a momentary alarm, which was succeeded by an expression of resignation.

¶ 16 "I am sure she pinched your arm most cruelly," he murmured, rather disconcerted now at what he had done.

¶ 17 It was a great comfort to hear her say:

¶ 18 "It wouldn't have been the first time. And suppose she did—what are you going to do about it?"

¶ 19 "I don't know," he said with a faint, remote playfulness in his tone which had not been heard in it lately, and which seemed to catch her ear pleasantly. "I am grieved to say that I don't know. But can I do anything? What would you wish me to do? Pray command me."

¶ 20 Again the greatest astonishment became visible in her face; for she now perceived how different he was from the other men in the room. He was as different from them as she was different from the other members of the ladies' orchestra.

¶ 21 "Command you?" she breathed, after a time, in a bewildered tone. "Who are you?" she asked a little louder.

EXERCISES

I. In the two preceding selections, Rebecca West and D. H. Lawrence use the methods of fiction, but write matter-of-fact narratives. Joseph Conrad is writing fiction. Like Lawrence he seeks to create the "effect" of an event (in this case an imagined event) by building up a series of "impressions" which, as one merges into the other, gradually create a unified and dramatized picture of life in motion. His diction, like Lawrence's, is often "sensational." In the words of his famous preface to *The Nigger of the Narcissus,* he is trying "by the power of the written word to make you hear, to make you feel . . . before all, to make you *see.*" As he succeeds in doing this, Conrad says, the reader will find in his story "encouragement, consolation, fear, charm—all you demand—and, perhaps, also that glimpse of truth for which you have forgotten to ask." In achieving this purpose, Conrad is much more indirect and roundabout than Lawrence. The hidden, often mixed *motives* of human action are what he particularly likes to explore—the scruples and hesitations of fine consciences, the reasons for acts that a person may find it difficult to explain. His prose, therefore, is much more complex than Lawrence's.

In this selection, Conrad is presenting the "state of mind" of Axel Heyst, the leading character in the novel *Victory*. Heyst is a philosophical recluse. By following a philosophy of non-action, he is trying to escape the human involvements that lead to commitments, trouble, and even tragedy. His natural generosity, however, leads him to violate his code if he encounters some deserving person who is in distress. One such encounter has just led to trouble and disaster. And now—in the present incident—he is on the verge of making another commitment.

II. The key to Conrad's method here is implied in the last sentence of Par. 6: ". . . Heyst felt a sudden pity for these beings, exploited, hopeless, devoid of charm and grace, whose fate of cheerless dependence invested their coarse and joyless features with a touch of pathos." In Heyst's eyes, the members of Zangiacomo's "ladies' orchestra" have no status as individual personalities. They are simply units of a mechanism that Zangiacomo and his wife (as also the hotel-keeper Schomberg) "exploit" for their own ends. It is therefore appropriate (1) that the "music" of the orchestra, to Heyst's outraged senses, should seem only "noise" and (2) that the rhetorical figure of *synecdoche* (use of a part to represent the whole) should be employed to give Heyst's impression of the orchestra members.

A. Note all words and phrases in Pars. 1 and 2 which through specific images convey the impression of unpleasant noise. To what extent does Conrad use *adjectives* or *adjectival constructions* to create this impression? To what extent does he use nouns, verbs, and adverbs? Is the effect of the "uproar" further accented by Conrad's use of these images in cumulative series? Does he use repetition? Are there any examples of *onomatopoeia* (words imitating the actual sound referred to)?

B. What other senses, besides the sense of hearing, does Conrad appeal to in order to build up the effect of the unpleasant sensations that Heyst encounters in the concert-hall? Is there any implication in these two paragraphs that such "noise" is to be associated with the vulgarity and materialism of such a "concert-hall," such an "audience," such a "conductor" as Zangiacomo?

C. In Pars. 4, 5, and 6, how is the difference between Heyst and the throng developed? Would the "audience" understand Heyst's distaste for the "noise"? Would they regard the "noise" as "music"—"good music"?

Is there any indication that Heyst is "isolated" from humanity at large? Or that he is "superior" to the common run of people in the hotel concert-hall at Sourabaya?

D. The first example of *synecdoche* appears in Sen. 3, Par. 2: "The small platform was filled with white muslin dresses and crimson sashes slanting from shoulders provided with bare arms, which sawed away without respite." This visual impression—the image that Heyst's eye receives—is used by Conrad to indicate the underlying reality of the situation. The orchestra women are not individualities, but mere "functions" dressed up for Zangiacomo's use—"clothes" rather than human personalities. Thus Heyst's eye, in Conrad's fictional representation, is making a true report to Heyst's intellectual and ethical judgment. Therefore it is also true, in fictional terms, that Zangiacomo is "horrible"—not a human being but "the male creature with the hooked nose."

Point out all other instances of synecdoche in the selection and comment on their appropriateness.

E. Discuss the function of Par. 6 as a transitional paragraph.

F. Trace out the stages by which the girl is gradually transformed, in Heyst's view, from another "white muslin dress" into an individual whom Heyst feels he must befriend.

G. What passages suggest that the girl is as much isolated from the world at large (in the sense of being "different") as Heyst himself is? See especially Pars. 15–20.

III. Comment on the effectiveness of the following:

A. "A grand piano, operated upon by a bony, red-faced woman with bad-tempered nostrils" (Par. 2)

B. "there is an unholy fascination in systematic noise." (Par. 4)

C. "glad enough, no doubt, to stretch their legs while resting their arms." (Par. 6)

D. "Their crimson sashes gave a factitious touch of gaiety to the smoky atmosphere" (Par. 6)

E. "a brusque, impatient action of her ugly elbows." (Par. 7)

F. "He looked at her anxiously, as no man ever looks at another man" (Par. 10)

G. "an assembly of middle-aged brides with free and easy manners and hoarse voices." (Par. 13)

H. "She was looking down, very still, without colour, without glances, without voice, without movement." (Par. 13)

IV. Select for close study a paragraph or group of sentences that you think representative of Conrad's style at its best. After you have made a careful analysis, write out a statement in which you set forth the significant features of Conrad's prose. Support your points with quotations.

A WORLD OUT OF CHAOS*

by ELIZABETH MADOX ROBERTS

LESSON XVII

¶ 1 Sam and Reuben sheared the sheep in April, working in the barn-shed beyond the milking place, ripping the coats from the backs of the sheep with great shears. Diony helped wash the fleeces at the wash place, making a rich hot lye suds in the great iron washing pot, and each fleece was beaten about in the hot foam with battling sticks of wood. Then the wool was drained of the water and rinsed once and hung to dry on scaffolds. Her thought penetrated the wool and went with the fleece through the hot foamy bath and lay stretched with it on the scaffolds in the shade of the greatest oak. In the night she dreamed of planes of white frothy matter which the sheep had shed and of the sheep going back to their pasture, their yield gone beyond their power to recall. When the wool was dry Polly called her to help pick it free of sticks and burrs, and if one of the fleeces was of a richer whiteness and softness than the rest she had a peculiar pride in it, as if she shared of some right with the flock. Sam would be singing a song, his falsetto voice that he used among the barns and cow-pens:

Many hist'ries have been read and many stories told
How Moss caught his mare. It was in the days of old . . .

¶ 2 In summer the cloth-making was of the wool, making garments for winter wear; in winter it was of the linen, the wear of the summer. Now, soon after the first meal of the day, Diony would be busy with the wool, and Polly's plans for it would run forward even while they sat at breakfast in the great kitchen room where Sallie Tolliver had put a trencher of ham and a fine wheat loaf on the board. Spinning the wool, she would work in the west end of the room, running back and forth to the rhythms of the great wheel. Out the small window she could see the garden patch along

*From *The Great Meadow,* by Elizabeth Madox Roberts. Copyright, 1930, by The Viking Press, Inc. Reprinted by permission of The Viking Press, Inc., New York.

the creek, the flowing water beyond, and the hill. Stepping back and forth in the dance of spinning, she would recall words from her father's books, from one book: "It is evident to anyone who takes a survey of the objects of human knowledge, that they are either ideas actually imprinted on the senses or else such as are perceived by attending to the passions and operations of the mind . . ."* This would blend anew with the flow of the wool in her hands until the words and the wool were spun together and all stood neatly placed in her thought ready to be woven into some newer sort . . . . "It is evident to anyone who takes a survey . . . ." She would hear Betty and Sam in a rough frolic in the dog alley. Sam's voice:

¶3 "I'm a torn-down Virginian. I'm a Long Knife. And iffen Virginia goes to war on Pennsylvania I'll offer Lord Dunmore my sword . . . ."

¶4 "Don't be so antic with that-there cut-tool," Betty cried out in defense. "I'm not Pennsylvany. Keep off, keep offen my head . . . ."

¶5 The wool was soft in her fingers, but heavy in bulk, being great in quantity and requiring much service of her. She would return to the words of the book and heed what they said, in substance: that all knowledge is of three sorts, that derived by way of the senses, that by way of the passions, and lastly, quoting now the words of the text, "ideas formed by help of memory and imagination." She could easily see the truth of this since she had discussed all fitfully with her father and had turned again to the book for renewal of faith when the words grew dim in memory. The whirr of the wheel came into her thought of the book as she fitfully remembered. "And beside all that, there is likewise something which knows or perceives them and exercises divers operations, as willing, imagining, remembering . . . . This perceiving, active being is what I call mind, spirit, soul, MY-

*This and other quoted prose passages in the selection are from *A Treatise Concerning The Principles of Human Knowledge,* by George Berkeley, the English philosopher (1685–1753).

SELF . . . . Some truths there are so near and obvious to the mind that man need only open his eyes to see them. Such I take this important one to be, namely, that all the choir of heaven and furniture of the earth, in a word, all those bodies that compose the mighty frame of the world, have not any substance without a mind, that their being is to be perceived or known . . . that, consequently, as long as they are not actually perceived by me, or do not exist in my mind, or that of any other created spirit, they must either have no existence at all, or else subsist in the mind of some Eternal Spirit."

She could hear her mother walking in the room above where she had gone to search out the dye pots to make ready for coloring the yarn, and she heard her calling to Sallie Tolliver down the stairway to ask after the logwood, Sallie Tolliver going mutely up the steps by way of reply. In the smith-shop behind the house some strong hand hammered, blow after blow, her father mending a plow. She clung rather to the words of the book, letting the iron shriek pass, Sam outside singing: ¶ 6

Many hist'ries have been read and many stories told
How Moss caught his mare. It was in the days of old.
He got up early one morning thinking he'd find her asleep,
And all about the barnyard so slyly he did creep . . .

She turned the thought of the words that the book used over and over with a pleasure in knowledge, restating all for her own delight. "They, these things, or any small part of the whole mighty frame of the world, are withouten any kind or sort or shape until somebody's mind is there to know. Consequently, all the ways you wouldn't know, all you forgot or never yet remembered, mought have a place to be in Mind, in some Mind far off, and he calls this Eternal Spirit." Her thought leaped then beyond articulation and settled to a vast passion of mental desire. Oh, to create rivers by knowing rivers, to move outward through the extended infinite plane until it assumed roundness. Oh, to ¶ 7 make a world out of chaos. The passion spread widely through her and departed and her hands were still contriving the creamy fibers of a fleece.

EXERCISES

I. In "A World Out of Chaos," we have a picture of a few moments in the life of a Virginia family, some members of which are soon to follow Daniel Boone and migrate westward across the mountains into the wilderness country—the "great meadow" of Kentucky. Here again we have a style based on the use of images that at first glance may seem to be mainly physical and sensational, as in the prose of Lawrence and Conrad. The sensational images, however, are called up in the *mind* of Diony as she works at household tasks and recalls passages that her father had read aloud from Berkeley's philosophical treatise on human knowledge. It is therefore the "thought" or "idea" of the physical objects that is paramount here, not just the "perception" or "sensational experience" of those objects. The dreamy quality of the prose and its innocent simplicity derive from the application of Berkeley's "subjective idealism" to what might be called the "crude facts" of pioneer life. Sam, singing his ballad, and Betty and Sallie are no doubt more on the level of mere perception. But Diony's "thought penetrated the wool." She wished "to create rivers by knowing rivers, to move outward through the extended infinite plane until it assumed roundness." Diony's reverie is therefore "physical" and "metaphysical" at the same time. It deals with something very substantial and solid, but is all the same pre-eminently idea—it is a Berkeleyan vision.

II. The pattern of Elizabeth Madox Roberts' prose in this selection may perhaps best be understood if we refer to the passage in Par. 2 where Diony, remembering the words of the book, is experiencing both "ideas imprinted on the senses" and ideas "perceived by attending to the passions and operations of the mind." The two aspects of her thought "would blend anew with the flow of the wool in her hands until the words and the wool were spun together . . . ."

Trace the "flow" of Diony's thoughts in this dual pattern throughout the selection. By "dual pattern" is meant: (1) the "flow" of sensations (and thoughts) having to do with real objects; (2) the "flow" of thought on the ideal plane—Diony's reverie-like generalizations about the objects and even about her ideas.

A. Distinguish the passages that deal with the "real" objects (substantial, physical things) and those that are "ideas" (the "fanciful," "dreamlike," "imaginative").

B. Fix in each case the *exact* point at which Diony shifts from "physical reality" to "ideal reality." Would you have noticed the transition from one plane to another if you had not been searching for the point of transition? Does the smoothness and unobtrusiveness of the transitions contribute to the "flow" of the prose? Does Elizabeth Madox Roberts use many "transitional devices" of the sort common in expository composition?

C. What grammatical type of sentence (simple, compound, complex) does Elizabeth Madox Roberts seem to prefer? Does her preference for a type of sentence structure contribute to the easiness and "flow" of the narrative?

D. You will also note a fairly high prevalence of participial phrases formed upon *-ing* participles ("stepping back and forth") and of gerundive constructions ("in the dance of spinning"). (See Par. 2.) Often the participial phrases appear as elements *added* at the end of a predication ("Diony helped wash the fleeces at the wash place, making a rich hot lye suds . . ." Par. 1) What effect does this preference for *-ing* constructions have upon the prose? Does this preference, as an element of style, contribute to the "easy flow"? Does it give the effect of thought flowing actively, rather than of a picture fixed and motionless? What difference would it make, in the sentence just referred to, if Elizabeth Madox Roberts had written: "In order that she might help wash the fleeces . . . Diony *made* a rich hot lye suds . . ."? Try similar alterations in other sentences. Does the author often prefer participial constructions at a point where other writers might use subordinate clauses?

E. How much does simplicity of diction contribute to the "flow" of the prose? What is the nature of this simplicity? Does it consist in refusal to use modifiers? In choice of plain and simple words? In rejection of metaphorical language and highly colored effects? Does the author, in this simplicity, intend to convey the effect of rendering the thoughts of an unsophisticated or unspoiled mind? That is to say, does the diction fit the character whose thoughts we are following? Do you think a girl who can quote Berkeley's philosophy would have a "simple" mind?

III. Is Elizabeth Madox Roberts historically correct in attributing a knowledge of Berkeley's philosophy to a girl of a pioneer family during the latter part of the eighteenth century? Does it matter whether she is historically correct if she is artistically plausible? Can you see any connection between the ideas of Berkeley and the ideas of American frontiersmen?

IV. Write a narrative in which, adhering to the point of view of a single character, you follow a dual pattern similar to that used by Elizabeth Madox Roberts. The narrative should proceed on two "planes" or "levels," but, taken together, the two must make a unified, harmonious composition.

LESSON XVIII

Principles of Criticism.
Major and Minor Art.
The Eclectic Style.

SEEING THE POINT *

by STARK YOUNG

All style in art begins with essential idea. When a painter says that another painter has style, or when we say that Mounet-Sully had style, we use the word in a somewhat special sense. Style in that sense means a certain heightening, a certain added elaboration, something that can be isolated from the content of the work of art though it is not false to it. Style in that sense is not necessarily the soul of the thing so much as it is the lustre of the artist. But style in any large and general sense comes back to Buffon's remark that the style was the man, or to Spenser's "soul is form and doth the body make." Style is the medium by which the idea finds expression. Style is what appears between the content of a work of art and its appearance in a form. Style is what arrives at that precise point at which the work of art comes into existence. Before this point at which it achieves its style, the work of art does not exist. In a work of art the artist has a certain underlying essential idea or characteristic in the treatment of his material, a certain point, which he sees as the soul of it. This point he puts through every part of it. Complete style arrives in a work of art only when the idea is translated into the terms of every part. ¶ 1

The difference between an artist and a man who has in- ¶ 2

* Reprinted by permission of the publishers, Charles Scribner's Sons, from *Glamour: Essays on the Art of the Theatre,* by Stark Young.

tentions but cannot create them into art, appears in the absence of the style that might accomplish this translation of idea into form. Minor artists and imitators, apart from the significance of such ideas as they possess, are what they are because they are able to put the essential characteristic not through all the parts of a work, but only in this part or that. Mr. Paul Manship, beautiful and learned as his work may often be, has a statue of a girl with fauns that we may take as an example of such incompleteness. The turn of the girl's head, the lines and folds of her garment are in the manner of the early Greek marbles; the fauns, in the management of the ears, the nostrils, the little chasings to indicate the hair above the tail, the hoofs and eyes, remind us of that lovely pair from Herculaneum, pseudo-archaic, exotic, charming past all words. But the girl's hands and her ankles and feet are almost modern in their character; in those two details the idea that characterized the rest of the work has not found expression, and they are therefore dead, and, in fact, never lived; they are apart from the rest of the statue.

¶ 3 Artists that are almost wholly eclectic and not very original get the form without the content. They learn from other instances of their art and from masters of it a manner of working; they take on bodies for which they have no fulfilling souls to contribute. They take over a style which says something not their own and is almost free of them. A highly eclectic sculptor, for example, may get the surface, the external manner, the character that he has derived from another, but he cannot get the essential sculpturesque solidity which derives from the true relation of the modelled mass to its idea. And it may happen in all arts, also, that a style gets fixed, outstays its meaning; the form remains, but half the fundamental idea beneath it is lost; as at the Théâtre Français, for one illustration, where much of the tradition is, at the hands of bad actors, lacking in idea; or as in some of Michelangelo's followers, who got only his mannerisms without the ideal necessity behind them.

¶ 4 No style at all, then, to repeat, can arrive until the artist gets the point, the characteristic. The completeness of the style—and of the work of art—depends on the extent to which this characteristic extends through every part. An actor creating Oedipus can learn from the play itself the character of every detail confronting him. He can discern, for instance, that his make-up requires a beard, and the obligation for a beard will serve to comment on his whole problem. That he must wear a beard the actor knows not so much from tradition as from every separate aspect of the drama. To begin with, the very story itself is not personal with Sophocles but was a racial myth ready to his hand. This story—and the final form of it that he uses in his play—consists mostly of outline, a large, general pattern in which the shadings of incident, character, and emotional and ideal reaction are included. The characters themselves are, first of all, types, large forms, and afterward more or less individuals. The emotions and ideas are not so much personal as typical, powerful visitations within these human vessels of forces larger and more lasting than they, passing through them, shaking and revealing and leaving them. The images created, the diction employed in the play, are kept within the bounds of a certain size and a certain pattern of simplicity. From all this the actor learns, then, at the very start that his own features will too greatly individualize the rôle; just as in turn he knows, in so far as he is an artist, that the reactions he expresses and the gestures he employs must have about them a certain outline quality, a pattern of universality; and just as in turn he knows that in his recitation he must strive for line forms rather than words and phrases, and so must move toward a sonorous and impersonal and formal manner of delivery. Sophocles as a dramatic artist succeeds and attains greatness by reason of the fact that the characteristic quality is carried greatly and completely through every part of his drama, the story, the ethical theme, the characters, the reactions, the imagery, diction, the verse. His play possesses an absolute totality in style.

The defect of Euripides, on the other hand, great poet ¶ 5

and dramatist that he is, consists, in so far at least as the Greek dramatic form is concerned, in his not being able to create or to introduce a style that could express his quality amply or completely; Euripides leaves no little of his thought and content undramatized, uncreated, and conveys it to us as more or less separable moments of literature or philosophy; it is as if Velasquez in his Surrender of Breda, instead of carrying into his very brush and into the outlines of his forms the quality that in the art of words we should speak of as gracious and most suave, had attached written words to the canvas to express further the idea in his mind.

¶ 6 In many a production of *The Merchant of Venice,* the casket scene has had a mass of gilding and tricking out, with every sort of detail, cushions, canopies, throne-chairs and costumes, coming and going, everything but the point; which visually is the relation of the caskets to the suitors, to Portia and to the whole scene; which orally is the poetic rhythm and imagery; which in sum is the pattern of idea, picture, and sound that underlies the scene. In the Hopkins-Jones-Barrymore production of *Hamlet,* on the contrary, the scene where Hamlet comes upon the king at prayer was acted with the king on his knees near the front of the stage, his hands lifted to heaven. Behind him stood Hamlet with his drawn sword in his hand. The two figures, one behind the other, the lifted hands, the sword pointing, expressed for the eye the exact pattern of the scene's idea, the precise theme of relationships. Visually, at least, the essential of that scene had been achieved, and had been freed of every characteristic not its own.

¶ 7 An actor, therefore, is an artist only in so far as he can first see the point of characteristic quality and then put this through every detail of his performance. His manner, his gestures, his walk, his diction, and quality of mind will differ in *The School for Scandal* from what they must be in Ibsen's *Ghosts;* in Regnard's play of *le Légataire Universel* he will eat grapes, make love, wear his clothes, or fight a duel in a style that differs from his necessary style in Beaumont and Fletcher as Regnard's precision and swift cold elegance differ from the gallantries and lyrical whimsies of the two Elizabethans. And it is through this principle that the actor will know how to approach the question of naturalness in acting, and to dispose of the usual nonsense on the subject. He will know that in acting, as in any other art, the only naturalness involved—and the only meaning that the word could have—arises from the essential nature of the work of art which he has in hand.

¶ 8 All purity in art begins with the translation of the essential idea. A work of art is pure in so far as it compels the ideas within it to stick to its own terms; it is pure in so far as the ideas within it find expression solely in these terms, without relying on anything else. In a work of art that is pure the idea—and every manifestation of it—discovers a body that is free of all characteristics not those of the art employed. A painting of a majestical scene or of some heroic and austere vista is not a painting at all—however stirring it may be as a visual memory or as poetry—unless this characteristic that, in the art of words, we call magnificent austerity exists in the color, the line, the brush, the composition of the picture. And so with music and every art. And that purity which we discern in the great artists' natures—and to a lovable extent in most minor artists, too—and in great saints, arises from this; what they dream and desire is for its own end and perfection, free of considerations outside itself and untouched by the intrusions of another world of aims. For them the idea or dream can alone be important; and by the side of it they are not even aware of "all other idle and unreal shapes attendant on mortality."

¶ 9 Criticism of art that is a matter of personal preference and individual taste and private responses is not without value, however variable these may be. But the aspect of criticism that is most constructive, useful, and not to be debated, is that which arises first from the critic's ability to perceive the characteristic quality underlying a work of art. He abstracts this characteristic from whatever embodiments of it may be apparent; he carries it to some ideal completion, and then judges the work of art by this ideal, by the extent to which this complete realization of its idea is achieved. Where the critic can do this he transcends individual accidents of mere choice. And no small part of his cultivation will derive from his training in the perception of and the acquaintance with many characteristic qualities.

¶ 10 And, finally, in every man the delight and happy nurture of all art—as of all other experience—will depend at length on his seeing the point, on his discovery of the last necessary characteristic. With the growth and cultivation of this faculty he will go learning to see the point of what he considers and exercises himself upon, taking a kind of delight in finding what seems for him to be the soul of the thing observed. From the body of it the essential idea emerges like a soul; from the circle its circularity and its perfect cessation within itself; from the moonlit plain what in language he calls its stillness and infinite peace, the dream of it that there are no words to describe; from the rose its roseness, by which it lingers in the memory; from Mozart his quality, and from El Greco his; and from the poet of the *Eclogues,* the *Georgics,* and some of the *Aeneid,* that character of poignant and lyrical reflection and ornate quietness that we call Virgilian. These essential qualities of things emerging out of them take on a permanence in the man's life that seems to survive them, and to achieve a kind of constancy; and so, out of the flux of all things, to offer to us something immortal in mortality.

¶ 11 Through this development in a man it may come to be that his pleasure in a work of art does not depend so much on the discovery of superlative instances and hot enthusiasms often soon past. It relieves him of the sense that he must acclaim the work of art as the best in the world or the best he has ever seen; and allows him the pleasure, always possible, even in an inferior thing, of discerning what the essential quality within it is and the extent to which this quality has been expressed. And in his own mind at least, if not always in the work of art, these essential ideas may dilate themselves toward perfection. This will add to that development and perfecting within himself of conceptions, qualities, essential ideas, by which not only he understands art, but he lives as well. From them he gets light for his own experience, and out of his experience he adds elements to the sum of them. Art becomes—as the rest of life is—the field for his immortal search and continuity. And through this, art can reveal those in whom life is a passion of oneness and duration; and can, as Plato said of a certain music, from the divinity of its nature make evident those who are in want of the god. In great art a man seeks even more than in his own flesh a body for that which he most wishes to preserve in himself.

EXERCISES

I. What distinction is Stark Young making when he says (Par. 1), "Style in that sense is not necessarily the soul of the thing so much as it is the lustre of the artist"? In answering the question, be sure that you grasp and state the antithesis between "soul of the thing" and "lustre of the artist."

II. Give other relevant illustrations of "minor" art—from painting, music, poetry, fiction—comparable to the example cited by Stark Young in Par. 2.

III. Give the derivation of *eclectic* (Par. 3) and the meaning that applies in the context of Stark Young's discussion. Of the following, which are "eclectic" in style, and which are not: a painting by Leonardo da Vinci; a painting by Landseer; a symphony by Beethoven; a symphony by Brahms; a play by Sophocles or Shakespeare; a play by Chekhov; a play by Eugene O'Neill; the Chartres cathedral; the buildings on your campus?

IV. State in your own words, after studying Par. 4, the reasons why a good actor, playing the part of Oedipus, would know "that he must wear a beard." What is the meaning of Stark Young's statement that the story of Sophocles' *Oedipus Tyrannus* "is not personal with Sophocles but was a racial myth ready to his hand"? How does Sophocles' drama differ in this respect from a play by Ibsen or George Bernard Shaw or Noel Coward? Are any of these (or other modern dramatists) comparable to Euripides, if considered in the terms that Stark Young uses in Par. 5?

V. In Shakespeare's *The Merchant of Venice,* what is the point that Stark Young wishes to emphasize with regard to "the relation of the caskets to the suitors, to Portia and to the whole scene"? (Par. 6)

VI. Consider carefully Par. 8, and in your consideration apply the meaning, both stated and implied, of the word *pure.* Does Stark Young mean by *pure* any of the following: "moral"; "virtuous"; "good"; "objective"; "abstract"? Is a painting "pure" if it is "poetical"? Is a poem "pure" if it only "paints a picture"? Is a piece of music "pure" if it imitates the sound effects of a storm? Which is nearer pure art, by Stark Young's definition: Tschaikovsky's *1812 Symphony* or Beethoven's *Fifth Symphony?* Give other examples of purity and impurity in art. Choose examples from this textbook if any will serve.

VII. How may a student apply in his college studies and in his mature life the principles set forth by Stark Young in Pars. 9, 10, and 11?

LESSON XIX

Vocabulary: Saxon and Foreign Elements in the English Language.

THE LANGUAGE OF THE KING JAMES VERSION OF THE BIBLE *

by JOHN LIVINGSTON LOWES

Utter simplicity, limpid clearness, the vividness of direct, authentic vision—these are the salient qualities of the diction of the men who wrote the Bible. ¶ 1

Now let me return to what was said a few moments ago. The Hebrew of the Old Testament (and to a less degree the Greek of the New) is supremely translatable, and it is so largely because of just these salient characteristics of its diction—its simplicity, its clarity, its directness, and its universal and immediate appeal. And that brings us to another aspect of the subject. For it is the translation into English with which we have to do. And as regards possession of these same qualities, the English vocabulary, as it happens, can meet the Hebrew upon equal terms. ¶ 2

There are in the English vocabulary, as everybody knows, two chief elements—the one native, the other complexly foreign. And it is the fusion of these two which constitutes the unrivalled flexibility and variety of our speech. To its native, Saxon element it owes a homely vigour, a forthrightness and vividness and concreteness, an emotional appeal, in which it matches the Hebrew itself. To its foreign element—chiefly the Latin component, which will concern us in a moment—is due, among other things, a sonorousness, a ¶ 3

* Reprinted by permission of the publishers, Houghton Mifflin Company, from "The Noblest Monument of English Prose," in *Essays in Appreciation.* by John Livingston Lowes. Copyright, 1936, by John Livingston Lowes.

stateliness, a richness of music, a capacity for delicate discrimination which makes it an instrument of almost endlessly varied stops. Now one element is predominant, now the other; more frequently there is an intimate fusion of the two. Every page of English literature, whether prose or poetry, illustrates the possibilities of infinite variety inherent in this fundamental character of English diction; but it is its bearing on the translation of the Bible which concerns us now, and to that I pass at once.

¶ 4 For reasons too complex and far-reaching for discussion here, the language at the period during which the Bible was being translated into English was in its most plastic stage. It was a time of intense living, of incomparable zest in life. England was literally, in Milton's words, "a noble and puissant nation rousing herself like a strong man after sleep, and shaking her invincible locks." Without being too crassly figurative one may put the thing in Biblical phrase: "The winter was past, the rain was over and gone, and the time of the singing of birds had come." This is no place to linger on the glory of those spacious days. The one thing which I wish to emphasize is this: with the new quickening of every phase of life, the language itself kept even pace. There was a fresh consciousness of its possibilities, a sovereign and masterful exploitation of its hitherto undreamed resources. For the Elizabethans dealt with their speech as they dealt with life —with an adventurous zest in exacting from it all it had to give. "The lady shall speak her mind freely, or the blank verse shall halt for't," says Hamlet to the players—and to say its mind freely, to the top of its bent, this particular period proposed; and if the language cabined, cribbed, confined it—why, then, the language must expand! And expand it did, with palpable growing pains now and then, but with an ultimate gain in freshness, in vividness, in raciness, in flexibility which it has never wholly lost. And so far as their medium was concerned, the King James translators fell upon lucky days.

¶ 5 They had at their disposal, then, on its Saxon side, a

vocabulary scarcely less concrete and vivid than that of the Hebrew itself. Here is a paragraph from a book printed a hundred years before Shakespeare began to write, but widely read in Shakespeare's day—Malory's *Morte D'Arthur:*

> And as the king lay in his cabin in the ship, he fell in a slumbering, and dreamed a marvellous dream: him seemed that a dreadful dragon did drown much of his people, and he came flying out of the west, and his head was enamelled with azure, and his shoulders shone as gold, his belly like mails of a marvellous hue, his tail full of tatters, his feet full of fine sable, and his claws like fine gold; and an hideous flame of fire flew out of his mouth, like as the land and water had flamed all of fire. After him seemed there came out of the orient a grimly boar all black in a cloud, and his paws as big as a post; he was rugged looking roughly, he was the foulest beast that ever man saw, he roared and romed so hideously that it were marvel to hear. Then the dreadful dragon advanced him, and came in the wind like a falcon, giving great strokes on the boar, and the boar hit him again with his grisly tusks that his breast was all bloody, and that the hot blood made all the sea red of his blood. Then the dragon flew away all on an height, and came down with such a swough, and smote the boar on the ridge, which was ten foot large from the head to the tail, and smote the boar all to powder, both flesh and bones, that it flittered all abroad on the sea.

There is no lack in that diction of vigour, of concreteness, of picturing power! And when the translators of the Bible came to their task, they found a medium ready to their hand: ¶ 6

> Blessed above women shall Jael the wife of Heber the Kenite be, blessed shall she be above women in the tent. He asked water, and she gave him milk; she brought forth butter in a lordly dish. She put her hand to the nail, and her right hand to the workmen's hammer; and with the hammer she smote Sisera, she smote off his

head, when she had pierced and stricken through his temples. At her feet he bowed, he fell, he lay down: at her feet he bowed, he fell: where he bowed, there he fell down dead.

¶ 7 Or take another passage from Malory, and one from the Bible again.

> Ah, Launcelot, he said, thou were head of all christian knights; and now I dare say, said Sir Ector, thou Sir Launcelot, there thou liest, that thou were never matched of earthly knights' hand; and thou were the courtiest knight that ever bare shield; and thou were the truest friend to thy lover that ever bestrode horse; and thou were the truest lover of a sinful man that ever loved woman; and thou were the kindest man that ever strake with sword; and thou were the goodliest person that ever came among press of knights; and thou was the meekest man and the gentlest that ever ate in hall among ladies; and thou were the sternest knight to thy mortal foe that ever put spear in rest.

¶ 8 Now hear the other:

> The beauty of Israel is slain upon thy high places: how are the mighty fallen! . . . From the blood of the slain, from the fat of the mighty, the bow of Jonathan turned not back, and the sword of Saul returned not empty. Saul and Jonathan were lovely and pleasant in their lives, and in their death they were not divided: they were swifter than eagles, they were stronger than lions . . . . How are the mighty fallen in the midst of battle! O Jonathan, thou wast slain in thine high places. I am distressed for thee, my brother Jonathan: very pleasant hast thou been unto me: thy love to me was wonderful, passing the love of women. How are the mighty fallen, and the weapons of war perished!

There is in the translation from the Hebrew a majestic rhythm, of which I shall speak later, and which the prose of Malory lacks; but the two agree in the simplicity and the directness of their diction. And those qualities of the native element of English have met and merged with similar, often identical, qualities of the original. For no less than the Hebrew, the native English is the language of the eye, the hand, the heart, and one of the supreme merits of the Jacobean translators is their sense of that fundamental fact. Let me choose three other brief passages to make still clearer what I mean: ¶ 9

> Intreat me not to leave thee, or to return from following after thee: for whither thou goest, I will go; and where thou lodgest, I will lodge: thy people shall be my people, and thy God my God: where thou diest, will I die, and there will I be buried: the Lord do so to me, and more also, if ought but death part thee and me.
>
> Set me as a seal upon thine heart, as a seal upon thine arm: for love is strong as death . . . . Many waters cannot quench love, neither can the floods drown it: if a man would give all the substance of his house for love, it would utterly be contemned.
>
> And God shall wipe away all tears from their eyes; and there shall be no more death, neither sorrow, nor crying, neither shall there be any more pain.

There are no nobler passages in English prose. And out of the 144 words that I have just read, only ten are not of native origin. And the far-reaching and pervasive influence of the King James version of the Bible upon English style is very largely due to this happy coincidence of qualities in two languages in other respects as far apart as the East is from the West. ¶ 10

But simplicity is not the only quality of the diction of the King James version. It has majesty and stateliness as well. And that lofty grandeur of the diction of the English Bible ¶ 11 is due in large degree to still another remarkable convergence of kindred qualities in two otherwise alien tongues. For centuries the ear of the English-speaking people had been attuned to the sonorous diction of the service of the church —to the majestic Latin of its offices and of its hymns. And for sheer splendour of verbal music the Latin of the Church —if I may express my own opinion—has never been surpassed. Let me read a brief passage from the lines of Bernard of Cluny on which the familiar hymn "Jerusalem the Golden" is based:

> Urbs Sion aurea, patria lactea, cive decora,
> Omne cor obruis, omnibus, obstruis et cor ora.
> Nescio, nescio, quae jubilatio, lux tibi qualis,
> Quam socialia gaudia, gloria quam specialis . . . .
> Urbs Sion inclyta, turris et edita littore tuto,
> Te peto, te colo, te flagro, te volo, canto, saluto . . .
> O bona patria, num tua gaudia teque videbo?
> O bona patria, num tua praemia plena tenebo? . . .
> Pax ibi florida, pascua vivida, viva medulla,
> Nulla molestia, nulla tragoedia, lacryma nulla.
> O sacra potio, sacra refectio, pax animarum,
> O pius, O bonus, O placidus sonus, hymnus earum.*

¶ 12 Or listen to the clangor of this:

> Mortis portis fractis, fortis
> Fortior vim sustulit;
> Et per crucem regem trucem
> Infernorum perculit.

* Zion, city of gold, land of milk, of beauteous citizenry,
Every heart thou dost subdue, all hearts, all lips thou dost make speechless.
I know not, I know not what rejoicing is thine, what kind of light,
How many share thy joys, yet how thy glory is but one . . . .
Zion, glorious city, thy tower and its heights on the safe shore,
Thee I seek, thee I cherish, thee I adore, thee I wish, sing, salute . . . .
O good land of my fathers, shall I behold thy joys and thee?
O good land of my fathers, shall I clutch thy full rewards? . . . .

Lumen clarum tenebrarum
Sedibus resplenduit;
Dum salvare, recreare,
Quod creavit, voluit.†

¶ 13 Or to the mellower music of this—from the original of the hymn we know as "Jesus, the very thought of thee":

Jesu, dulcis memoria
Dans vera cordis gaudia,
Sed super mel et omnia
Eius dulcis praesentia. . . .

Jesu, dulcedo cordium,
Fons vivus, lumen mentium,
Excedens omne gaudium,
Et omne desiderium. . . .

Mane nobiscum, Domine,
Et nos illustra lumine,
Pulsa noctis caligine
Mundum replens dulcedine.‡

Peace is there, flowery, fields of living green, the marrow of life,
No harm there, no tragedy, no tears.
O sacred drink, sacred feast, the peace of souls,
O reverent, O good, O calm sound—the hymn they sing!
(This and the two following notes are more or less line-by-line translations by the editor. The mediæval Latin, however, cannot be translated literally with full satisfaction.)

† When the gates of death were broken, He, the Stronger One,
Bore up the strength of the brave;
And by His cross he quelled
The savage king of Hell.
Light shone clear
Upon the houses of darkness;
And, what he created,
He willed to save, to recreate.

‡ Sweet memory of Jesus
That giveth the heart's true joys,
But more sweet than honey, than all,
His sweet presence . . . .

Jesus, hearts' sweetness,
Living fountain, light of minds,
Excelling all joy
And all desire. . . .

Dwell with us, Lord,
And illumine us with Thy light,
Beat back the darkness of night
And fill the world with Thy sweetness.

¶ 14 I have read these because I want to make at least reasonably clear the sort of thing that had trained the ear, and had become through generations part and parcel of the subconscious possession of those who listened, even without understanding, to the service of the church. And it was in the majestic Latin of the Vulgate that the Bible, in that service, for centuries was heard. And the sonorousness of the Latin, no less than the simplicity of the Hebrew, found in English its apt and adequate vehicle. For through its enormous Latin element the English vocabulary had become an instrument capable of scarcely less stately harmonies than Latin itself. And so, in the King James Bible, we find the plangent organ music of passages like these:

> And after these things I heard a great voice of much people in heaven, saying Alleluia; Salvation, and glory, and honour, and power, unto the Lord our God. . . . And I heard as it were the voice of a great multitude, and as the voice of many waters, and as the voice of mighty thunderings, saying, Alleluia; for the Lord God omnipotent reigneth.
>
> Who shall separate us from the love of Christ? Shall tribulation, or distress, or persecution, or famine, or nakedness, or peril, or sword? . . . Nay, in all these things we are more than conquerors through him that loved us. For I am persuaded, that neither death, nor life, nor angels, nor principalities, nor powers, nor things present, nor things to come, nor height, nor depth, nor any other creature, shall be able to separate us from the love of God, which is in Christ Jesus our Lord.
>
> For this corruptible must put on incorruption, and this mortal must put on immortality. So when this corruptible shall have put on incorruption, and this mortal shall have put on immortality, then shall be brought to pass the saying that is written, Death is swallowed up in victory.

¶ 15 In a word, the supreme qualities of two vocabularies—the

Hebrew of the writers of the Bible, and the Latin of its most influential version—found their counterpart in English; and to this complex of correspondences is largely due the marvellous felicity of diction which has made the English Bible a potent factor in the ennobling of the English speech.

EXERCISES

I. John Livingston Lowes' "The Language of the King James Version of the Bible" is a portion of an essay of considerable length which was originally delivered as a lecture.

A. Explain the origin and character of the "native element" (Par. 3) of the English vocabulary? What is the "foreign element" and how is its presence to be explained? What does Lowes mean by describing this element as "*complexly* foreign"?

B. In Sens. 3 and 4 of Par. 3, identify, first, all words that belong to the "Saxon element." Of these words, which are *content words*—i.e., nouns, verbs, adjectives, adverbs—and which are *functional words*—i.e., pronouns, prepositions, conjunctions? Are any of the functional words foreign in origin? Next, identify all words in the two sentences that belong to the "foreign element." To what extent do these belong to "the Latin component"? From such a sampling (in which, if you wish, other sentences can be included) formulate a generalization as to the use to which the two vocabularies are put in a literary essay of the type before you. In arriving at this generalization, take into consideration Lowes' statement (Par. 3): "Now one element is predominant, now another . . . ."

II. In Par. 4, Lowes says that "the language at the period during which the Bible was being translated into English was in its most plastic stage." Assuming, as Lowes does, that the period referred to was approximately "Shakespeare's day" (1564–1616) and that the extracts from Malory (Pars. 5 and 7) appropriately represent the "Saxon element," answer the following questions:

A. How large is the proportion of "Saxon" words in the extracts from Malory as compared with the proportion of such words in the quotations from the Bible (Pars. 6 and 8)? As compared with the proportion in Lowes' own writing?

B. In the passages from Malory, what words are now *obsolete* or *archaic?* Are there any obsolete or archaic words in the passages from the Bible? Are there any words or forms in the passages from the Bible that would not be readily understandable to a present-day reader or hearer?

C. What peculiarities or defects of syntax appear in Malory's prose? Do you find similar peculiarities or defects in the passages from the Bible?

D. From such an inspection, what conclusions would you draw as to the meaning and implication of Lowes' phrase, "in its most plastic stage"?

E. What similarities of sentence structure and rhetorical pattern do you find in the prose of Malory and the prose of the Bible?

F. What is the nature of the "majestic rhythm" (Par. 9) which, according to Lowes, "the prose of Malory lacks"?

III. Lowes states that the original Hebrew and the prose of Malory "agree in the simplicity and directness of their diction." Further on, he says that "no less than the Hebrew, the native English is the language of the eye, the hand, the heart."

Analyze the diction of the three passages (Par. 9) from the King James translation of the Bible by way of testing Lowes' statement. Do the strength and general effectiveness of the passages quoted depend merely upon "simplicity and directness of diction"? What part do rhetorical patterns play in making the prose effective and memorable? What are the ten words in these passages that are "not of native origin" (see Par. 10)? Look up their derivation.

IV. In Par. 11 Lowes says that the "lofty grandeur of the diction of the English Bible is due in large degree to still another remarkable convergence of kindred qualities in two otherwise alien tongues." What are the "two otherwise alien tongues"? Does Lowes mean to omit from consideration here the Greek of the New Testament (see his reference, Par. 2)? What specific Latin influences does Lowes mean to include in his phrase, "the Latin of the Church"? Was the Latin of the Church the same as the classical Latin of Vergil, Horace, and Cicero? What was "the Vulgate"? On what grounds can Lowes call it "the most influential version" of the Bible? Analyze the passages quoted from the New Testament (Par. 14) to demonstrate (1) the degree of their Latinity; (2) what Lowes means by the terms that he applies to the diction—"majesty and stateliness" . . . "lofty grandeur" . . . "sonorousness" . . . "plangent organ music" . . . "stately harmonies."

V. What writers in this book could you use to support Lowes' final statement (Par. 15) that the English Bible has been "a potent factor in the ennobling of the English speech"?

VI. Compare the prose of the quotations that Lowes gives from the King James translation of the Bible with the versions given in any available *recent* translation of the Bible. Sample other passages from such a recent translation. If Lowes had had such a modern translation before him and had made a similar comparison, what do you think would have been his opinion concerning the modern translation?

LESSON XX

Analysis of Sentences and Passages.

SPECIMEN ANALYSES OF SENTENCES

1.

(I) A rim of the young moon cleft the pale waste of sky line, the rim of a silver hoop embedded in grey sand: (II) and the tide was flowing in fast to the land with a low whisper of her waves, islanding a few last figures in distant pools.

—James Joyce, *A Portrait of the Artist As A Young Man.*[1]

This is skilfully constructed compound sentence in which the two independent clauses—(I) "A rim... cleft the pale waste..." and (II) "the tide was flowing in...."—are artfully balanced to convey two related aspects of the sea-shore at twilight. Clause I gives, in terms of visual impressions, the look of the sky, which is quiet and motionless. Clause II, in unobtrusive images of sound and movement, presents the sea with its flowing tide and its whisper of waves. The two clauses describe complementary aspects of the same scene, and together they make one effect. Therefore the balanced compound structure is highly appropriate.

The main elements of both clauses are in normal order: (I) "rim" *(subject)*—"cleft" *(verb)*—"waste" *(direct object);* (II) "tide" *(subject)*—"was flowing" *(verb)*—"in... waves" *(adverbial modifier).* But each clause contains as its final element an additional modifier in the form of an elaborate phrase that qualifies the subject. In each instance this modifying phrase serves a non-restrictive, adjectival function; it adds to, but does not restrict, the meaning of the substantive to which it distantly adheres. And in each instance Joyce has given this adjectival modifier a figurative cast. In Clause I, "the rim of a silver hoop embedded in grey sand" has an appositive relationship to the subject "rim." Thus the first element of

[1] Reprinted by permission of the publishers, The Viking Press, Inc.

the sentence, "the rim of the young moon," which is a plain, rather matter-of-fact phrase, receives a delayed modification from its appositive and is transformed into a metaphor. The rim of the young moon (which was actually there) becomes the rim of a silver hoop embedded in sand (an imagined likeness). In Clause II, the added phrase is built upon a present participle ("islanding") which modifies the subject "tide." The matter-of-fact assertion, "the tide was flowing in," is altered by this metaphorical addition into a pictorial image.

The placing of these two modifiers illustrates a principle defined by Richard Weaver as follows: "One of the common mistakes of the inexperienced writer. . . is to suppose that the adjective can set the key of a discourse. Later he learns. . . that nearly always the adjective has to have the way prepared for it. Otherwise, the adjective introduced before its noun collapses for want of support." * In the light of this principle, the sentence would have been less effective if Joyce had given the large adjectival phrases a leading position in each clause—if, for example, the sentence had read: "Like the rim of a silver hoop. . . the young moon cleft the sky . . .; and, islanding a few last figures. . . the tide was flowing in fast. . . ."

One should note also that the static or unmoving condition of the sky area is partly suggested in Clause I by the tense forms used: "cleft" (past tense—a metaphorical term); "embedded" (past participle, passive). And in Clause II the effect of the flowing tide is carried out in the use of the progressive form of the past tense ("was flowing") and the present active participle ("islanding"). In this clause the idea of movement, which implies vitality, is subtly underlined by Joyce's use of the personal pronoun "her" to refer to "tide." The verbs carry a large strength of meaning without much need of adverbial assistance: "cleft," "embedded," "islanding." These are "verb epithets"—in Mr. Weaver's phrase.†

Linkage of elements and of clauses is achieved through repetition of identical or assonant sounds as well as through the logical structure of the grammar: (1) "rim". . . "rim";. . . (2) "moon". . . "hoop". . . "few" . . . "pools"; (3) "cleft". . . "embedded"; (4) "pale". . . "waste". . . "grey" . . . "waves"; (5) "sky". . . "line". . . "tide". . . "*i*slanding"; (6) "silver" . . . "in". . . "with". . . "wh*is*per". . . "f*i*gures". . . "d*i*stant"; (7) "sand". . . "and". . . "isl*and*ing". . . "dist*ant*"; (8) "fast". . . "last." The total effect is a harmony of sound, of logical meaning, and of figurative overtones. One can hardly doubt—once the analysis reveals it—that Joyce deliberately sought such a harmony.

* From *The Ethics of Rhetoric*, by Richard M. Weaver, p. 130. Reprinted by permission of the publishers, Henry Regnery & Company.

† *Ibid*, pp. 135–136.

2.

(I) I went to the woods | (I′) because I wished to live deliberately, | (A) to front only the essential facts of life, | (B) and see if I could not learn what it had to teach, | (C) and not, when I came to die, discover that I had not lived.

—Henry David Thoreau, *Walden.*

In this complex sentence, the rhetorical emphasis falls upon the intricate adverbial clause introduced by "because," not upon the principal clause, "I went to the woods," which seems like a plain and simple statement of a commonplace action. Although "I went to the woods" ranks grammatically as the principal clause, it really serves as little more than a directive or introductory clause pointing to the subordinate clause—"because I wished. . . ."—in which the reasons for going to the woods are given an elaborate and subtle development.

The "because"-clause may be parsed as an adverbial clause modifying the phrase "to the woods," which, in turn, may be parsed as an adverbial modifier of the intransitive verb "went." Through the adverbial clause Thoreau makes a large qualification which must be added to the meaning of "woods." This large qualification distinguishes Thoreau's "woods" and his action in going to them from all other "woods" and all other goings to the woods, whether of a casual, recreational, or commercial nature. Thus "woods," which might otherwise be a commonplace, undifferentiated objective, is distinguished as a place where one may go "to live deliberately" and is accordingly set in implied contrast with all places where men cannot live "deliberately," such as cities or towns in which there must be a great deal of involuntary or undeliberate conformity to a more or less servile routine.

The assertion contained in the subordinate clause—"I wished to live deliberately"—is indeed, the "rhetorical subject"—that is, the true theme or topic of the sentence, as it is also of Thoreau's *Walden.*

Examining next the internal structure of the "because"-clause, we perceive that "wished," the main verb (or "simple predicate") of this clause, takes as its complements a series of infinitives: "to live. . . to front. . . and [to] see. . . and not. . . [to] discover." Grammatically considered, these four infinitive constructions seem to be coördinate. Rhetorically considered, all but the first of the series are appositive constructions, added to explain, amplify, and refine the meaning of the first infinitive construction, "to live deliberately." "To front only the essential facts of life" is the first positive stage of living deliberately; and it is therefore a modifier, at least in a rhetorical sense, of "to live deliberately." "And [to] see if I could not..." the second positive stage of living deliberately, is a second rhetorical modifier. The third modifier of the series—"and not...[to] discover..." —being thrown into negative form, introduces a sudden and very impressive contrast. The rhetorical "coördination," therefore, is a coördination of the groups lettered A, B, and C. These three rhetorical groups extend the meaning of I′, the rhetorical subject. The pattern of the rhetorical coördination thus does not exactly follow the pattern of the grammatical coördination, which would make the four infinitive phrases "equal"—that is, all complements of the verb "wished."

In the "if"-clause the precise balance between "learn" and "teach" gives Group B a striking amount of firmness and weight. The strongest surprise, however, appears in the paradoxical opposition in Group C between "came to die" and "not lived." "Not lived," which suddenly infuses a metaphorical content into "lived," is anti-climactic in its negativeness, but, because of its placing, is climactic in rhetorical force, with reference to the total meaning of the sentence. One should furthermore note that "if I could not learn," though negatively expressed, is positive in logical meaning; Thoreau intends to learn, not to fail to learn. The placing of the true negative, "not lived," has a powerful retroactive influence upon "to live deliberately," since this true negative implies that to live non-deliberately (unthinkingly, involuntarily, mechanically) is nothing but a mockery of life, indeed a death-in-life of man as man.

Out of a total of 44 words in Thoreau's sentence, 39 are words of one syllable; only 5 are words of more than one syllable. The language is extraordinarily simple, and it is also very abstract. Yet the sentence is tremendously assertive and sharp. Thoreau takes as strong a position as a man can take. The strength of the sentence, the feeling of intense conviction and purposefulness that it carries, derives to a very great degree from the carefully controlled branching off of important qualifying ideas from the simple trunk, "I went to the woods," with which the sentence begins.

SENTENCES FOR ANALYSIS

1. Now, at the name of the fabulous artificer, he seemed to hear the noise of dim waves and to see a winged form flying above the waves and slowly climbing the air.

—James Joyce, *Portrait of the Artist As A Young Man.*[1]

2. For fountains they are a great beauty and refreshment; but pools mar all, and make the garden unwholesome, and full of flies and frogs.

—Sir Francis Bacon, "Of Gardens."

3. Men come tamely home at night only from the next field or street, where their household echoes haunt, and their life pines because it breathes its own breath over again; their shadows, morning and evening, reach no farther than their daily steps.

—Henry D. Thoreau, *Walden.*

4. His mount, an untamed sorrel, exploded from the rodeo chute, rearing and chopping at the air, twisting its body with a whiplike motion, then settled down to a series of earth-pounding bucks.

—"Champion Cowboy," *Time,* March 8, 1954.[2]

5. There is nothing that God hath established in a constant course of nature, and which therefore is done every day, but would seem a miracle, and exercise our admiration, if it were done but once.

—John Donne, *LXXX Sermons* (22), 1640.

6. It may be to some purpose but has all the air of irony that as we travel the long road of our life it is in the beginning, when we would appear to need most those who might go along with us, we are most unaccompanied.

—Stark Young, *The Pavilion.*[3]

7. Then a gleam of sand, a flash and glint of water; the white rail streamed past in one roar and rush and rattle of planking and they were across.

—William Faulkner, *Intruder in the Dust.*[4]

8. It was a game, precious and obsessive, with cunning and awareness matched against cunning and awareness, a game played for ultimate stakes,

[1] Reprinted by permission of the publishers, The Viking Press, Inc.
[2] Reprinted by permission of Time, Inc.
[3] Reprinted by permission of the publishers, Charles Scribner's Sons.
[4] Reprinted by permission of the publishers, Random House, Inc.

like the game that had been played not long back in this land when it was a land of dark forests and beasts and savages, a game of hunter and hunted.

—Robert Penn Warren, *World Enough and Time.*[1]

9. It is infinitely wiser to use the statutes presently available to us than to clamp a new control over every community in order to fashion a trap for improper law enforcement in a few communities.

—John Edgar Hoover, "The Basis of Sound Law Enforcement," *Annals of the American Academy of Political and Social Science, January,* 1954.[2]

10. Tragedy, then, is an imitation of an action that is serious, complete, and of a certain magnitude; in language embellished with each kind of artistic ornament, the several kinds being found in separate parts of the play; in the form of action, not of narrative; through pity and fear effecting the proper purgation of these emotions.

—Aristotle, *Poetics* (translated by S. H. Butcher).

11. The work of a correct and regular writer is a garden accurately formed and diligently planted, varied with shades, and scented with flowers; the composition of Shakespeare is a forest, in which oaks extend their branches, and pines tower in the air, interspersed sometimes with weeds and brambles, and sometimes giving shelter to myrtles and roses; filling the eye with awful pomp, and gratifying the mind with endless diversity.

—Samuel Johnson, "Preface to Shakespeare."

12. He was a fair, tall man, in a snuff-colored suit, with a plain sword, very sober and almost shabby in appearance—at least when compared to Captain Steele, who loved to adorn his jolly round person with the finest of clothes, and shone in scarlet and gold lace.

—William Makepeace Thackeray, *The History of Henry Esmond.*

13. There were fat old ladies in fine silk dresses, and slim young ladies in gauzy muslin frocks; old gentlemen stood up with their backs to the empty fireplace, looking by no means as comfortable as they would have done in their own armchairs at home; and young gentlemen, rather stiff about the neck, clustered near the door, not as yet sufficiently in courage to attack the muslin frocks, who awaited the battle, drawn up in semicircular array.

—Anthony Trollope, *The Warden.*

[1] Reprinted by permission of the publishers, Random House, Inc.
[2] Reprinted by permission.

14. The two great points of difference between a democracy and a republic are: first, the delegation of the government, in the latter, to a small number of citizens elected by the rest; secondly, the greater number of citizens, and greater sphere of country, over which the latter may be extended.

—James Madison, *The Federalist,* No. 10.

15. The original power of judicature, by the fundamental principles of society, is lodged in the society at large: but as it would be impracticable to render complete justice to every individual, by the people in their collective capacity, therefore every nation has committed that power to certain select magistrates, who with more ease and expedition can hear and determine complaints; and in England this authority has been immemorially exercised by the king or his substitutes.

—William Blackstone, *Commentaries on the Laws of England,* Book I, Chap. VII.

16. For the key to this regional America will be found in its richness and reality whether it is reflected in the observations of our foreign visitors who marvel at its bigness, expanse, and complexity; or whether it is reflected in the enthusiastic admiration of each region by the vividly writing First Lady of the Land; or whether measured in terms of Babson's appraisal of prosperity and financial prospects; or reflected in the professor's or the administrator's verdict that the nation is too big for any single administrative unit to be successful; or in the enthusiastic but puzzled student of literature in search of the great American novel; or, as is everywhere in evidence, in the quest of the traveler and the tourist and the searcher after new frontiers, for the enjoyment of a richer life in America.

—Howard W. Odum and Harry Estill Moore, *American Regionalism* (1938).[1]

17. He developed the acute exasperation of a pestered animal, a well-meaning cow worried by dogs.

—Stephen Crane, *The Red Badge of Courage.*

18. Of such mighty importance every man is to himself, and ready to think he is so to others, without once making this easy and obvious reflection, that his affairs can have no more weight with other men than theirs have with him, and how little that is, he is sensible enough.

—Jonathan Swift, "Hints Toward an Essay on Conversation."

[1] Reprinted by permission of Henry Holt and Company, Inc., publishers.

19. I had not been long at the University before I distinguished myself by a most profound silence; for during the space of eight years, excepting in the public exercises of the college, I scarce uttered the quantity of an hundred words; and indeed do not remember that I ever spoke three sentences together in my whole life.

—Joseph Addison, *The Spectator.*

20. Irresponsible rulers need the quiescence of the ruled more than they need any activity but that which they can compel.

—John Stuart Mill, "Considerations on Representative Government."

21. They went noiselessly over mats of starry moss, rustled through interspersed tracts of leaves, skirted trunks with spreading roots whose mossed rinds made them like hands wearing green gloves; elbowed old elms and ashes with great forks, in which stood pools of water that overflowed on rainy days and ran down their stems in green cascades.

—Thomas Hardy, *The Woodlanders.*

22. She was somewhat like those small dull, compact apples that in the flush of the harvest are passed over almost with scorn, but late in the winter, when the fine, brightly colored fruit has grown too mealy and insipid, can stir the appetite as though in the darkness of the storage cellar they had managed to keep and augment the ripe, full, winey richness of the last sunshine of the summer.

—Robert Penn Warren, *Night Rider.*[1]

23. A great brush swept smooth across his mind, sweeping across it moving branches, children's voices, the shuffle of feet, and people passing, and humming traffic, rising and falling traffic.

—Virginia Woolf, *Mrs. Dalloway.*[2]

24. You did not love the floor of a flat-car nor guns with canvas jackets and the smell of vaselined metal or a canvas that rain leaked through, although it is very fine under a canvas and pleasant with guns; but you loved some one else whom now you knew was not even to be pretended there; you seeing now very clearly and coldly—not so coldly as clearly and emptily.

—Ernest Hemingway, *A Farewell to Arms.*[3]

25. In the porch stood the porter in a green livery, girt about with a cherry-colored girdle, garbling of pease in a silver charger; and over head

[1] Reprinted by permission of the publishers, Random House, Inc.
[2] Reprinted by permission of the publishers, Harcourt, Brace & Co., Inc.
[3] Reprinted by permission of the publishers, Charles Scribner's Sons.

hung a golden cage with a magpie in it, which gave us an All Hail as we entered; but while I was gaping at these things I had like to have broken my neck backward, for on the left hand, not far from the porter's lodge, there was a great dog in a chain painted on the wall, and over him written in capital letters, BEWARE THE DOG.

—*The Satyricon of Petronius* (translated by William Burnaby).

26. As for jest, there be certain things which ought to be privileged from it; namely, religion, matters of state, great persons, any man's present business of importance, and any case that deserveth pity.

—Sir Francis Bacon, "Of Discourse."

27. What song the Sirens sang, or what name Achilles assumed when he hid himself among women, though puzzling questions, are not beyond all conjecture.

—Sir Thomas Browne, *Urn Burial.*

28. Many a man lives a burden to the earth; but a good book is the precious life-blood of a master spirit, embalmed and treasured up on purpose to a life beyond life.

—John Milton, *Areopagitica.*

29. When men do not love their hearths, nor reverence their thresholds, it is a sign that they have dishonored both, and that they have never acknowledged the true universality of that Christian worship which was indeed to supersede the idolatry, but not the piety, of the pagan.

—John Ruskin, "The Lamp of Memory," *Seven Lamps of Architecture.*

30. To reverse the rod, to spell the charm backward, to break the ties which bound a stupefied people to the seat of enchantment, was the noble aim of Milton.

—Thomas Babington Macaulay, "Essay on Milton."

31. The professor of anatomy, Dr. Oliver O. Stout, was himself an anatomy, a dissection-chart, a thinly covered knot of nerves and blood vessels and bones.

—Sinclair Lewis, *Arrowsmith.*[1]

32. No person shall be held to answer for a capital, or otherwise infamous crime, unless on a presentment or indictment of a grand jury, except in cases arising in the land or naval forces, or in the militia, when in actual service in time of war or public danger; nor shall any person be

[1] Reprinted by permission of the publishers, Harcourt, Brace & Co., Inc.

subject for the same offence to be twice put in jeopardy of life or limb; nor shall be compelled in any criminal case to be a witness against himself, nor be deprived of life, liberty, or property, without due process of law; nor shall private property be taken for public use, without just compensation.

—*Constitution of the United States of America,* Article V.

33. The fountains of her great deep were broken up, and she rained the nine parts of speech forty days and forty nights, metaphorically speaking, and buried us under a desolating deluge of trivial gossip that left not a crag or pinnacle of rejoinder projecting above the tossing waste of dislocated grammar and decomposed pronunciation.

—Samuel L. Clemens, *Roughing It,* Chapter II.

34. With each homey crásh-crásh crásh-crásh of the wheels against the rails, there would steal up at me along the bounding slopes of the awnings the nearness of all those streets in middle Brooklyn named after generals of the Revolutionary War.

—Alfred Kazin, *A Walker in the City.*[1]

35. As a result, the game has been taken over by a type of critter who, although differing in design, has the same basic construction as a $1.48 bridge table with a deficient thyroid.

—Red Smith, "The Missing Link," *Out of the Red.*[2]

36. I fell in with the world's way; and if my "puffing" was more persistent, my advertising more audacious, my posters more glaring, my pictures more exaggerated, my flags more patriotic, and my transparencies more brilliant than they would have been under the management of my neighbors, it was not because I had less scruple than they, but more energy, far more ingenuity, and a better foundation for such promises.

—Phineas T. Barnum, *Struggles and Triumphs.*

37. Then Sir Bedivere departed, and went to the sword, and lightly took it up, and went to the waterside; and there he bound the girdle about the hilts, and then he threw the sword as far into the water, as he might; and there came an arm and an hand above the water and met it, and caught it, and so shook it thrice and brandished, and then vanished away the hand with the sword in the water.

—Sir Thomas Malory, *Morte D'Arthur,* Book XXI, Chapter 5.

[1] Reprinted by permission of the publishers, Harcourt, Brace & Co., Inc.
[2] Reprinted by permission of the publishers, Alfred A. Knopf, Inc.

38. And Ruth said, Entreat me not to leave thee, or to return from following after thee: for whither thou goest, I will go; and where thou lodgest, I will lodge: thy people shall be my people, and thy God my God: where thou diest, will I die, and there will I be buried: the Lord do so to me, and more also, if aught but death part thee and me.

—*Ruth,* Chapter I, 16, 17 (King James translation).

39. And at the end of the days I Nebuchadnezzar lifted up mine eyes unto heaven, and mine understanding returned unto me, and I blessed the most High, and I praised and honoured him that liveth for ever, whose dominion is an everlasting dominion, and his kingdom is from generation to generation: and all the inhabitants of earth are reputed as nothing: and he doeth according to his will in the army of heaven, and among the inhabitants of the earth: and none can stay his hand, or say unto him, What doest thou?

—*Daniel,* Chapter IV, 34, 35.

40. Behold, I shew you a mystery; We shall not all sleep, but we shall all be changed, in a moment, in the twinkling of an eye, at the last trump: for the trumpet shall sound, and the dead shall be raised incorruptible, and we shall be changed.

—*I Corinthians,* Chapter XV, 51, 52.

PASSAGES FOR ANALYSIS: SENTENCES IN CONTEXT

I

There was a singular absence of heroic poses. The men bending and surging in their haste and rage were in every impossible attitude. The steel ramrods clanked and clanged with incessant din as the men pounded them furiously into the hot barrels. The flaps of the cartridge boxes were all unfastened, and bobbed idiotically with each movement. The rifles, once loaded, were jerked to the shoulder and fired without apparent aim into the smoke or at one of the blurred and shifting forms which, upon the field before the regiment, had been growing larger and larger like puppets under a magician's hand.

—Stephen Crane, *The Red Badge of Courage.*

II

Georgia started off on Cousin Hester's making her husband learn to knit in order to keep him at home on winter evenings. She told of Cousin

Hester's sleeping without taking off her starched collar on summer afternoons, when everybody else was down to slips and ribbons and fans, and powdering with rice-flour from bags made of pieces of white stockings, and lying straight out on the floor on a pallet instead of burying yourself alive in a bed, and keeping between windows, trying to survive the frightful heat. But Cousin Hester lay on her couch like a stiff little statue pushed on its side, the darling old thing.

—Stark Young, *Heaven Trees.*[1]

III

In the serene weather of the tropics it is exceedingly pleasant—the mast-head; nay, to a dreamy meditative man it is delightful. There you stand, a hundred feet above the silent decks, striding along the deep, as if the masts were gigantic stilts, while beneath you and between your legs, as it were, swim the hugest monsters of the sea, even as ships once sailed between the boots of the famous Colossus at old Rhodes. There you stand, lost in the Infinite Series of the sea, with nothing ruffled but the waves. The tranced ship indolently rolls; the drowsy trade winds blow; everything resolves you into languor. For the most part, in this tropic whaling life, a sublime uneventfulness invests you; you hear no news; read no gazettes; extras with startling accounts of commonplaces never delude you into unnecessary excitement; you hear of no domestic afflictions; bankrupt securities; fall of stocks; are never troubled with the thought of what you shall have for dinner—for all your meals for three years and more are snugly stowed in casks, and your bill of fare is immutable.

—Herman Melville, *Moby Dick.*

IV

Count Greffi was ninety-four years old. He had been a contemporary of Metternich and was an old man with white hair and mustache and beautiful manners. He had been in the diplomatic service of both Austria and Italy and his birthday parties were the great social event of Milan. He was living to be one hundred years old and played a smoothly fluent game of billiards that contrasted with his ninety-four-year-old brittleness. I had met him when I had been at Stresa once before out of season and while we played billiards we drank champagne. I thought it was a splendid custom and he gave me fifteen points in a hundred and beat me.

—Ernest Hemingway, *A Farewell to Arms.*[2]

[1] Reprinted by permission of the publishers, Charles Scribner's Sons.
[2] Reprinted by permission of the publishers, Charles Scribner's Sons.

V

He crouched there a long time, in the stillness of the night, feeling his muscles cramp and the chill grow in his bones. But that did not seem to matter. He scarcely troubled to make a slight shift now and then to get relief. He had the fancy that he was growing into the ground, was setting roots like the plants of the thicket, was one of them groping deeper and deeper into the cold, damp earth with fingers of root and tentacles like hair. He let his cheek rest against a thick, dry stalk of lilac, but the silk of the mask came between. So he raised the silk to give his cheek that companionship. And he remembered how, on the morning of the great and glittering frost years before, when he had been but a boy, the morning when all the world was covered with brilliant ice in the sun, he had touched the bough of the ice-ridden beech and had felt his being flow out into the shining tree, as though the bough were a conduit, and into the sunlight from every lifted twig, and down the trunk into the secret earth so that he was part of everything. That memory was important to him now, for it seemed to verify him, to say that all his past was one thing, and not rags and patches, and that all had moved to this moment.

—Robert Penn Warren, *World Enough and Time.*[1]

VI

How many million times she had seen her face, and always with the same imperceptible contractions! She pursed her lips when she looked into the glass. It was to give her face point. That was herself—pointed; dartlike; definite. That was her self when some effort, some call on her to be her self, drew the parts together, she alone knew how different, how incompatible and composed so for the world only into one centre, one diamond, one woman who sat in her drawing-room and made a meeting-point, a radiancy no doubt in some dull lives, a refuge for the lonely to come to, perhaps; she had helped young people, who were grateful to her; had tried to be the same always, never showing a sign of all the other sides of her—faults, jealousies, vanities, suspicions, like this of Lady Bruton not asking her to lunch; which, she thought (combing her hair finally), is utterly base! Now, where was her dress?

Her evening dresses hung in the cupboard. Clarissa, plunging her hand into the softness, gently detached the green dress and carried it to the window. She had torn it. Some one had trod on the skirt. She had felt it give at the Embassy party at the top among the folds. By artificial light the green shone, but lost its color now in the sun. She would mend it. Her maids had too much to do. She would wear it tonight. She would take her

[1] Reprinted by permission of the publishers, Random House, Inc.

silks, her scissors, her—what was it?—her thimble, of course, down into the drawing-room, for she must also write, and see that things generally were more or less in order.

Strange, she thought, pausing on the landing, and assembling that diamond shape, that single person, strange how a mistress knows the very moment, the very temper of her house! Faint sound rose in spirals up the well of the stairs; the swish of a mop; tapping; knocking; a loudness when the front door opened; a voice repeating a message in the basement; the chink of silver on a tray; clean silver for the party. All was for the party.

—Virginia Woolf, *Mrs. Dalloway.*[1]

VII

It is agreed that "the end of all government is the good and ease of the people, in a secure enjoyment of their rights, without oppression;" but it must be remembered, that the rich are *people* as well as the poor; that they have rights as well as others; that they have as clear and as *sacred* a right to their large property as others have to theirs which is smaller; that oppression to them is as possible and as wicked as to others; that stealing, robbing, cheating, are the same crimes and sins, whether committed against them or others. The rich, therefore, ought to have an effectual barrier in the constitution against being robbed, plundered, and murdered, as well as the poor; and this can never be without an independent senate. The poor should have a bulwark against the same dangers and oppressions; and this can never be without a house of representatives of the people. But neither the rich nor the poor can be defended by their respective guardians in the constitution, without an executive power, vested with a negative, equal to either, to hold the balance even between them, and decide when they cannot agree.

—John Adams, "A Defence of the Constitution, etc." *Works,* Vol. VI.

VIII

There seem to be but three ways for a nation to acquire wealth. The first is by *war,* as the Romans did, in plundering their conquered neighbors. This is *robbery.* The second by *commerce,* which is generally *cheating.* The third by *agriculture,* the only *honest* way, wherein a man receives a real increase of the seed thrown into the ground, in a kind of continual miracle, wrought by the hand of God in his favor.

—Benjamin Franklin, "Positions to Be Examined, Concerning National Wealth," *Works,* Vol. I.

[1] Reprinted by permission of the publishers, Harcourt, Brace & Co., Inc.

IX

All sorts of limestones are composed of more or less pure carbonate of lime. The crust which is often deposited by waters which have drained through limestone rocks, in the form of what are called stalagmites and stalactites, is carbonate of lime. Or, to take a more familiar example, the fur on the inside of a tea-kettle is carbonate of lime; and, for anything chemistry tells us to the contrary, the chalk might be a kind of gigantic fur upon the bottom of the earth-kettle, which is kept pretty hot below.

—Thomas Henry Huxley, "On a Piece of Chalk."

X

The style is the mirror of the mind, and Macaulay's style is that of a debater. The hard points are driven home like nails with unfailing dexterity; it is useless to hope for subtlety or refinement; one cannot hammer with delicacy. The repetitions, the antitheses, produce an effect of mechanism; and, indeed, the total result is a kind of fatal efficiency which suggests the operations of a machine more than anything else—a comparison which, no doubt, would have delighted Macaulay.

—Lytton Strachey, "Macaulay, Philistine on Parnassus." *Books,* New York Herald Tribune, January 15, 1928.[1]

XI

There are no universal geniuses in art: the thing is a contradiction in terms. But there are geniuses whose energy is too colossal to permit of their confining themselves to any one form of intellectual activity. Goethe was not satisfied to be a poet: he had to be a politician as well, an administrator, a theatre producer, a critic and aesthetician, a speculator in purely scientific territories such as those of botany, geology, and the theory of colour. The result was, as Brandes has pointed out, that, for all his greatness, he achieved hardly a single perfect work of art on the large scale. Wagner's was really the more remarkable artistic mind of the two; no matter in how many directions he might waste the surplusage of his vast energies, he gave to each of the completed works of his maturity the finish, the organic unity, that one expects of an artist who has never thought of anything else but his art. But when, as was so often the case, the creative impulse was lying dormant in him, wisely biding its appointed time, some other outlet had to be found for his inexhaustible intellectual and physical energy, some other means of gratifying his considerable self-esteem, some other channel through which he could exercise his lust for shaping men and things to his own end. In the whole course

[1] Reprinted by permission.

of his life he never seems to have doubted himself. He was as certain that he could solve the knottiest problems of art, of science, of politics, or run a kingdom, or guide a strayed civilization to the new Jerusalem, as that he could write better music than any of his contemporaries.

—Ernest Newman, *The Life of Richard Wagner,* Vol. I, 1813–1848.[1]

XII

Unfortunately the histrionic sensibility is seldom recognized, as the ear for music is. Ear-training is required wherever music is studied, but the actor's sensibility is supposed to be incorrigible. Perhaps that is because we are all actors so much of the time—imitating ourselves or others; feeling our way histrionically through the tangle of personal relationships; trying to judge people by our direct sense of their motivations, while discounting the rationalizations they offer. We recognize the histrionic talent of diagnosticians, children, and practical politicians; but we think of it as a completely unintelligible gift. Nevertheless the histrionic sensibility can be trained.

—Francis Fergusson, *The Idea of a Theater.*[2]

XIII

As the stream of commodities flowing from the factories broke every barrier, the business of selling goods employed an ever larger army of commercial officers and privates, swelling the ranks of the middle classes with recruits of the mercantile color. Huge areas of American social power were now occupied by huckstering shock troops who, with a technique and a verbiage all their own, concentrated on ogling, stimulating, and inveigling the public into purchases. By raising the business of advertising to the intensity of a crusading religion, embattled vendors gained an almost sovereign sway over newspapers and journals, as they pushed goods, desirable and noxious alike, upon a docile herd that took its codes from big type and colored plates.

Under this economic drive the psychology of the salesman—as distinguished from that of the warrior, organizing capitalist, and creative inventor—became the dominant spirit of an immense array of persons who, in the view of "thoughtful editors," constituted the "sound heart of the nation." In this intellectual climate, trades which the landed gentry had formerly scorned as vulgar were crowned with respectability: real estate agents became realtors, undertakers assumed the role of morticians, and clerks expanded into salesladies. When the second census of the

[1] Reprinted by permission of the publishers, Alfred A. Knopf, Inc.
[2] Reprinted by permission of the publishers, Princeton University Press.

twentieth century was compiled there were seen to be at least four million people engaged in trade, including retailers, sales agents, and collateral forces under this general head.

—Charles and Mary Beard, *The Rise of American Civilization,* Vol. II.[1]

XIV

For this offering of their lives, made in common by them all, they each of them individually received that renown which never grows old, and for a sepulchre, not so much that in which their bones have been deposited, but that noblest of shrines wherein their glory is laid up to be eternally remembered upon every occasion on which deed or story shall fall for its commemoration. For heroes have the whole earth for their tomb; and in lands far from their own, where the column with the epitaph declares it, there is enshrined in every heart a record unwritten with no tablet to preserve it, except that of the heart.

—Thucydides,"Pericles' Oration on the Athenian Dead," *The Peloponnesian War,* II, 43. (Crawley translation)

XV

Commitment to a political and administrative system, such as federalism in the United States, is something more important than a convenience. It is a basic political principle, which is broader than any one activity, such as forestry. When state action is weak or slow, as it has been in forest fire protection, or in the development of cutting practice control in the opinion of the U. S. Forest Service, a plan to supersede the states is not solely a forest problem. Such a change is a constitutional amendment of our federal system. While foresters or welfare workers, or school men, or road builders, or public housers, or health authorities may each in their own field propose a small whittling away of state responsibility, or a purchase of state sovereignty through federal aid, presidents, governors, legislators, and citizens generally must be alert to recognize that the underlying problem is general and not special, and that federalism will not long survive unless in each functional area the effort is made to maintain and develop local responsibility and enforcement as far as this is practicable. For forestry this means a vigorous effort to develop effective state forest administration together with the public opinion required in its support.

—Luther Halsey Gulick, *American Forest Policy.*[2]

[1] Reprinted by permission of the publishers, The Macmillan Company.
[2] Reprinted by permission of the publishers, Duell, Sloan & Pearce.

XVI

The snow was about four inches deep when I started; and when I got to the water, which was only about a quarter of a mile off, it looked like an ocean. I put in, and waded on till I came to the channel, where I crossed that on a high log. I then took water again, having my gun and all my hunting tools along, and waded till I came to a deep slough, that was wider than the river itself. I had crossed it often on a log; but behold, when I got there, no log was to be seen. I knowed of an island in the slough, and a sapling stood on it close to the side of that log, which was now entirely under water. I knowed further, that the water was about eight or ten feet deep under the log, and I judged it to be about three feet deep over it. After studying a little what I should do, I determined to cut a forked sapling, which stood near me, so as to lodge it against the one that stood on the island, in which I succeeded very well. I then cut me a pole, and then crawled along on my sapling till I got to the one it was lodged against, which was about six feet above the water. I then felt about with my pole till I found the log, which was just about as deep under the water as I had judged. I then crawled back and got my gun, which I had left at the stump of the sapling I had cut, and again made my way to the place of lodgment, and then climbed down the other sapling so as to get on the log. I then felt my way along with my feet, in the water, about waist deep, but it was a mighty ticklish business. However, I got over, and by this time I had very little feeling in my feet and legs, as I had been all the time in the water, except what time I was crossing the high log over the river, and climbed my lodged sapling.

I went but a short distance before I came to another slough, over which there was a log, but it was floating on the water. I thought I could walk it, and so I mounted on it; but when I had got about the middle of the deep water, somehow or somehow else, it turned over, and in I went up to my head. I waded out of this deep water, and went ahead till I came to the high-land, where I stopped to pull off my wet clothes, and put on the others, which I had held up with my gun, above the water, when I fell in. I got them on, but my flesh had no feeling in it, I was so cold. I tied up the wet ones, and hung them up in a bush. I now thought I would run, so as to warm myself a little, but I couldn't raise a trot for some time; indeed, I couldn't step more than half the length of my foot. After a while I got better, and went on five miles to the house of my brother-in-law, having not even smelt fire from the time I started. I got there late in the evening, and he was much astonished at seeing me at such a time. I staid all night, and the next morning was most piercing cold, and so they persuaded me not to go home that day. I agreed, and turned out and killed him two deer; but the weather got worse and colder, instead of better. I staid that night, and in the morning they still insisted I couldn't get home. I knowed the water would be frozen over, but not hard enough to bear me, and so I agreed to stay that day. I went out hunting again, and pursued a big *he-bear* all day, but didn't kill him. The next morning was bitter cold, but I knowed my family was without meat, and I determined to get home to them, or die a-trying.

I took my keg of powder, and all my hunting tools, and cut out. When I got to the water, it was a sheet of ice as far as I could see. I put on to it, but hadn't got far before it broke through with me; and so I took out my tomahawk, and broke my way along before me for a considerable distance. At last I got to where the ice would bear me for a short distance, and I mounted on it, and went ahead; but it soon broke in again, and I had to wade on till I came to my floating log. I found it so tight this time, that I knowed it couldn't give me another fall, as it was frozen in with the ice. I crossed over it without much difficulty, and worked along till I got to my lodged sapling, and my log under the water. The swiftness of the current prevented the water from freezing over it, and so I had to wade, just as I did when I crossed it before. When I got to my sapling, I left my gun, and climbed out with my powder keg first, and then went back and got my gun. By this time I was nearly frozen to death, but I saw all along before me, where the ice had been fresh broke, and I thought it must be a bear straggling about in the water. I, therefore, fresh primed my gun, and, cold as I was, I was determined to make war on him, if we met. But I followed the trail till it led me home, and I then found it had been made by my young man that lived with me, who had been sent by my distressed wife to see, if he could, what had become of me, for they all believed that I was dead. When I got home, I wasn't quite dead, but mighty nigh it; but I had my powder, and that was what I went for.

—From *Narrative of The Life of David Crockett.*

INDEX

OF

AUTHORS AND TITLES

INDEX OF AUTHORS AND TITLES

(Untitled material is entered under the name of the author only, with a reference to the source. When no author's name is used in the text, the entry generally is for the source only.)

INDEX OF RHETORICAL AND GRAMMATICAL TERMS

INDEX OF RHETORICAL AND GRAMMATICAL TERMS

(This index refers to terms used and questions raised in the exercise material accompanying the selections. Entries in capital letters refer to the larger forms of prose composition which constitute units of study.)